FUTURE PERFECT NOW

365 visionary tapas
on life, love, art
and everything in between

LEWIS EVANS

Copyright © 2020 Lewis Evans

Published by InsideOut Media: info@insideoutmedia.net

Cover design and layout by Lewis Evans: https://lewisevans.net

All rights reserved. No parts of this book may be reproduced or used in any manner whatsoever without prior written permission from the publisher, except for brief passages or quotations used in a book review or other publication. For permission and all other requests, please contact the publisher.

Publisher's Cataloging-in-Publication Data

Names: Evans, Lewis, 1952- author.

Title: Future perfect now : 365 visionary tapas on life, love, art and everything in between / Lewis Evans.

Description: Horsefly, BC : InsideOut Media, 2020.

Identifiers: LCCN 2020919962 (print) | ISBN 978-1-928103-16-5 (paperback) | ISBN 978-1-928103-17-2 (ebook)

Subjects: LCSH: Short stories. | Future, The--Fiction. | Quality of life--Fiction. | Visions--Fiction. | BISAC: FICTION / Short Stories (single author) | FICTION / Visionary & Metaphysical. | GSAFD: Short stories.

Classification: LCC PR9199.3.E93 F88 2020 (print) | LCC PR9199.3.E93 (ebook) | DDC 813/.6--dc23.

Foreword

Have you ever wished you could fast-forward to your ideal life? Artist and author Lewis Evans has done just that, vividly creating it in his imagination, pre-living and pre-loving it in exquisite detail, until it materialized in physical form.

Quantum physics tells us we are an integral part of the seamless consciousness that pervades our cosmos, connecting us to the infinite possibilities of universal intelligence. Since our individual electromagnetic fields are part of this interconnected energy, we are constantly transmitting and receiving, broadcasting information to the world around us. Our sense of self is informed by our thoughts, which are electrical, and by our emotions, which are magnetic. This means that what we think and feel matters—and *becomes* matter if we powerfully focus our thoughts and feelings on the vision we wish to realize.

In this unique futuristic projection, Lewis takes you on a very personal journey, sharing his profound wisdom, insights and breakthroughs as he envisions his ideal reality, bringing it alive for the reader as it gradually takes physical form in his own life.

A collection of inspired journal entries spanning 365 consecutive days, this book represents an intimate conversation in which you get to know the man behind the pen and the paintbrush. The captivating narrative establishes a special relationship that also enables you to discover and more deeply relate to yourself. As the revelations unfold, the sharing becomes more intimate and profoundly philosophical, creating a friendship and a shared vision of what is possible for our world.

Future Perfect Now is an invitation to expand your sense of self, to embrace your own limitless possibilities, and to engage your higher faculties in creating your own vision for the world you wish to see. It is an invitation to a quantum upgrade—to fully live your life and to truly love living it.

—Olga Sheean, author of
The Parents: How far would you go to save your world?

Create a vision and never let
the environment, other people's beliefs,
or the limits of what has been
done in the past shape your decisions.
Ignore conventional wisdom.
—Anthony Robbins

FUTURE

Every day, for a whole year, I settle down to write.

I have no agenda, no forethought, no story, no plan.
My mind is empty, save for a vision of my perfect future and
the blank page in front of me, which I fill,
right down to the very last square of the grid.

They say that thoughts become things, and I certainly
agree. Everything we create begins with a thought.
To create something we want, we must think of it
in the present tense, seeing it as a done deal.
If we put it in the future, that is where it will remain.

I let my mind roam in this space as I explore my perfect life.

Now.

Am I writing about a future life or
having realizations and feelings about my present?
Human experience is only in this present moment,
so vision and reality merge in a seamless flow.

PERFECT

This book contains 365 visionary tapas—snippets of unfolding reality for me; perhaps some inspiration for you. These pages can be read individually, in any order, because there is no plot, no timeline. Only now.

Now. Our most precious gift and our only true reality.

Which came first: the chicken or the egg? The vision or the life? In my experience, they co-exist. They are inseparable.

As an artist, writer and lover of life, I appreciate the magic of the moment, the power of stillness, and a focus on our fragile existence. What I create is also for you, and vice versa. Our co-creations merge, out there in the ether, with my vision supporting yours and yours mine.

Sample, savour and share whichever tapas appeal. May they inspire, bring fresh perspectives or ignite a spark on your journey, lighting the way towards your vision and enriching those who see you shine.

NOW

1

I love these moments. After a good lunch up at the house, we step down to the beach and walk along the surf. It's such a gentle slope at the water's edge that we are both able to soak our feet as we walk. That's when we dream. That's when we remember past times and look forward to new ideas that surprise us still. That's when we connect in creativity—and gratitude. Today, we are remembering. That was such an incredible day, not so long ago. You hated it but loved the anticipation when I insisted that you wear a blindfold. You knew roughly where we were after an hour's drive from the airport. And, of course, you could smell the sea and hear the breakers. But did you have any inkling as to what was about to be revealed when I stopped the car on gravel, and opened the door to the blast of heat and warm breeze? When I opened your door, took your hand and walked with you, eventually placing your hand on the iron knob of a heavy gate… "Turn it," I said. The hinges creaked a little as the gate opened. We walked a little more, flip-flops on warm gravel, before I stopped you again. I could hardly contain my emotions. "Lewee, where ARE we?" you said, smiling under your blindfold. I turned to face you. I felt so proud, and so much love. I felt humble and had a slight sense of worry in case the effect wasn't as I'd anticipated. Would it be another Milestones[1] moment? I gently removed your blindfold. You blinked. "Welcome home."

2

You are still sleeping as I tiptoe downstairs and charge up the Gaggia. It's taken a few goes for me to get it right. But, then, trained baristas devote a lot more time—or, at least, they used to, when all the Gaggias were purely mechanical—to get the pressure exactly right, the exact amount of grounds, freshly milled in the machine that stands beside it, and the perfect pump action on the handle. So satisfying. All that chrome, all that engineering focused on creating a perfect, slightly frothy espresso. In my case, it's a double. I withdraw the little white cup and place it on its curved white tray with one—no, let's make it two—almond biscotti. I admire the arrangement on the beautiful gift you gave me so many years ago. Sitting on our lush wooden worktop. I tie my bathrobe and take the coffee, slide open the patio door and place the cup on the wall. The seagulls are up to their usual tricks. I instinctively place my hand over the biscotti. Just in case. As I breathe in the warming sea air and watch the last of the mist evaporate over the still ocean, I am so grateful … and somewhat smug, I have to say, that after everything that has happened—all the struggles you had with your health and the fight to find a safe place—here we are. Safe, secure, fully paid up, huge income in place, and a beautiful home where we are already getting creative.

3

I stand at the front door, looking out across the gravel courtyard towards the gate. A beautiful curved wooden double gate that echoes the shape of the doorway where I stand. The gateway, framed with rambling wisteria that extends along the newly renovated wall that it serves to mask on our side, leads onto the coast road a short distance beyond. It's a quiet road as it doesn't lead anywhere that tourists want to go—to the south. And, to the north, there is just the village. From the village, you wouldn't even know the coast road was there, unless you had spent some time studying the map. No visitors yet. But there will be very soon. Carefully and lovingly, they will be welcomed to share in the beauty of our new world. Our front door, a bridge. Our protector. Our stargate. It's strong, weighty, but moves on the perfect mechanism in effortless balance and firm resolve. It knows what it does and is proud of it. You are safe here, but you are no prisoner. You shine and grow stronger by the day. Sea air. Long walks on the beach. Good food. The boundaries are in place, but they are laughing with those who understand, those who love, because they provide the freedom in which we now revel. I go back inside. Each step appreciative of where we have been, our journey, our struggle, those who have loved us along the way; knowing you are there with your heart aimed fully at mine. The door closes, my heart opens.

4

My restless mind is both a blessing and a curse. When I got up this morning, it was as if nothing was in sync. I did the five rites[2] all wrong and forgot to put my cup on the coffee machine, having pressed the button to deliver the coffee. And I didn't even notice for a few seconds. I was somewhere else. I was thinking about the planet. Turning one turn each day. And, as it does, people rise, have their day and go back to sleep. Like a Mexican wave, eternally rising and falling, opening like a flower to greet each day and then closing up as the light fades. It seems such an impossible and at best unlikely process, unique—as far as we know—to this one rock, floating round this sun of ours, with its own gravity, ecosystem and consciousness. And then I look around me at the stuff we have for living, and outside at the garden and the beach and sea. I am not of this, I think. But then the eternal question butts in. Okay, then, what am I? I have asked this too many times, so I take my partially rescued coffee and sit on the warming terrace for a few minutes while I drink it. And forget the question for a while longer, knowing that, in doing so, I am re-entering the illusion where I have striven and been fortunate to become comfortable and to have found love—and to know the question will come back.

5

It's all about mark-making. This life. We make marks, not knowing what on earth we are doing and how it relates to or affects anything else, or how the picture will develop. The first mark on the canvas. My life without a real plan. Even if I have an idea as to how this painting will work out, I know it may change significantly along the way, either by dint of my skill limitations or my choosing to change things, my choice of colours, shapes, materials. It's all the same. All a choice. And what does it all matter in the end? I don't even go there. The search for meaning becomes too tortuous. But, somehow, I tread a path between aesthetics, meaning and some idea of decorative acceptance. Or do I? What is my courage? I take a quick break to re-hydrate. I am safe here in the cocoon of my studio, to explore beyond—but only in my head. Outside, the world of living, relationships, eating, shitting, busying, finding interesting and entertaining ways to fill time before death. And there is so much beauty there already. There is you, this place, tastes, smells, sex, love. So, what am I trying to do in my private space? Why do I always question? Why cannot I simply enjoy—a reflection, a reflex to what happens beyond these walls, a celebration in abstract expression. How can I usefully use my energy and enjoy the rest of my life?

6

I press the button and a wedge of blinding white light starts to spread across the concrete floor as the door slowly rises. Eddies of dust and sand swirl, dramatically thrown into contrasty detail that fades as the door nears the top of its travel. My eyes adjust to the light. The bright white sand resumes its sand colour. At the back of the room, I grab the hook on the end of the cable and pull. As it unreels, I walk out onto the beach and down to the water. A momentary chill as my feet are submerged by the slight swell. "How was it today, Manuel?" "Good, thank you. I think you will be pleased." I am still embarrassed that this simple handyman has perfectly mastered my language while I have done so little to learn his. I attach the hook to the bow and we take up our normal positions—one on either side as I press the remote for the winch. The boat lurches as the cable takes up the slack and we glide it up the beach to the runners, then inside onto the rollers. I cut the winch motor and turn on the lights as Manuel closes the door. Together, we haul the box out of the boat and lay it on the floor to inspect its contents. It has indeed been a productive morning. He gives me the two Dorada and a snapper that I choose and quickly lay on ice in the fridge. We haul the box to his van so he can get the rest to market. I know he has no time for a coffee, so we shake hands and he leaves.

7

How come ants are so organized? And how did they find our barbeque, anyway? I didn't clean up properly last night, so I am watching as a neat line of them commute both ways, with purpose and amazing mountaineering skills, from the barbeque, down to the floor, across the terrace, up and over the containing wall before they disappear into the shrubbery beyond. An entire city mobilized with one simple aim—to get food and take it home. Compare that with the chaos we humans create at the supermarket, just before national holidays or in times of crisis. Mind you, ants don't have to battle with trolleys or line-ups at checkouts, or park and load shopping into the backs of SUVs. All the same, I am struck by the seamless flow, the apparent cooperation, the seeming absence of self-interest and the pure athleticism of what they achieve. Bring it up to human scale and we'd need to be iron-man fit and then some. And we'd need climbing equipment and goodness only knows what to tackle the terrain. And we'd have to cooperate, every single one of us, without ego or baggage or complaints or discussion of any aspect of it, and simply get on with it. What are the chances of that, I wonder. Will humans ever achieve the level of efficiency and cooperation that ants achieve constantly? Each one of us has a brain the size of a planet, quite literally, compared to the brain of an ant. And they will survive long after we have all destroyed ourselves.

8

Being at last stationery, rooted, settled in our place, has given us the opportunity to see our lives afresh. No more rushing from one temporary place to another. Some of the effects of this have surprised us in a nice way. We had been concerned that we might get bored—repetitive journeys, the same beach, the same house, year after year—but the reverse is true. We have calmed our adrenaline-fuelled tendencies and stilled our minds. Every day brings fresh surprises, new experiences and new joy, in ways that, perhaps, we would have missed before, in our race to be somewhere else. Now, we are present and time has become elastic and full of wonder. In our stillness, we see, taste, feel, experience so much more. Sometimes it's mind-boggling—even sad—to see how much of life we have missed by being constantly in a state of flux, in our heads; missing. They say that travel broadens the mind, but stillness enriches it because it has less impetus to interfere with the now. We are relieved and gratified to have discovered such new wealth and happiness. I open my eyes and become super-aware of the sea, lapping gently against the rocks where I sit. "Time to go." Your breath is warm as you lean down to kiss my lips. "I can't get any more in the bag." You lift the bulging string bag to show me, bursting with glossy black shellfish. I feel so alive and I am bursting with love—so happy you are well—as we walk back along the beach.

9

I have to say, it was a piece of genius to make the connecting room into the garden with its spring. What a fabulous discovery—that clear mountain water was just a few feet below the surface when they dug the foundations. That bench, set among the rich foliage, is still one of your favourite spots to sit and read, with the water gently trickling in the background. Our cool retreat for days when we actually want to get out of the sun for a while, but we don't want to be in the dark, behind the storm shutters. I still remember Dee's reaction when she first walked from our lounge, across the stepping stones, to the guest house when she first arrived. "I'll sleep here!" she burst out with admiration and enthusiasm. "How utterly gorgeous!" And, of course, the water is heaven to drink. No more Berkey[3], no more bottled stuff, just the best—the real thing—which is so rare in our world now. "Have you nearly finished?" I ask you, stepping carefully around papers scattered over the desk as I bring you a glass and some chocolate. "Almost." You keep your focus on what you are reading. "They're sending an agent to pick it up, this time. He should be here any minute." Wonderfully old-fashioned, I thought, how they still also like to have the physical paper version along with the digital. But they knew you'd make last-minute changes before publishing.

10

We all have notions of greatness and whatever success is for us. And they change. All the time, if we are honest about it. Success can simply be a great breakfast, or it can be lots of money in the bank. Greatness can be influence over others or the admiration of millions, or it can simply be feeling whole and content. We are dynamic beings and, as soon as we try to grasp and hold on to singular concepts, we shut the door on a million others. And, so, along the way, lack of focus can be a blessing. Contemplation without purpose can lead to creativity. And we are meant to be creative. It's at the very core of us and its evidence is all around us and has been since the beginning of man on earth. My ideas about such things have shifted considerably, especially as I entered my third phase. Maybe this was brought on by my relative lack of success in my second phase, when I was supposedly meant to be establishing and solidifying my position in this world. It doesn't matter. What happened, happened, for whatever reasons. And I am at peace with that, because what I did or didn't do has left the doors wide open for my potential to form and change as it will, when many others have stopped that process and are content to fill time in other ways. Not only that, but I am in the unique position of being married to the most incredible, wise and perfect person for me. I know and really appreciate that. And I know that however this all eventually plays out, my success and greatness are assured.

11

It is done. All of it. This game of life is simply to find the key to knowing that, and then ride the wave. How much do we actually learn from others? Very little, I suspect. When I look at the myriad blind alleys I chased in my life, I am convinced that we actually have the knowing inside us. All the preachers, intellectuals, influencers, seers, so-called leaders—they know no more than any of us. They are just as lost and confused as the next man – probably more so, since they wittingly or unwittingly seek recognition and some sort of elevated position in society, to try to convince others of the partial answer they think they have found, and thereby use it as a springboard to 'change the world'. What does that even mean? Change the world? The world would be fine, if only we would stop trying to change it. Our efforts to change the climate, in the name of prosperity on a material level; or to change people, to align them with our egotistical wants and thereby control and manipulate them, are as transparent as they are ill-informed. Changing the world is truly us on the road to nowhere. Why didn't we realize, when we first arrived on this planet, that the world is done. It was perfect. Nothing needed changing. Everything was in balance. Everything worked. The world turned, seasons came and went, and the whole thing operated like a giant free supermarket. Then it changed, when we introduced pricing. It may be too late, but I really hope we all start knowing soon.

12

I realize now that the only thing that stopped us from getting to where we are now was that we didn't have a dream. We weren't clear about what we wanted the universe to give us, so it didn't know what to give us. Once we'd got that sorted out, we allowed the universe to help us achieve everything we wanted. And once we had 20/20 vision (so to speak), we stopped running away—from microwaves, people, places, uncomfortable beds, the wrong walks, rain, cold, unsatisfactory shops, the wrong coloured stone in houses, false dreamers and self-responsibility—towards what we wanted, and what we now have. It was flipping a switch from 'off' (negative) to 'on' (positive). It sounds banal now, like some sort of inspirational speaker's spiel, but it really was as simple as that. "That was easy." I'm glad we kept that button[4], by the fireplace. It is a constant reminder of the key to a wonderful life. I don't need to be reminded about being grateful. Gratitude is always there. It has been, for a long time. I roll over on our dream-filled mattress. You stir, deep in slumber. I carefully run my fingers across your cheek. That skin! That beauty! You smile, your eyes still closed as you plant a leg firmly over mine as if to say, "Don't you dare move. Don't even think about getting up yet. Keep doing what you are doing." I smile, knowing there is no place I would rather be—ever!

13

One small fear that had been lurking in my subconscious had been that, once we were fully installed in this beautiful place, I would get lazy. Yes, there was a period of two weeks when I simply basked. I would sit, for hours, on the terrace, gazing out to sea, or spend an hour wiping down the Gaggia until it gleamed like new, or I would stand at different positions around the Aston Martin to simply admire the lines, the reflections, the colour, the presence of the thing. All because I could. No one was telling me to do something else. But, most of all, *I* wasn't telling *me* to do something else. There was a vast, indulgent stillness that came over me. A release from all the anxious years of never having enough, never giving enough, never being enough. What a fool I had been. But I was in no mood to fall back into admonishing myself. Here I am now. Congratulations! I walk down the stairs into the cool of the lower floor, with its workshop, garage, boathouse, storage, machine room and gym. It's the only part of our complex, apart from my studio, where I cannot be distracted by the sea and sky, or the ever-shifting patterns of sand. High windows in the gym cast enough light during the day that I don't need to switch on the LEDs. Now that I have a new rhythm in life, this is where I re-energize my body, get stronger, more alert, faster and enjoy the physical challenge that denies aging its descendance.

14

We really are peculiar beings. We live in this incredible manifestation and we are often miserable, sometimes bored, occasionally angry, unfulfilled, ungrateful, scheming—and, well, totally mad. I look for inspiration for my art. When I think about that, it is ridiculous in the extreme. Here I am, living a wonderful life: I have a beautiful home, a wonderful wife, health, hands, paint, canvas. Each day, there is an inspirational download—if that's how I want to think of it—of such incredible variety and colour and vibrancy, should I even care to open my eyes, that if I truly got started on it, I would never stop. I would have no time to stop. It would consume me 25 hours of every day. Instead, I look for meaning, search for an issue, work up some angst, look for some way to create impact. In other words, I am looking to serve the dysfunctional interests of others who also cannot see the incredible beauty, inspiration and richness that is set before us and inside us every waking moment of our lives. Yet still I have questions. Such is the tortured complexity of the human mind. How do I celebrate all this in my painting and in my writing? Still, there is a voice that tells me that these activities are a communication with others, not simply an expression of me to no audience other than the hearts, behind the minds, that know the truth.

15

It's been a great evening. My favourite kind of evening. I take one last look at the fantastically creative words arranged on the Silly Scrabble[5] board as we pass by the long wooden dining table and make our way to the stairs. The last of the sunset, dotted with lazy dark clouds, is the only light casting a cool glow over the aged wooden surface that has been such a convivial meeting place for so many meals with remarkable people. Somehow, we have gained a remarkable cachet across the globe, and great people travel huge distances for the opportunity to be in our company for a few days. But this evening it was just us. My favourite kind of evening. You clasp my arm in both hands as we pad our way, barefoot, across the tiles and make our way upstairs. As the wide vista that we see from our bed slowly disappears, I light the soft lamps and switch on the clever mechanism that lifts the projector from under the bed and points it at the white ceiling. It's a clever bit of technology—all fully shielded. It suspends the projector three feet above the bed and gives us cinema-quality imagery. The sound is theatre-surround-sound built into the walls and everything is controlled from the headboard. As you undress, I am impossibly distracted, but I try to focus on choosing a nice film. We sink into our wonderful mattress, my arm around you, your head resting on my shoulder, as we settle in to watch again, the movie of my novel, *Hominine*.

16

I'm so glad that I'm no longer chasing the dreams of others. All those things that are designed to make you feel less than, in order to have power over your heart. All those things that appeal to your sense of unworthiness, in order to feed the bottomless pit of a false, expansive economy. Marketing, after all, is all about discovering 'pain points' and then pressing those points relentlessly until your target succumbs, through desperation or manufactured desire. After all, what do we as humans ever really need and desire other than love, food and a level of comfort and good health? I am amazed at the way those basic needs have been exploited and distorted, along with the massaging of ego, purely to create and sustain an expansive and unsustainable system that brings only discord and envy and sadness, as well as ill-health. All the opposites of what we truly want and what we are designed to enjoy. I could not be happier with what I have, now that I have discarded that poisonous need. It all reduces down to incredibly beautiful simplicity. I have love in infinite abundance. I have health. I have comfort and good food, and I have a beautiful home. How come it has taken most of my life to realize, to come full circle from the day of my birth, when all was well in equal measure, before the strange, mysterious and disruptive journey began? Okay. Now is all that matters.

17

We are much less about doing than we are about being, if only the majority of us could see that. Years ago, on a brand-building course I devised, I said that if we don't know how to be, we cannot know what to do. Pat on the back to my former self. Without being connected to being, we are animals. That seems to show itself all the time, in the world and in our entertainment—be it books, films or whatever. The eternal dance, or struggle, between our animalistic selves and our higher selves that we misguidedly suppress, in the delusion of the reality that we perceive on the physical plane. And it's so damned attractive and powerful, if we let it be. Yet if we let go to the higher and disengage from it timelessly, we can be in a much better place. That's what I strive for now, every minute of every day. The triggers to go there are many and plentiful, if I choose to take notice. They start at sunrise and finish... when? If I think about it, they are always there – even in my dreams at night. Perhaps especially then, and particularly when I am dozing in the early morning, when dreams and first thoughts intermingle imperceptibly, into fantastic stories, scenes and feelings. I guess the trick is to keep that unaware awareness as we progress through the day, somehow not allowing the physical reality to take over and take us away from being the amazing beings that we truly are.

18

She's unmistakable in the distance—as much because of her statuesque figure as the fact that there is no one else on the beach. She's casually wandering back to the house. Big hat, long beach wrap, camera clasped loosely in one hand as the gentle surf splashes around her feet as she walks. "ETA?" you say. "I'd say we have about 10 minutes, at the rate she's going." The table is almost ready. Gleaming white bowls and plates, bright serviettes —your favourite breakfast ones with the multi-coloured jungle prints—even candles in tall glass holders. "I'll get the glasses," I say, as I open the unit along the back wall. You're at the cooker, preparing this momentous breakfast. I fill the Gaggia with water and switch it on, then fill the holders with organic decaf, smoothing off the tops before I twist them tight in the machine. Clara has excelled today. Fresh spelt croissants! How on earth did she get them so light and fluffy? But she knows what you can and can't eat[6], and she has never let you down. "Oh, I nearly forgot!" You look up from the cooker and glance nervously ahead. The pressies... "I'll get them!" I say, and I dash upstairs. They're sitting on the bed, wrapped in the most incredible paper and tied with ornate bows. I bring them down and arrange them carefully on the table. We're ready—and not a moment too soon, as she comes up the steps from the beach. "Happy birthday, Dee![7]"

19

I used to wonder if my senses had become dulled over the years, but now I know they hadn't. The world has changed, but if you know where to look, you can find again those senses that I thought were lost. That's what I had done, and it was a revelation. Thankfully, there were people who took the trouble, years ago, to store ancient seeds. Now, we are reaping the benefits of their good deeds. As I dig up a few potatoes for our evening meal, and gently rub off the dirt, I can even now smell the rich sweetness they will release when we boil them. It's a taste I remember from my childhood that was lost with the advent of supermarkets and chilled food distribution, extended shelf lives and plastic packs. Now, I hold that richness again in my hands. Reaching back into history to find healthiness and a way forward that the rest of the world may never know. True balance. The way we are meant to be. And, after all our struggles, I am so, so grateful. A humble potato. A revelation. I pick up the basket. The breakers lunge methodically and eternally at the beach, releasing their energy and drawing back, as if to say: "There you are, another miracle for you. Now, wait, I'll do it again." As I walk through the terrace back towards the house, I cannot resist picking a couple of heritage tomatoes—gnarled and bulbous and so incredibly scented that they almost make me dizzy. And you are picking some herbs outside the kitchen. My miracle. Another day, another meal, another opportunity to give thanks.

20

"Do you miss the snow?" I say as I open my eyes and see Jack gazing out to sea. He turns. "No, not really" "What about your friends?" "Yes, a little bit." He considers this further. "And my mom and dad." "I'm sure you do," I reassure him, "and you'll be seeing them all again soon." He smiles. "So," I say, as I get up from the recliner. "What have you got for me? Is it finished?" He looks sheepish. "Yes, I think so." "How do you know?" I smile. I'm teasing him. "Let's go and have a look." He leads the way back to the studio. He looks unsure. The drawing is on the small easel. He really has come a long way in the two weeks he has been on this scholarship. "I think…" I look at him. He's hanging nervously on every word. "I'm really proud of you. And you should be proud of you, too." He smiles. He's got Becky's structure, the feeling of her, the proportions—everything! "Now you're ready for Emily Carr[8]—if that's what you want." And I feel a huge satisfaction as well. Being in a position to take four school students a year out of the Canadian winter and into an intense life-drawing course that wasn't available for them anywhere else, and show them a taste of Europe—its history and its art—is deeply satisfying for me. And their parents don't have to pay for a thing—just get them to the airport. The kids are all verified and they win this. We have friends in Canada who do a great job of vetting them. And I get to help develop some of the rising stars that this world needs so much, nurturing the soul and spirit and revitalizing traditional art skills.

21

It's only when I took action that things started to work and we realized our vision. I am aware, or I often had the feeling, that my well-entrenched programming had held us back for a long time. Patterns that I had reinforced as I went through life – negative patterns that were reductionist, certainly not expansive, had seriously impacted my life, the lives of those close to me, and our progress. Once broken, the patterns became clear and I could see them for what they were, rather than the *fait accompli* that I saw my life as, for so long. And, by action, I discovered that I meant something different to what I had been taught in the past. It's not about manufacturing a burning passion, working all hours or following a 12-step program to emulate someone else's journey that brought them the dream that they had and now, for various nefarious reasons, peddle to desperate souls in the guise of an answer. No, the new action surprised me somewhat. The action was in being still. One of the most challenging actions to take in a world that claims that true action is anything but still. Yet in this stillness is all action. Because unless I am in that stillness, there is no clarity and therefore no direction and therefore, without it, all action is useless – or simply a lottery. But the action in the stillness is profound. It encompasses all possibilities and potentials in ways that I could not have imagined before. And it realizes my vision.

22

The air has a fresh scent after a good downpour. This time of year, we get almost nightly rain, so we don't need to use the desalination or irrigation systems. We're both out there working the moistened soil before the sun gets too hot for gardening and the earth hardens. I'm weeding one of the raised beds that promises to yield a bumper harvest of an ancient variety of strawberry. You are up the hill on the flat part, in your element, kneeling down, bare-footed in the rows of leeks. Working your way along, piling up the soil on either side to ensure long white stems when we eventually harvest them. You came out before the rain stopped. Your straw hat is steaming as you start to dry out. Your T-shirt is soaked. I cast my mind back to the beach at Langkawi, when you walked up the beach from the sea, your breasts proudly visible through your T-shirt after a swim in that warm water. You are just as beautiful now. Nothing has changed and I still want you every day —although my body cautions me to cool it! You still have that wonderful elegance, square-shouldered lightness of being that tells me you will never age. You have kept your sparkle, your inquisitiveness, your creativity, your 'can do'—when I haven't figured out that you plan to do something differently and better than I had thought of. And you still know how to lovingly deal with my quirks and annoyances in ways that leave us both laughing and loving. I cannot imagine any ending, only your eternal embrace.

23

I pick my way through the brambles and brush aside branches and tall grasses. My jute-soled shoes are wet through as I tread softly through the undergrowth. My legs are scratched, furry little seeds cling stickily to my shins. The air is scented and clammy. My shirt is running with sweat. I found a small forest just a few minutes' drive from the house, and now I am the intrepid explorer, miles from anywhere, hemmed in by green, no sense of direction save for the sun glimpsed through the canopy, and my watch, so I can relate its position to the time and guess my north. There are no paths. No one comes here. Nature owns the land and the air. I am a foreigner. And then I see it. A small clearing where the broad-leafed trees have denied seedlings an opportunity to crowd out their territory with a thousand lesser species. A place of peace and shade. Quiet, once I stop trudging forward. Moss and sand; rocks and exposed roots are the only inhabitants. A world on pause, regardless of elsewhere. Its own meditation, claimed through years of diligent growth, safely locked away from all activity beyond its own stuffy stillness. A place to hear the sounds of the rock, the stories of the roots, the settling of sands blown in from continents afar. A place to sit in full contact with the entire mass of this planet that these roots and we humans cling to for fear that we disappear and mean nothing.

24

I switch the fan on again and open the skylight a bit further. It's a routine I seem to have adopted once I have completed a section or a colour, or I have re-defined a shape, or I simply need to step back and contemplate. Luckily, the paint dries quickly with the additives and the heat of the day, but I always need to get rid of the fumes. I have a love-hate relationship with those fumes. I know they are not good for my health, but they are also a reminder of the earthy artist I have become. Nothing plastic or chemical about my work. It's all done with materials that are as close to the earth as you can get. It's also the reason why my sophisticated clientele love the work that I do. These are people who have nothing to prove. They are not flashy, just richly educated, sensitive and great company. I take in the work from a distance. Trying not to think. Just being with it. A movement on the monitor in the corner catches my eye. The gates are opening. I wipe my hands and walk out into the sunny courtyard just in time to see your bright yellow bug of funkiness—your C1—sweep into the driveway and circle to a stop by the front door. It's a move you've refined over the years. Fast, confident and timed to perfection, you stop firmly, inches away from a large plant pot I strategically placed to protect our flowers from your F1 tendencies, should you make a wrong move any time. But, of course, you never do. You smile—no, beam—at me as you get out, knowing full well I was waiting for a sickly crunch. "How did it go?" I feign relaxation. "Fine!"

25

There are many values of black and white. Seen one at a time, they are simply accepted by their names as absolutes. They are either black—or white. But when you get to work with them, they are very varied, and they fulfill many different purposes. It's the same with silence. This place has taught me subtle differences that exist as what we call silence. I am experiencing one of those this evening. There is simply absence of noise—which can be empty, even scary. Add peace and it can be a huge relief. There is the silence of the mind, which is so elusive and that we misguidedly chase down in meditation until we understand that we simply must surrender. Then there is the silence of nature, which is what I am experiencing now. It's a very loud silence, yet a profound one. If I listen, as I sit here on our balcony, this silence is speaking to me all the time, caressing my soul, feeding my imagination with its rich murmurings and gentle songs. Accompanied by warm breezes, sweet smells of herbs, flowers and trees, the taste of salt on my lips, the flicker of a candle's flame on the table beside me. And, above it all, the delicious knowing, as I glance towards you, soaking up the stars, that it also carries our richest, most powerful, loving communication with such purity and simplicity, that even to say "I love you" is as unnecessary as it is true.

26

The creation of an abstract is a complex business for me. Today, I got started, after days of reflection and consideration, scribbling down thoughts and ideas, trying (and trying not to try) to achieve some intuitive connection with what may be subject matter; curbing emotions, generating emotions, stretching beyond tired old concepts of shape and colour, emptying my mind of things seen, other art, great works of the past, searching for a new voice and a construct that speaks clearly and powerfully in non-words and deep emotions. I start with a blank canvas and a mess of imagery on paper on the floor. The white is oppressive, so I have previously washed it with what I believe will be a complementary colour to the image that will evolve. I scrawl the basis of the form or arrangement in charcoal, in swift, broad strokes. Step back, drink some water. Face the other way, watch the image in the paint-spattered mirror across the studio. Be careful not to edit or 'tidy up', but see it for what it is, with its comfort or discomfort, aggression or reassurance, balance or disturbing vertigo. Whatever. I start to think how I can work with this and, at the same time, get out of its way so it can emerge in its own way. I mix colours, precisely, intuitively, in varying volumes. A palette develops as its own artwork. I choose a brush and start.

27

How do I measure it all? Shock, intrigue, alarm, love, inquiry, impact. All the qualities, as well as a binding relationship that I seek to imbue my work with, are all abstract. All mists; uncontainable, indefinable, amorphous. It's so much easier, and in some ways more attractive, to hit for the base. Go for the obvious, strive to strike just a little beyond the cliché. Because, if I go too far, the audience reduces to a pinhead, and the haystack is huge. Then it becomes a task of mass communication before that little pinhead sees daylight again, and I stack up a complete sewing kit in an over-stuffed studio of unknown mysteries that even I forget. The heart, the clear place, the fine point and the strong message is an elusive and time-bound thing that may work one minute and be lost in the pandemonium of existence the next. So, is the answer to produce quickly, manically, and expose immediately; hoping that eyes coordinate minds and hearts before the moment is lost and as energy and money are exchanged? It seems we have no time to digest, ponder and meditate on a piece that has taken days, weeks or months to prepare while somehow maintaining the original measured emotion. And so I continue my search for a universal language in art.

28

Where did the past go? Our visitors keep me lightly tethered to the world. I'm a helium-filled balloon, most of the time, dancing in the breeze, enjoying the view, just occasionally looking down. What was it that kept me so low down for so long? I listen to their concerns when they arrive, see the tension in their expressions, their movements. I feel their victim mentality and I don't want to go there. Selfish? I don't think so. They are here for something else, something better. Not an escape, but a deep transformation in themselves. It had taken a while for us to reach this point, these universal realizations, this lifting of our souls from all the madness that had kept us bound to simply surviving. No one goes back in the same state of mind. Hearts open. "She's incredible." Someone sits at the table beside me and puts their plate of food there. I look up. I don't really know what to say. Of course, I know you are incredible. I have lived with your incredibleness for so many years that a simple "Yes, she is," or "I know" is just not sufficient. The transformation of our lives, under your guidance and wisdom, has been something that there are no words for – or to say them would take a lifetime. But there is a part of me that needs, wants to stay in this world because, from this standpoint, it is indeed a truly magnificent place. I don't know how long I have left to love you, but it feels like the beginning of a perfect eternity.

29

I always remember, from when I was a teenager, my cousin was at college studying architecture, and he told me something really interesting. It was that one of the best parts of the course was where they talked about designing feelings into buildings. What was the sensation you would experience in a space? A good architect designed this home. It was as if he'd had us in mind right from the initial site survey, through his inspired scribblings, to the finished haven of peace that this now is. This place FEELS like our home. I remember the huge relief and knowing when we first walked in. It was as if we knew it already. It was as if IT knew US! And then a skillful and sensitive interior designer had known how to enhance that feeling, what furniture to perfectly occupy the right spaces, what parts to leave open, where to hide things away in enclosures. There are just the right spaces on walls to fill it elegantly with an ever-changing tableau of canvases, and there is still space for extraordinary sculptures. And then there is the gorgeous light. Casting sunlight on a mobile vista of shadows and colour as it weaves its lazy way through the day. And the evenings, when the light takes on its cozy hues and defined focus, its gentle flickering and calm highlights, in ways that define anew the areas and rooms, matching our relaxed moods, meals and whatever reading we may do. Every day, pictures of you, placed and posed in perfection.

30

When I look at you, I feel whole. In this instant in time, that expands infinitely beyond the crude limits of physicality that wants to confine it to a moment that will pass sooner than I can register it with my mind, I see you. A snapshot, held forever, stored somewhere inside the extended me that has no limits, it is there, and always will be. This delicious fraction of the whole that I record has a beaming smile, sandy hair fluttering across your forehead, touching an eye, abundant freckles cover your tanned face as you turn your head, shiny with the sea, little rivulets running down to your neck. Our eyes meet. "Lewee…" You've done it again. A new moment. Do I have the storage capacity for yet one more instant? Of course I do. That's the miracle of now. No photos, no clinging to past memories, no yearning for then or when. Just now. With you. And it is all-consuming. I can hardly move or speak. Intense. Beautiful. Is this why we are here? To truly experience this?! I can hardly believe my luck. Thank you. Thank you. Whatever impossibly strange and gracious being or thing or accident of circumstances made this moment, I thank you. And I spend more and more of my time in this moment. Flying high in a sort of universal connection, but also being here, as a true observer, detached and yet my body and mind are somehow participating. Everything changes all the time, yet, somehow, the universal truths are constant as the colours swirl around them.

31

We'd given visitors a lot of thought before we moved here. We were aware of the serious addictions they would have when they arrived, but we were often pleasantly surprised when they left—which some had, just today. I opened the main gate, which automatically unlocks the phone box as well, to check it again. A traditional red phone box. I brought it from London and had it fully shielded, and kitted out with power plugs. This ensures that no cellphones enter the property and they could be fully charged when their owners leave. As usual, there was one still there, left by an owner who had no further use for it. This place opens people's eyes again—to nature, to being present, to themselves. These are the lucky few who have the realization and come seeking help to get their lives back—to get themselves back. Cold turkey never tasted so good after a few days of your care and understanding. As the techno-madness increases, so do the requests for help, because more and more are being affected and are feeling it. I remove the battery, bin the phone and walk back into the kitchen where you have your hands in a salad, mixing in wild strawberries and herbs from the garden. "Look at the miracles you perform," I say. You smile coyly. You KNOW how good you are, but you are still too modest to fully admit it. It's so, so wonderful to see you shining like this, and so perfectly healthy and strong. Our hearts fill as we eat.

32

There were always so many images of you that I wanted to somehow capture, and now I have the opportunity to at least attempt it. Even on a daily basis. I keep the small digital 'sketching' camera close by a lot of the time, and spend hours sifting through the images on my computer, always looking for those magical moments that somehow work. Trying every day to stay open to new ways of seeing, new moods, new compositions. Drawing every day. Making fresh marks and letting the work develop. I have let go of the idea of progressing in my work—as an intention. I can see it happening with each new piece, as the work gets more and more personal, and increasingly energized. And there is so much of it! Photos, drawings, lightly scribbled in seconds or poured over for hours, paint thrown at the canvas with new passion. I even find that the proportions and details are becoming more accurate, more fluid. And the less I think, the more it comes. Yet there is a thinking process going on somewhere. Thankfully, it doesn't burden me now. In the same way that the mechanics of mark-making, and the decisions that I have to make, seem to flow from me now, I can relax more into the moment, and the energy of what I am doing. Letting go of the spectre of end results and flowing with whatever comes. And, all the time, I am so grateful for this place, the way our lives turned, all the good in it and, especially, my muse.

33

It's amazing how we are all communicating—all the time, even without realizing it. And it's not just us. Everything does, in its own way. What is the sand telling me? We think we are so smart, but I cannot tell you that. And when we don't understand, do we listen harder, look for signs or ignore, perhaps with contempt, as I know I have done in the past when another person has not made their communication clear, or when their words are unwelcome, as in so many e-mails. But sand, and rocks, and grass, this pen (well, maybe that's obvious!), the table. I have no idea. I could easily say, therefore, that they are not communicating. They are inanimate, of course. Yet I have seen the energy, the connective universal consciousness that binds everything into one. So it's reasonable to assume that communication is here. Surely it has to be, in order to connect. It's easier to understand when I look at my art—an inanimate communication—or a book. Or watching birds and animals and, especially, Jake, our dog. Another language, supported by my own, that has developed into a complex, deep understanding and relationship. Through touch, as well. I wonder, then, if everything that touches another is just as much in communication as I am with you. It's a mind-boggling concept but one that is manifest throughout nature, perhaps best demonstrated by a tree with its roots in the soil and its body in the air. We are all conduits in the whole.

34

Gurus ain't what they used to be. Time was, they resided in mysterious, not-easily-accessible places, where they received seekers of truth in quietness after long and eventful journeys. And the seeker would have realizations about the journey that got them there, and they would already understand the teachings they were given along the way. And there would be reverence, silent respect and misty landscapes viewed from the tops of mountains, stories and artefacts that had real meaning. Contrast that with today's gurus, the 'successful' ones plying their trade through devoted and well-paid teams in ever-larger halls, ever-more high-tech. Lots of air punching, slow waves, teary private revelations on show to sway the crowd—a crowd drawn there through social media, advertising, air travel, endless e-mail streams and the trick of high-cost commitment. "This isn't for everyone." "You must really want this." Seduce and entrap, assisted by the devoted hysteria of those who have convinced themselves. I have always felt uncomfortable following the crowd that has been magnetized by hype, however clever. Surely the truth doesn't need all that, and forums to discuss it. The truth, surely, supports itself. And it cannot be complex, intellectual or a process that takes years; or it cannot be universal. Just as any religion cannot, in itself, reveal the truth, through divisive self-interest. The truth is that we are all gurus—if we want to be. We are all magnificent, and there is nothing to sell.

35

This is how 'going against the grain' really pays off. We did it! You did it with your commitment to consciousness when all the world wanted to talk about technology. I did it by imbuing my work with consciousness and rejecting the high-tech art movement for an immersive physical experience. Some said I was falling behind the times; others that I was a sentimentalist. But none of them knew what was really happening inside me and my work until they saw it. Then the few could not wait to own it. But we weren't ever really 'going against the grain'. We weren't rebelling. Well, not in the conventional sense of the term. We were searching, discovering, getting back to the truth of who we are in a world where insufferable pressure is brought to bear for everyone to comply. The political and economic systems, the education, the media, the technology and the chips embedded everywhere. Somehow, amidst all this, we found some reality and, because it is now so rare, it shines out in the world. Many people, although they are attracted by it, don't understand it or know how to find it for themselves. They haven't made our journey, preferring instead to stay with the crowd, dipping in from afar, every now and then, living in a duality that gets more painful each time they taste the truth. I am so proud of you. I am now proud of me. Despite all my resistance, all my previous conditioning, everything, you stayed true, with me, loving me so magnificently into our beautiful paradise by the sea.

36

There's a deep, primal satisfaction that I get from all of this. I think they call it a paddle. The broad, flat wooden spatula that I slide into the hot clay and brick oven just outside the back door. It scrapes over the surface. I dip my head and peer into the glow, locating the loaf—as much by its delicious smell as by seeing it—and I push the paddle underneath it and slowly draw it towards me. The long incision you made in it before we put it in here is now spread wide over the loaf's bulging golden surface. I carefully lift it onto the rack with gloved hands and bring it back into the house. The table is set, the rich aroma of coffee wafts from the kitchen. Eggs from our chickens, tomatoes and lettuce from our garden, bread mixed and kneaded by your own hands, fresh from a naturally heated oven. The perfect breakfast on our long wooden table, in our own beautiful house. It makes a man proud. More than the trappings of wealth and the social status that is so often sought, the empty highs of meaningless things; our table is born of love, and that love is the root of all good. And I cannot believe my good fortune that I have been blessed with so much of it. Who would have thought, given the way we are conditioned to crave expansion, wealth, status and stuff, that a simple loaf of bread would come to represent the pinnacle of achievement, and that love could be the only thing that provides the perfect expansion to fill me up.

37

I've never been much good at remembering names of plants but I really should look up this flower. It's stunning, like a bird of paradise displaying its colour and exotic design with such pride, with its flash of orange pointing into the distance, swathed in a blue collar and surrounded by the perfect green enclosure, all mounted on a gracefully curved yet sturdy stem. And I am in awe of the way nature trumps all our attempts at emulating its beauty. What is the point, anyway, of trying to paint this? Yes, I can make a hyper-real copy, with embellishments, perhaps. And, yes, people may be impressed by the skill, and amazed to have this small fraction of the whole brought into sharp focus so they can stop and begin to actually see it. But what then? No, I have to keep exploring new languages to create my own beauty, my own terms of reference. And all I can do is silently ask for help. I cannot think it into existence with a mind that is so cluttered by what has gone before and the crude network it has built to keep me captive. I must use other faculties and then, somehow, draw down into the physical that which cannot be known or thought. And, then, will I know it when I see it? Will anyone? I am guessing that we all have that deep connection to it, deep inside. I'll know. In fact, that is where I have to start. I know. I thank the flower and, with a renewed sense of calm, I walk back into the studio and start again.

38

I open another bottle of red and dig a San Pel out of the ice. I pause to look back from our kitchen to the broad deck where everyone is relaxing, chatting happily in the soft glow of the lights. Alfonso is gently strumming his guitar. Abby is gently swishing her skirt to and fro to the rhythm. Greg is quietly beating rhythm with the maracas. I consider, for a moment, that I might get my sax, but think better of it. It would dominate, changing the mood of conviviality on the deck. All the snacks on the table have been pretty much devoured and the energy is a little more subdued, but very happy. I glance over at you. You raise your fizzy grapefruit drink to me and mouth something at me that I don't quite get—although I know it is a lovely sentiment. I mouth back, "Go on!" You turn away, grinning, and carry on talking to someone close by you. The sparkle in your eyes makes me think you just might. But it's never straightforward, however much you may feel you want to enjoy and show your amazing talent. I watch you. Golden shoulders, beautiful neck, hair swept up to keep you cool, always smiling in elegant conversation. Then you turn to Alfonso and touch his shoulder. My heart skips a beat, as he starts to strum, and you lift your head, close your eyes and sing us to heaven.

39

You are lying on a white sheet that covers a firm mattress. Naked and oh so beautiful. After completing several quick sketches, I've set the easel where I want it. I take one last walk around you, taking in all the angles, striving to fully understand the three-dimensional aspects of this pose, so that when I take up charcoal and then brush, I fully understand the seen and unseen. I am a bit nervous at this beautiful moment. Stage fright or something like it. It feels like such a huge responsibility to honour you and all that you are, with pigment and oil on ancient thread. But then, I remind myself, as I lay down the first bold strokes on this unknowable journey, that I can really enjoy this process. Flow with it. Flow with you. Sure, there will be challenges, but no suffering. I used to believe that worthy work only came out of struggle and that joyous work was somehow lightweight and not as worthwhile. Not now. Not with you. Now I can combine the joy with the artistic value, in ways that I could never have imagined when I was younger. There's the key. The years passing have been my rite of passage to a new level of awareness and practice. Age does bring benefits! A lifetime with you has been and continues to be my greatest gift. You are my rock, but a rock that is so light that it floats in my hand. I see you lying there, but what I see transcends the physical form, way beyond. And that is my challenge. What it comes down to is that this painting is simply another way to love you.

40

I realized, today, that I have no real sense of history. Living here, I am living now, and building a future. I also realize that whole chunks of my life have gone from my conscious mind. Irretrievable. Does it matter? What does our history represent? I find that, while I love old architecture, the art of the past and some objects, I don't crave knowledge or experience of them. I love the new equally. History is just stories, to me. I think that, sometimes, we search for clues and truths about ourselves that are related back to us through stories. But that's all they are. Stories. What I crave, and what I am more and more present to, and what is real to me—is now. That is what I strive to make better. Each moment. Each sparkling, incredible, mysterious now. Seamlessly following one after another. And does any of that matter? Probably not, but it is what I have, and I have been blessed with you and all of this to enjoy. So, when I start a painting, it is an infinite process because there is no time. It's a magical state of being that somehow intertwines the physical act with feelings, sight, shape and form, materials, the turning of the world on its axis, light and shade that inform us of place and the natural rhythms of which we are all a part, and the sounds that form the musical backdrop to our lives. And, always, in this little existence of mine, this rolling, cascading, impossible, ravishing, exotic ride, there is your smile that washes over me. A heavenly tsunami.

41

I stand up for a better view as you open the heavy wooden door down our stairs to the beach. It's a lovely crisp morning and you've decided to take a quick swim before breakfast. It's a particularly enchanting time of day. The air is still. A seagull perches nonchalantly on the wall near me, sniffing the air, scanning the horizon. All is quiet, save for the gentle lapping of the waves on the shore. Even the sea is resting this morning. I smile as you emerge onto the sand. You wear your bathing cap and nothing else. The last vestige of a restricted upbringing, soon, I suspect, to be abandoned as well. Of course, there is a reason for it—to protect your hair from whatever… But it is so gorgeous to see how you have freed yourself from everything, how you have grown so confident—yet without ego, and so sensual, yet still with your innocence and delicacy perfectly intact. I watch you as you walk your beautiful walk to the water's edge. The years haven't touched you. If anything, you just got better. Stronger, somehow more powerful in your presence. You rose to the challenges gracefully, and the fame and the media attention didn't spoil anything about you. You test the water, crouch down and push off, gliding effortlessly and efficiently as you breast-stroke to and fro, knowing I am watching. I sip my coffee, slip off my bathrobe and head down the stairs. Your gift to me this morning will be to simply stand in the surf and make your gorgeous way back to me on the beach.

42

There's a little eddy of dust in the corner, on the floor, being brought to life by a breeze blowing in from the sea. I see it because this is the time of day when the house is brightly lit by the sun rising on the horizon. A huge warm yellow orb lifting itself weightlessly from the ocean to start the cycle again. I glance across at you, perfectly upright, lotus position on your burnt-orange yoga mat. I close my eyes but the glow persists with pinks, oranges, dissolving patterns on the inside of my eyelids. I rein in my thoughts, but all I do is give way to something bigger. It seems to be unavoidable but, then, this is why we do it. A few feet apart yet joined in the most fundamental and awesome ways, we begin the morning's journey—inside. At times like this, I feel intimately included as a part of everything. In fact, I am not sure where I begin and end. The boundaries dissolve into irrelevance. The shadows dip down the walls, carefully caressing my eyelids until the cool blue brings peaceful timelessness and the breath merges with the rhythm of life, within and without. I am on the edge of this fantastic globe as it curves and rotates through darkness and light and everything—ridiculously, wonderfully, incredibly happening. Through life cycles, love and hate and everything in between. I am one of the fortunate ones. So, so fortunate, to know I am truly part of this incomprehensible beauty, forever held still, yet travelling with you, the love of my life.

43

I still don't understand why we have to go on such a long journey only to arrive back at the beginning. As I massage your scalp, working the shampoo suds through your hair as you bend over the edge of the bath, I marvel at your neck, your shoulders, the ever-gentle presence of you. And I am truly here. Not thinking beyond, or into the past or future. All the same, pictures still swirl and butt into this exquisite experience. There was that other time I did this in a darker chapter that you went through, yet still I felt the same love, tinged as it was with fear and sorrow. But all that is past. As a child, I can still remember this kind of presence of mind—the smell of spring grass, the taste of new potatoes, the pungent aroma of sage on a Greek hillside. So many forgettable experiences that somehow keep their place in my psyche. And now this. Again. But new. Because this has never happened before. And I wonder if it will stay with me as those other gifts did. I let it go. It will be as it will be. This is beautiful right now. I look down at you, blond hair on golden skin, as I shower away the shampoo. Water on your skin. Always a feast for the senses. A riot of passion passes through me. I keep it in check, with loving consideration, but keep it there, sliding my hands over your silken skin, just in case you feel it too. We keep growing in love, and I have come to understand its delicate sensitivities and teasing clues, its humour and lightness and passion in you.

44

I love oil paint. I didn't realize just how much I love it until recently. I lay down a broad area of cadmium red. Just for the satisfaction of seeing it light up the canvas. Next to it, the deep blue block throws it into sharp relief, intense and guttural in its living enthusiasm. The brush squishes over the surface as the canvas gives slightly under the pressure, receiving the paint into its weave, absorbed by the gesso surface I rolled on and then sanded down to a fine stipple. Is this process about creating an image? An illusion? Something that represents something else? No. This is about my love of oil paint. (How can anyone truly love acrylic? That is beyond my comprehension. Plastic is dead. Just showy. Not of this world. Not of my world.) I wipe the brush and stand back. Contemplation. Trying not to rationalize or judge, design, arrange or tidy up. Just be with it. The paint is as much, if not more, of the active partner in this. I simply apply it, sincerely and with some hope. It radiates and gives back as I respond in a dynamic dance of effort and emergence. I am given this painting as much as I create it with intention, love and little else. And if I interfere, I know it will stiffen, become lifeless, because I would suppress its life in attempting to supplant it with mine—my ideas, thoughts, reason. If I had applied that way to my life with you, what kind of journey would it have been? As it is, each has fed the other, and I have been gifted the perfect existence.

45

Someone, somewhere in time, decided that this balmy day in February[9], this blip on the arc of time, each year as the earth took up its position, is when we express our love for whoever is the most special in our lives. I wonder why and how you could only dedicate one day per year to this essential, life-giving activity. Especially when that expression forms the background music and the foreground, in-your-face, perpetual game of ping pong played with kaleidoscopic laughing balls every moment of every day. I wonder, as I scribe words in the sand with a stick, if that is why you and I enjoy ping pong so much. "To you" and "back at you!" Over and over again. I look up and see you. Isn't that incredible! I write 'Olga' in the surf. It stays for one wave and is given back to the sea. I look up again. You are still there. Even more incredible! That's what I love about this. Whatever we write, however we express ourselves, it passes, dissolves, moves on. It gets interpreted, reasoned, thought through by minds that are forever moving, dissolving images and words that it processes and mainly forgets as the world and our needs scramble for attention. And they have chosen just one day to give perfunctory attention with commercial icons to the one thing that is constant in our lives – in my life. How ridiculous! I scratch your name again in the sand. It disappears, of course, but you – and love – remain.

46

I remember expending vast amounts of precious energy in being somewhere else, doing something else, not being present. That seems to be the education we are handed down. Strive, don't be content with what you have, what you are. That is not enough. You are not enough. You have potential, you can do good, get more, give back. Why are we taught this? Rather than appreciation, love, relationships, truth? Yet, among all the rushing to achieve and survive on a higher physical plane, there is a natural human quality that begs attention. Rich people often return to it once they have ravaged the planet and exploited whatever they can do to achieve lofty status in the eyes of others. Now I see why I was confused for all those years. Spreading my resources, dispersed and lost in a battle that, quite honestly, didn't interest me. Accumulation. I think I was clever enough to do that, if I had wanted to but, as they say, my heart wasn't in it – and it wasn't in my heart. Mutually exclusive worlds. So, to at last arrive in this eloquent stillness, intact bar a few physical nagging conditions, I feel I have achieved what many may envy. I have somehow circumnavigated a lot of the madness with my heart intact. I am younger than my years and so looking forward to every moment with my even younger wife. Two kids, playing in the sand, expressing our energy by expending it only on what we truly want to, and on what we truly love. A wonderful ending and a magical beginning.

47

I don't think we will ever be able to appreciate the true nature of energy. What is it? How does it transform and how does it ultimately balance out in the universal scheme of things? On a rare cool evening, I am sitting by the log fire, watching the flames lifting from a log in momentary yet unique patterns. No two are exactly alike. What are they? What are those yellow and orange tongues that can consume everything? I could not even lift the amount of dense wood that it takes to provide heat for just one evening. Wood that took decades to grow, ring by ring, withstanding the seasons and harmonizing with natural energies and events to become tall and strong. Only to be cut down with machines, sliced up and delivered to my door to give their all to keep us comfortable. All that will remain of the many cubic metres in the woodpile will be a few bucketsful of ash, to provide protection for growing potatoes. And so the cycles continue. A seed, a tree, warmth, ash, food, us. What real and useful part do we play in all this? What do we do to return the favour of warmth and potatoes without bugs, that have cost an environment-nurturing, shade-giving, carbon-dioxide-converting tree its existence? I do wonder, sometimes, if we are the most useless, ignorant and destructive species on the planet. So, I am grateful, when I am conscious of this, for everything.

48

Birdsong. First thing on a sunny morning. An orchestra of difference where the land birds meet the sea birds for a joyous chorus. I watch the sky above our vegetable patch as I cut today's lettuce and gather sweet-scented fresh tomatoes. The little land birds darting here and there, settling on branches, full of twitchy energy and bursting with song. The sea birds, soaring high, fluttering and adjusting to catch some lift, swooping, calling—somehow more businesslike and purposeful. I am grateful to be seeing, hearing and fully experiencing this. Too much of my life it has been a background that I ignored in my mad dash to fill a bank account, on the ever-elusive path to what they called financial security. Yes, we live in a cocoon, these days. And I am proud of that – that I achieved this with you so we can live protected, in touch with it all. It's hard to believe that we lived so long in the numb world, the dumb world, and that it took so much focus, intention and energy to simply get back to reality, nature, truth. I have come to the conclusion that most people are blind. You can see it in their eyes and the choices they make in life. Such a shame. So many of us led into living a life in a disconnected state that is dressed up to look so attractive, so compelling and true that it is not questioned, even when it is painful, wasteful, pointless. And I could never even start to convince most of them that to pick up a pen and describe on paper the curve of your body, is just pure heaven.

49

"This is how you buy fish!" I say, with a flourish, as I swing the coolbox off the dock and into the boat. "Ya!" You smile down at me and I reach up to give you my hand and help you climb down. The sun is behind you. You reach down and, in that moment, a deep, luscious feeling washes over me—it almost punches me in the chest—almost primeval, animalistic, urgent. A wonderful realization—that I have more and more, although it is like new every time—that I have you. I HAVE you! Please let me keep this second for a second second, then a third. It's just so delicious, I never want it to pass. But it does, and the miracle of it is that it is followed by more. Abundance is just that, after all. The universe just keeps giving. Then you are in the boat, steadying yourself as you find a place to sit. And, as you do, you gift me with such an exquisite, beautiful, delicate smile, that I just want to ravage you there and then. "We did it!" I say, keeping my emotions in check. You laugh and dip your hand in the cool water. I yank the outboard motor into life and we putter out of the harbour, seagulls darting about us, sensing our fresh cargo. Past the sea wall, the water is a deeper, clearer blue with gentle waves nudged by a cool breeze. I open up the engine and we surge forward. In a few minutes, we'll see home around the headland. As we thwap, thwap, thwap across the waves, my attention never leaves my mermaid sitting at the bow. Gorgeous!

50

Food doesn't travel. I've always felt that. Ever since I experienced the difference in food prepared in, say, Italy, when I was in my teens, and the same food prepared in England. I now know it's true. We live in a world of instant satisfaction, sophisticated international commerce, pre-packaged convenience and mass production, but nothing matches picking your own food from your own garden, having planted it, nurtured it and watched it grow. Whatever comes via that route is always healthy, always naturally in season, always fresh and so much more tasty. Loving what you put into your own body, with confidence and the satisfaction it brings, even beyond its value for your health, must be good for your spiritual existence. It's officially winter now, although the seasons are not so clearly defined here. I am kneeling in the soil, my knees sinking into the soft cool of the land, and the parsnip I am easing from its place gradually reveals its shape, size and length. Surely, this is more of a religious experience than any you can get in a church. The emergence of a living, growing being from its nest of earth that has, over several months, somehow configured this incredible vegetable and brought it into being. And all I had to do was push seeds into the soil, keep it watered and weeded, and wait for nature to work its magic. I look around at the abundance of plants that are simply growing and giving us their best. My head is swimming as I bring this gift into the kitchen to show you. "Look," I say, "a parsnip."

51

I just have to wonder at the power of words, thoughts, intentions, focus, visualization. When I think about that power now, as we sit together on the deck, simply looking out at the beach and the sea beyond, I am struck with the realization that those things are, in fact, more powerful than 'things'. They are the most powerful things in the world. Because they are the creators. They are the magical tools we have been given to craft our own reality. Why were we never taught this as children? Or were we? I remember, in my life, when that connection was broken, leading me on a long and wild journey of false hope, broken promises and false gods. A journey that I suppose I had to take, to find my way back to truly appreciating what really makes this world tick. My education for life got twisted when I succumbed to a fear-based reality that was not a reality at all. Words, thoughts, intentions, focus, visualization—all so much more solid than the second-hand notions of our weak captors. For me, art was always the true path, but fear took me elsewhere. Because art is a vehicle for all those real things, and my only hope for the life that I now lead. Just one minute of that realization, that practice, that satisfaction, makes the whole journey worthwhile. Now it is so strong in me that the negativity has been banished from my presence. I glance at you and I am transported by the incredible being that you are, just as I should be, for all of it.

52

We stand a few feet apart. 'Close but not touching' comes to mind—the instruction I used to give to my typesetter before the days of computers, to describe the spacing I wanted. The painting is eight feet by eight feet. I think I have finished it. It has taken a while, because I had to use the hydraulic platform to reach parts of it. It's a nervous moment for me, waiting for you to comment. Even after all this time, all the success and critical acclaim, your first word is the one that makes all the difference to me. I have learned, though, that I don't need to go into panic mode if that word is anything but wild enthusiasm. I don't need to search your face or analyse any hidden truths that you may not be telling me. Partly because you say what you feel and partly because I have learned to accept that you simply don't like EVERYTHING I do, and that has been an important development in me growing, as an artist. I have to be free to do the work without any hint of co-dependence causing me to edit. That freedom, after all, is what I am delivering. Freedom from concepts, judgements, expectations. New ways of seeing that may shock, anger, disappoint, love and so much more. I watch you—taking it in. Your body language and expression give nothing away. My heart warms as you tip your head slightly to one side. You're teasing me with your declared neutrality. It is all that I can do not to come over to you and wrap my arms around you. I ask the banal question to distract myself. "So, what do you think?"

53

"I should be working." I used to say that a lot. Yes, I remember that now. But I am working. I'm always working. But perhaps I need to re-frame that according to current circumstances. The word 'work' carries with it some pretty negative connotations; some guilt, maybe obligations, duties, a heavy weight, perhaps. It's hard to remember now, because, for me, working equals enjoying. So, of course I always want to work! What else would I do with these long elastic days of sunshine, sweet scents, good food and nature? You work all the time as well. I see it in the early hours as the orange light creeps up over our bed and into your dreams. I watch you then. Your hair tumbling down your neck, the gentle heaving of your chest under the sheet, the manic business of your twitching fingers. Whole novels in the making! No wonder you yawn when you wake up. Even from the bed to the coffee machine, each step is a new idea, a new painting. Maybe 'work' is the wrong word and it has transmogrified into 'function'. That I still function is a miracle indeed, and that I can still paint, walk with you on endless beaches, enjoy food and wine and deep, searching, hilarious, creative conversations with you—for that, I am eternally grateful. I now know why I used to find subject matter for painting so confusing. Time and space and our environment are so impossibly confusing unless you see it through the lens of love.

54

I feel as if I have been learning to let go all of my life. There is only one thing I cannot ever let go, and that is you. It's been quite a journey. Even before I met you, I had let go of the things that most would regard as essential—a home, some sort of regularity in life, many possessions. And it was only in shedding those things that the truth started to emerge. After the initial shock, there was no sense of loss, just a vague recollection of things that never brought me joy anyway. Often they brought the opposite. And, as we have travelled, I have released the notion that things are important. As we crossed the Atlantic many times, releasing, accumulating, releasing again, I gave less and less importance to the tangible, and more to the intangible. The intangible became my reality and what I valued most. And here's the kicker! As soon as I had that realization, I started to accumulate more than I had ever done before in my life. This beautiful house in this wondrous place and everything that we have bound by these smooth white walls and the environment beyond. Ironic. But now we are accumulating beautiful things with so much joy, as well as discernment, humour and enthusiasm. It has become a wonderful process now that my perspective is true. And that creative dance that we so enjoy has become the song that we live by, with every moment we live filled with contentment, satisfaction, laughter and deep fulfillment. And now we can truly say, "That was easy!"

55

Rein them in! Rein them in! Even here, I am occasionally plagued with mischievous thoughts, spectres of guilt, doubts, anger and sadness. The prattling monkeys appear at the most inopportune times—often when I think I am doing my best to ignore or suppress them—meditating, cuddling, walking, cooking, tending the garden. At least now I can live with them, in the little cage I have built for them, where I can keep an eye on them and not let them out to interfere with our life the way they used to. I also choose—I don't let THEM choose!—how I ignore them. They laugh and say I should get spiritual, meditate, do yoga. But I say, today, for instance, I'm taking a drive into the village, so suck on that, monkeys! I press the button for the hood. The roof unfolds like techno-origami and disappears under its cover behind me as the wind deflector silently sits in position to keep my orange hat from flying off. I rev the engine—so smooth and growly—and there's a satisfying crunch of gravel as the tyres gain their grip and launch me majestically forward. I swing onto the road. The monkeys can't keep up and I leave them behind in a cloud of dust. With my sketch pad on the yellow leather seat beside me, I cruise towards the village, and the dock, and the café, and the friends I have come to know and value so much. It's good for me, and I am so glad that, in removing the monkeys, I have also ascertained a wonderful day for you as well.

56

I really appreciate the luxury of being offline, these days. To re-connect with you, with me, with nature, with my art. And I am so glad I have been able to carve an existence that demands less and less of my presence in that other world. It used to be that luxury meant having all the tech. Now, the new luxury is being free of it. How stupid we have been as a race, to not see that—that, after so many millennia, we have learned so little about the true nature of things, the true nature of us and of life. For years, I felt like a square peg in a round hole, and definitely in the tiny minority. Now, I just don't care about all that, because I know what I know, and even if it is no one else's reality, it is certainly mine. Some may call it madness. I call it happiness. And I see my reality reflected in your eyes, in our love, in everything. Sometimes I want to shake the world of people, shout and try to penetrate their profound deafness. But I have tried that, and they still cannot hear. So, now, I paint, and those whose eyes and ears may be tempted to open can see what I am doing. I hope that doesn't sound arrogant. I do love people and I continue to learn, every minute, just as everyone does. But I imagine if you have trodden a path for so many years, you do get to know it a little. My art is certainly an imperfect voice, but it is the one that I have been given, and I offer it with sincerity and passion. The online world is a screaming, empty space that we were never designed to exist in. We can do better.

57

I understand Stanley[10] a little more now. Well, actually, a lot more. Why he drew his family close and hid away behind electric gates, containing his creative resources in his own compound, maintaining strong boundaries and being careful to only let good influences in. Being a powerful creative also makes you vulnerable, delicate. Other people only see the effect you create and may have little or no idea of what it took to create it. Being a powerful creative means taking on the feelings of others and presenting back scenarios that reside in the public subconscious, often blocked out and, more often than not, not fully formed. That's why, when a piece 'works', it hits a deep nerve, beyond the realm of the conscious mind, sometimes going to the very core, connecting the dots that we prefer to leave swimming free, in chaos. And that work takes a very special presence of mind that requires a certain distance, separation, exclusion, purification, certainty and risk. I understand that now, thank you, Stanley. If I had not seen it in you, I might never have craved, visualized and manifested this, our gorgeous home. And what were the chances, I wonder—they must be in the millions to one—that I would find and marry the perfect partner, who would truly see me, and want for me this perfect space, that also allows her to flourish. It has taken us so, so long to begin, but now we are truly on our way!

58

My mind roams free. Sometimes, it can be a bit disconcerting. Other times, it leads to magic. I am sitting on my favourite rock. Perched a few feet above sparkling pools with their crabs and other sea life, washed by the eternal rhythm. I am thinking of the names of things and how we have an inbred imperative to name things. I wonder where that came from. I can see where it got us. Naming, then remembering, then using that information that is born, gives power to the bearer over others. And so we evolved, from earliest cave paintings and the birth of language. But it is all illusory. This rock is still this rock, whatever that is—I may never know. All the beautiful flowers you have planted have names we have given them, but their names don't change anything about the experience they yield. In fact, I think that names can distract our minds, making us lazy in our observation and deeper experiences of life. I see this most in terms of visual memory as I draw the rock beside me. I struggle, with each glance, to convey through my eyes, into my head down my arms to my hands and through the pencil onto paper, the true nature of this rock. It's just a rock, you may say. Yet it is so much more than the name conveys. If you truly see, if you can see, if you take time to search with your eyes, with your whole being, at the depth, the mass, the life contained within it; the massive energy and weight, and then the ever-changing light on its surface, the myriad colours and shades, you would be in awe.

59

Freedom comes in many guises. I suppose we all have ideas of what freedom is. For the oppressed, it is freedom from oppression. For the lazy, it is freedom from work. For those in toxic relationships, it is escape. For a privileged, fortunate person, today, freedom has just let herself in the front door. Clara. I don't think she sees herself as a liberator but, in sacrificing her time for some money, she gives us freedom to break the routine, release ourselves from cycles of cooking, cleaning, refreshing our home. She gives us the freedom to explore, create, be children again or simply do nothing. And I am so grateful for that. Grateful for her, for our ability to pay her, and for the opportunities she presents. Not only that, she is a wonderful person with a sparkling personality that brings its own richness and joy into our lives. What, then, shall we do with this freedom today? There were times when such a choice felt like a burden, a confusing combination of possibilities that it took me some time to process so that I could make a 'worthwhile', 'good' or 'responsible' choice. In my mind, freedom was limited—something I had to grab when I could and ration my time to show my appreciation of it. But freedom is none of those things to me. Not any more. Right now, at this moment, as the sun starts to flood our bedroom and the sounds of the sea beckon us to a new day, freedom is to sit astride you and tickle you till you beg me to stop.

60

What do you change, and what do you keep the same, in your daily life? I almost said 'daily routine', but stopped myself just in time. Rich, successful people usually have some thing or things that they cling to, believing that what they have discovered is key to their success in their mad scramble to make a mark in the world. So, is it true? Or is habit simply a way to make things easier, take out some of the thinking involved, remove creativity and stick to a formula that will move the needle incrementally upwards? I find that, once I get into a routine, I start to dull down, to suffocate. Predictability is boring. I guess that someone who's driven by expansion and the measurable evidence of effort is turned on by that. I am driven by the ever-changing dynamic magic of existence, the eternal newness of things. I guess that is why I was never cut out for a career in one thing, and why art is my saviour. Risky, dangerous, unpredictable, passionate, unreliable, yet totally dependable. If I am not learning, not stepping into unknown territory, I am simply going through a process, making my technique ever more sophisticated, pleasing the ego. Sometimes it is frightening because there are constants in my life that I value so much. I am thinking of you, our relationship, our social code, if you like, that could be broken if I go beyond—should I ever be inspired to do so—and I do not please you. It's a balance, a habit in some small measure, not to keep the same, but to grow constantly. That is what I choose to keep the same, but nothing else.

61

I start, but I have no idea where I'm going. I start AND I have no idea where I'm going. There is a world of difference between those two sentences, and it only takes one small, three-letter word to make that difference. That word exchange is one that I have been conscious of making over the years, and it has made all the difference. It has helped me to throw off the old negative family conditioning that kept me trapped for too much of my life. It made the difference between being blindly confused as to why my life was always a struggle (while others seemed to cruise through it) and simply being there and enjoying it. I guess it's the fear that made me want to seek safety in strategies and plans. Now I know better. The first broad strokes come from a place I have yet to connect with for this painting. They come from a place that knows, so who am I to dispute them, or worry them, or try to make them look like other than they are, or tidy them up, make them more acceptable? Just as when you walked through that door at the auberge, I accept, with a sense of grace and excitement, that new discoveries, new experiences, new joy and more, are all being delivered to me with an exquisite perfection that my mind will never fully understand, and that I can only be with, accept or reject as I wish, but knowing that rejection so often means loss, and a closed door to what might have been had I not let my ego dictate. So, this new painting is, yet again, the start of a new and magical journey with me constantly present.

62

After all these years, you still don't really get it, do you. That's a fact that perpetually amazes me, but that is also one of your abiding and scrumptious qualities. You are beautiful. You always have been and you always will be. And not just in my eyes. The others feel it and see it, but don't say it as clearly, up-front and personal or plainly as I do. Maybe it's that family thing that gets in the way—when someone close to you gives their expert opinion, it's less believable. Or maybe it's simply self-image, innocence or delicate nature that clouds it for you. And, you might say, what are you supposed to do with that information? Just enjoy it, and let it inform all that you are instead of suppressing or hiding that quality that is bursting out for all the world to see. Celebrate it and value it. Let it in. When I see you and I tell you, it is no idle compliment. It's a rush, a deep realization, a tsunami that hits me full force in such a way that I have to express it, just to take the pressure off a little. The words, I know, may sound crass, manipulative, pathetic, but they are all I have—apart from my art. Forgive the inadequacy, the lack of poetry, the lack of sophisticated and nuanced word skills, and please just accept it from me, try to understand where it comes from, what drives it and how hopelessly lost I feel in the face of it. It is what you are, in every sense of the word and every aspect of your being. You are beautiful.

63

Digging deeper. That's one option. Numbing out. That's the other. I choose the first – the rockier path with highs and the occasional low to give the highs contrast, value and appreciation. You walk ahead of me, metaphorically and physically, on the cliff path. Up here, the air is clear, the wind presses your T-shirt against one side of your body, flapping slightly on the other. You occasionally grasp your hat with your right hand as wisps of your hair curl and tangle. And, through all the turbulence, there is that wonderful walk. All energy, smoothness, sensuality, athletic. It's a walk that employs your whole body in a subtle orchestra of movement and easy coordination, just as it always has. Down below, the eternal sea washes onto rocks, perpetually caressing the land with mighty motions. Seagulls and other birds circle above the spray. "Look!" You spot another sandy cove further along. And I know, in the way you say it, that, in 15 minutes or so, we will be scrambling down a steep path to discover its hidden secrets. You lead, I follow. I dig deeper now, conscious that my legs don't work quite as well as yours, but knowing I will be there with you, on the soft sand, as we curl our toes in the surf and talk about some new and amazing project. Just like we always do. Digging together and, then, after a whole load of work and preparation, releasing another precious gift to the world.

64

There's a different kind of silence as I come in from the studio for a break. You are not in the living area or on the balcony, but it's okay. This kind of silence—a calm, almost palpable one— means you are talking to a client online. Giving, giving, giving of your wisdom, caring, understanding and love. Changing someone's life for the better, for ever. It's still just as remarkable to me now as it ever was, the way you do that with such grace. This house—our house—has gained a frequency all of its own, an energy that people remark on whenever they visit. They feel it too. Shoulders relax, people breathe, they look a bit spaced out. They don't want to leave. There are times when we smile at each other as we gently ease them out the door. Your work, your presence, my art, our nest-building over the years have created a haven of peace and tranquillity that is somehow ancient, somehow filled with all the best that a human can be, can feel and can manifest from the heart. We love it. We appreciate every moment of it, we revel in it. And we also share it, because the more people feel it and experience it, the more they can find their own way to it, and own it for themselves. Silence has so many colours, so many heartbeats, so much richness and so many flavours. We have worked so hard to let go, if that is possible, and most of our time we limit our silent time to the best of those qualities. It's what we love; it's also our responsibility to ourselves and others.

65

I had so often wondered what it felt like to have certainty, solidity, confidence. Like a successful person. I bumped into it so many times in my early life, but less as I grew older. Maybe it was simply the experience of living through all the twists and turns and bumps along the road that showed me that so few people actually have that. Even for the seemingly rich, life is precarious, simply because of the precarious nature of its foundations for success. Sometimes you can even see the fear, the child, through the veneer. Now, I am one of those people that others see in this way, and I feel so grateful that I now understand the true nature of success, and where the certainty, solidity and confidence reside. All of this runs through my brain simply because, as I have a drink on the terrace with you, some young technicians who are probably earning far more than I did at their age, are overhauling the wind turbine. I see the envy, the searching, the innocent questions in their brash comments and nervously confident conversation. They have a handle on things, they know, but something inside them understands nothing of all this impossible complexity called life, and they have a deep yearning they don't know how to fill. And so the cycling continues. New souls, old souls, all grappling for the key, learning afresh the wisdom of ages, silently screaming for help. Don't ever believe that what you do is not the most valuable gift ever.

66

Today, the courtyard is full. It was just too nice a day to stay indoors, so the whole group took up their drawing implements, their donkeys and stands, and sunshades were raised, forming a soft warm glow beneath them. Our model is in the shady bit near the wall, under the wisteria that tumbles from it. The gate is closed. No traffic today. I arrange my course notes on the table by the studio entrance. You've provided drinks on the trolley by the front door. The stage is set, the model explores the space and thinks about poses for this day's exploration. My students quieten down as the energy stills and all we hear is the birds and a faint rumble of breakers beyond the wall. What a heavenly situation we have here. I glance at their faces and I can see they feel the same. The magnificence of our natural surroundings, a haven of peace that wraps itself around us, a beautiful, creative and skilled model. All willing conspirators in a brand-new creative process—because that is what it is, every time. There are always the unexpected twists and turns, revelations, surprises, highs and lows, struggle and the ease that flows like a universal gift when we learn to let it. Now. Only now can it happen. Only now does it exist. It almost makes me laugh out loud that we spend our entire energy looking for the present moment. I challenge them with yet another way to go and find it.

67

My father was born well over a hundred years ago. That fact suddenly astonishes me as I prepare to welcome three new young artists into the guest suite. You are talking with Clara, arranging flowers, making sure that everything is perfect for the arrival of these young souls. I am sweeping their terrace and imagining the evenings they will spend there—laughing and discussing the day or doing whatever comes to mind now they are away from home in this special place. It can be intoxicating for young minds. Each time they come, I am given new realizations and affirmations that the journey we take them on is the best possible thing for them at this delicate stage in their lives. I still remember the period of disconnect, and the separation I felt between myself and younger people as their world diverged mysteriously from mine. And I appreciate the effort I made, with your wonderful help, to get myself back—to reconnect with me and with everyone, in heartfelt, genuine ways. The disconnect that technology brings has been brutal, ruthless and non-discriminating. Now, many more are aware of what it has cost us and where it is leading. How it has taken from the souls and hearts of human beings, while masquerading as progress, convenience and even survival. It is a masterful deception, sadly without a master, and certainly not a wise master. But here we are, in a little bit of heaven, serving humanity one soul at a time, and bringing ancient wisdom, creativity and love back into their lives.

68

That we survived is remarkable in itself. That we now flourish is a miracle that is not lost on me. If we had had an outward focus for those crazy years, when the pressure on everyone was mounting, even though, in many ways, it was not apparent to many, we would not have emerged from this unscathed. I think of boiling frogs, and how the industry and governments get people worldwide to see increasing limitations on their liberties and humanity as a new normal. Exercise that kind of process over a long enough period, and it is, indeed, normal for those who have known nothing else. Add to the mix a carefully orchestrated media control, and the only information people receive is what is intended for them by those who disseminate it. But this story is an old one. The book, 1984, predicted it, as did so many intellectuals and seers over the centuries. Why, I wonder, are these people not heeded, when the perpetrators of these crimes against humanity are so obviously actualizing their predictions? All I know is that, on the fringes of society, there are people like us, here and there, who are rejected by the main stream and ignored as not being worthy of their attention as we have lost credibility for them. Thank goodness! And, now, we are free to happily live out our days in our own way, our own home, and in love.

69

I have always been mystified by the rarified worlds of high art. Yet there is something attractive about them for my anarchic mind. The opera, with its extreme voices and devoted followers who tend to be in a clique all of their own. Similarly, classical music, in big concerts, staged on open-air stages where the extremely comfortable and the aspiring extremely comfortable eat and drink with the knowing smiles of peer recognition. And, of course, art. The mysterious and the beautifully produced, nestled in the best galleries in the best parts of town where the moneyed gentry mingle. Some art is clearly passionate and born through years of development. Other art is carefully worked out, intellectually off-beat, usually with long commentaries behind perspex, on the wall next to them or in an expensively produced catalogue. I cannot take it all in. I cannot, often, even appreciate some of this music or some of this art. But I am fascinated, nevertheless. Perhaps it's the dynamic that fascinates me, more than the work; the carefully orchestrated presentation, often negotiated and planned years in advance over crisp linen serviettes and sterling silver cutlery. I have never been a part of that dynamic and now I would not want to be. Age, the passing of time, the disappointments and achievements leave me just dealing with me and what is in front of me now. And that, I find, is the best dynamic there is.

70

So here I am, walking with legs and feet around a miniscule part of the circumference of a huge ball, with the love of my life. We are walking on sand, in the midst of a stunning sunset. I am pondering impossible things for my mind to comprehend. The world, the universe, infinity beyond and within, probabilities and possibilities. What the heck is going on? Why am I? What is all this? And, even given that it all exists, which is just such a vast concept in itself, what is my part in it all? I block out, neutralize, blank the vast majority of it as my little brain cannot go there without blowing all its fuses. I am led to abstraction in my distraction. The whole thing is just too abstract for me. So, I am guessing that, in order to fully represent, express this whole mystery, I can only truly do abstract paintings. All I can do is chip away at tiny, insignificant bits of it and try to see, be enlightened in some small way. Try to escape the vastness of time and space and, just as a photograph captures one random moment, try to be present and do the same. But how do I do that for long enough to paint a painting while everything is changing all the time? I have no answers. Yet, somehow, in the midst of all this, I do have an answer. You. And there's another conundrum. To be with you, I have to be with myself—strong, certain, commanding, gracious, loving me, capable, present, with seniority. And so we walk this sunset, as always: individuals held together by the perfect elastic loving band.

71

I wonder if a vision can ever have a finite end, a complete realization and resolution. Now that we are living the life we set out to live all those short years ago, now that we are in our own home of our dreams, is this where it ends? No. I think that once you are a creative person, or a person who is fortunate enough to realize their own naturally creative nature, or a visionary, you never retire. You never put the slippers on, feet up and drink cocoa for the rest of your life. It goes on. Even if you are not fighting or being an activist, one is always an advocate for all that one believes and wants and craves for themselves and the planet. What is my vision now? I suppose many would see it as sentimentalism, backward thinking to an idealized existence that was never there. So, let's move the vision forward, where we have personally and spiritually grown out of the childish, destructive wants and desires of the techno- publicity-, advertising-, social media-, corrupt-government-driven world. The consumption-driven, expansive, greedy and depleting model has to break down since it is upsetting every human and planetary balance that ever existed. Those balances were there for a purpose, to allow us to continue, enjoy and grow in a paradise of incredible beauty, together, in love. That is my vision now, naïve as it may seem, because that is the only world that is, in truth, worthy of what we are.

72

A scruffy little dog sits near our doorway to the beach as I sit, leaning up against our wall, taking a break to fill my lungs with fresh air. He shivers, oblivious to my presence, looking intently at some distant point. It somehow feels significant. I can feel it in my chest. What is he thinking? What experience is he having in his continuum of days and nights, busyness, eating, crapping? Maybe scrapping. What makes a moment like this feel significant in some way? Why does it move me, stir me, still me in an effort to locate it and maybe keep it for a moment longer? Some are obvious. You stand facing me, smiling, naked, fresh from your bath. I explode inside. I cannot resist. Others are more subtle. You've left a coffee on the table for me and gone back to your office. It's in a mug from Langkawi[11]. The years evaporate before my eyes. A deep history of love, a shared journey resides in that moment. We are walking along the beach. I am troubled by some event or other. I feel your hand reach mine and gently grasp two fingers as we walk. And I am suddenly home, complete, breathing, universal. So we sit, this dog and I, sharing the stare at some distant point. Each with our own thoughts. And, in that sharing, I feel a connection. I wonder if he does. Preposterous to imagine, yet knowing we are all connected, everything is connected, why not? I glance across at him for something I can interpret as a sign. He ignores me, sneezes, and bounces off down the beach.

73

We have never liked clutter. Inevitably, we have some in our lives but, these days, we diligently remove it before it becomes a constant, unseen background. To some, I am sure that our home looks Spartan. To me, I celebrate open spaces, clean lines, good design. It helps me appreciate light and form as shadows move through the day and give way to our carefully placed lighting in the evenings. And I can appreciate more the dynamic shapes of people and things as they relate to and move throughout our environment. To truly see you, for instance, as you live in our spaces, is a privilege indeed—untainted by complex backgrounds and distractions. For me, in such a place, the present comes to the fore, in sharp focus, in such a way that it demands attention and invites respectful interaction, rather than presenting reminders of a dusty past, camouflaging the present in echoes and totems, icons and sentimentality. This was an unexpected benefit of our dislike of clutter—or was it always the driver behind it? We are already complex enough. I have spent the past two weeks with you in the studio, simply trying to get to grips with painting your lovely face. It seems like an impossible task. There is so much to see, so much to get down, and so little of it in the photo reference I took. I get frustrated. How can I possibly reveal, in one simple image, all that I feel, all that has happened, all that you are, to me?

74

Intellectually, I know that time is passing. Emotionally, spiritually, it doesn't. There is no time in spirit. Thank goodness for that! Days and nights pass but I stand still, just as I always wanted to. No more journeys of the mind and heart that stress and strain my systems. I have arrived where I want to be and have no intention of changing a thing. Yet, in this place, there is nothing but movement. I call it progress. A creative, exciting journey that occupies my whole being, perfectly. I realize that our wonderful home is the physical manifestation of this way of being. The culmination and realization of the vision we held in our hearts and minds for so long. What a miracle it has turned out to be! No more questioning. I now understand 'commanding' and 'seniority' in such profound ways. Everything has become hyper-real, somehow limitless and universal and truly connected. The words I use here cannot really describe this state, because it is beyond words. But all of this occurs to me in an instant—as long as I stay with it, and don't think it. You move your hand an inch across my chest. My awareness shifts and I am brought back – not that I have really been anywhere. I feel your breath, again and again. This amazing intimacy fills my heart, nurtures me like nothing else. And I fall into a heavy sleep. I dream, yet the dreams are what I am living now, with you. The boundaries blur, but the breath continues. We are living a sublimely beautiful life.

75

We're still risk-takers. We still love intellectual, probing conversations, taking things further, staying outside the box. It keeps us young. That and our love, singing, dancing, long walks on the beach, loving in creative ways, creativity, gratitude and so much more. The list is too long, so I am just talking about our creative conversations for now. Even that thought makes me smile. That we have a long list of all the things that make life wonderful and that we still make the effort to keep it that way. Not for us any moronic retirement, slippers and going gaga in comfy chairs. There is no 'old people' smell in our home. No medicinal support equipment making its sad institutional presence felt. We are too young for all that. Our life is all about colour and energy and creativity. And creativity doesn't get any easier. It probably wouldn't be so satisfying if it did. It would take on the dull routine of technique and shallow appreciation, easy point-scoring. An empty build-up of meaningless library of stuff for the sake of appearances. Not for us the smug satisfaction of the easy win. Not that we make things difficult. No. We just love the adventure. If life is just bean-counting, what is the point? If it revolves around completing each day with a neat conclusion, with everything neatly filed away, why bother to wake up the next day and do it all again? Yes, there are just so many reasons for us to be grateful, that I might be writing and discovering and creating and loving it for the rest of our lives.

76

I feel I am meant to be thinking deep thoughts, clever thoughts, wise thoughts. I am a mature man, after all, with something of a reputation with various groups of people around the world. It was hard-won—although, if I am honest, all I was doing to earn a sort of distinguished status, was having some fun and doing what I really wanted to do. Yet, here I am. And there is, I suppose, some equity there that is worth maintaining and/or expanding. I have to leave that to others to do, these days. The young, the urgent, the serious people who take it all seriously and make valiant efforts to make sure that my investment in them as gatekeepers and trumpeters is worthwhile. I can only hope that they also enjoy doing it. They seem to, or I would not be working with them, but you never really know. So, you are chopping onions in a bikini without the top bit. It's such a hot day. My thoughts have banished themselves to another planet where they can be worthy without me having to listen to their prattling. I am 100% consumed, so they can take time off, for all I care. I am just all eyes and feelings. Yet it feels more important, if that is the right word, even—as I said, I cannot think right now—to simply be here, with this magnificent scene. Definitely another one for the recipe book. After all, it's not just about the ingredients, as we know, it's also how it's all put together.

77

It's getting harder to find a piece of open road with no speed limit, cameras or radar. Maybe I'll have to find a racetrack. Just once, I'd love to find out what the Aston is capable of, and live to tell the tale—without a ticket, a ban or jail time. What is this desire for speed and performance? And I'm not talking straight-line pedal-to-the-metal here. That's for Americans in muscle cars. There's no interest in that for me. No, it's all in the handling and the skill—reading the road, compensating, anticipating, smoothly riding through the twists and turns with maximum efficiency. There's something delightfully satisfying about that and, after all, that is what this car excels at. I don't want to be a doddery windbag who can only show off such high-tech sophistication at a car show on the château lawn on a Sunday. I want to really drive the thing, be a part of it, use it for all it's worth, heat the disks to a glow, blacken the wheels, scuff the tyres and play, in perfect balance, in natural harmony with this beast. There is risk, I know, and my faculties aren't as sharp as when I was 20, but we all need to reach for the highs now and then, touch the stars, feel the surge and the rush and to know that I can say "I did it!" means something important, however silly that may sound. But living a life of caution has never been my preferred mode, so I once again embrace courage.

78

I often wonder about my place as an artist, and what I do. It was a watercolour painting, done by someone else, hanging on a kitchen wall, in a simple wooden frame. The painting was nice, naïve, warm. But I felt that its presentation didn't do justice to the artist—his skill, experience, the care he imbued this painting with. Low self-worth or simply economic limitations? Uncertainty of a sale or lack of care for the journey the painting might take. I imagined the painting in a gorgeous frame and multiple mats, giving it space, focus and respect. Singing its real value and pushing it way up there in terms of its appreciation. Would that be manufactured appreciation, or was it truly deserved? We behave like this on so many levels. Relationships, self-love, courage and hopelessness—all vying for breakthroughs and a chance to be somewhere better. It has taken me a lifetime to reach a point where I can be happy with at least some of my work. And I still get confused and blindsided by people's appreciation. I still try to find the real source of it. Is it simply because I am so well known, or are they connecting with the work? Is it the marketing or is it the image? I have to let it go and come back as quickly as I can to us, our home, our haven of peace to regain some clarity and connect with love again. And nature, and all that is true for me—never mind anyone else. Sometimes I feel I am only just surviving, but in a different way, on a different plane. But I would not change it for the world.

79

We did it! The vision held, and now we are here. Proof of our faith, our strength and perseverance. Yet, was it really us, or simply our connection, our asking, our knowing that all this was there for us, should we choose it? It's hard to know. And, anyway, why bother to re-think it? The fact is the fact. The vision became more real than whatever we were going through at the time. And we did it ourselves! There was a merging—not a point, specifically, when we unconsciously left behind the teachings, the books, the celebrity gurus, and simply did it ourselves. It was a subtle return to the subconscious, our bodies, our senses and spirit. A knowing is the only way I can describe it. It had no sides to it. No smug satisfaction, no fear, no needing, no entitlement. Just pure knowing, in peace. A lifetime searching for the switch that would turn on the flow of the universe and, when it happened, it was so quiet and perfect that, if we had been thinking it, we would surely have missed it and blundered on, searching for something unknown and wrapped in perceptions, thoughts and emotions. An imperfect thing sought out in an illusion of perfection that didn't even come close. I watch you, square-shouldered, leaning gently on the balcony wall, your hair touched by a light breeze. My angel in white flowing linen, set against the blue, the infinity that connects everything in its paradoxical emptiness; and all I can say is: "That was easy!"

80

I sometimes reflect on the imperfection of art. Its inability to be dynamically changing and in a constant state of evolution—as the rest of the world is, and as we are. The time it takes to produce a piece, freezing an experience, a thought, a construct, is in itself a challenge. To keep the energy fresh as I go. I guess that is one reason I have moved towards abstracts, for most of the time, as they allow space for evolution, more so than representative work. I see a lot of highly representative work following a sort of fashion or trend. Semi-naïve, big blocks of unnatural colours. And there's the political aspects that weave their way in—black people, indigenous and more. But I also see a healthy embracing of a wider cultural base that threatens the monetary values on big-name works and introduces fresh thoughts from all corners of humanity. So, people are finding hooks, as they always do, to define what is good and current. It still, even though this is an evolving environment, contains creative concepts in recognizable boxes. But, then again, sometimes that is helpful as too much choice can be overwhelming and confusing. So, where does that leave me and my work? In the same place it always has. Like any artist, I simply have to stay true to my own evolution. That may become a popular source for buyers. It may not. But my own journey is what it is, and it is all that I can do.

81

I even love it when it rains here. There's a sweet smell in the air. Water on hot stone, water on soil, on trees or herbs. So many scents for the senses. And, of course, there's a whole new vista in a storm. Dark clouds majestically, heavily, slowly moving above our heads and as far as the bright yellow glow on the horizon. They look as solid as the earth itself. Tumbling, shaping, opening and closing as they drift purposefully inland, stirring up thick grey waves beneath them, mysterious as an ancient homily that pounds onto friendly shores without fear or judgement, sifting and cleaning the edges of the land, cascading wild exotic sprays on the rocks. On days like this, all I can do is stand and watch in awe, as it speaks to me in deep resounding tones of its presences, its stories, its power and love. I am so small in the face of this riotous behaviour. Soaked through to the skin, stunned with admiration. What am I, what can I do, other than be a delicate observer? What has man ever really achieved? What is our place in all of this? The wind stings my face with fine droplets. I remove my clothes and surrender myself to its rough caress. I am silent, mute, subject to all that ancient anger that surrounds me. And I am grateful, yet again, for all that this is—this fantastic mystery, this incredible manifestation that shares its life with whatever I am, with its infinite energy, just for us.

82

We are at a turning point in our existence and nothing will ever be the same again. We cannot return to what we regarded as 'normal', as it was precisely that 'normal' that was the problem. And these statements are true, every day of our lives. That shows us what our impetus, our mode of existence, has to be. It has to be creativity. There is no other answer. Unless we embrace creativity every day, we are succumbing to a way of being that destroys our spirit and neutralizes our souls. Because the way we are designed dictates that we move forward, learn, experiment with a good and sincere heart. There is no other type of progress, and we would be fools to think there is. In a way, it is obvious, what I am saying here, yet we have so much in us that simply wants to stop, keep the success we have found, hang on to and repeat experiences that gave us comfort or joy, in the hope that this will be enough to sustain our psyche. But it never is. Second-hand experiences, repeated highs are only ever a poor sequel to the initial event. Who are we kidding? Not ourselves or anyone else. This is it, folks. The time is only now so we are compelled to think anew, constantly, and push ourselves beyond our comfort or coping zones, and really discover the best, the most amazing, the unexperienced fantastic potential of who we really are.

83

What is my vision now? Do I just stop envisioning? If I do, will I stop? The mind is a tricky adversary. It has me thinking all sorts of nonsense in ways that I cannot define what is nonsense and what is not. I guess that is the normal human condition. Now that I have everything I could possibly want, where do I go from here? Do I become some self-satisfied, boring retiree? M&S jumpers, beige wind-cheaters, Daks? Meekly frittering away the days in neatly organized routines that fade into a beige of their own? I don't think so. Even though the world would have me toe a predictable line, with marketing neatly organized to appeal to me, in my time of life, based on choices I have made on my recent path—smarmy shit! No, I have to keep going, as far off-grid as I can, to hold on to who I now know I am. They cannot classify me. They should not be trying to classify anyone, if they are honest. We need to encourage each other to find our uniqueness, not all the ways we can fit into boxes. And, so, I live in this charmed world with you, with a vision of growing old in our own unique ways, that may seem outrageous, anti-social, disgusting, impossible, too good to be true—to others. Who cares? The world will never find unity if it continues to avidly promote duality in everything. My vision is to achieve my own vision of unity and, for me, that is found in a constant, unending process of creativity, renewal, discovery, gratitude and acceptance. And I have the perfect partner to do that with, and truly live outside the box until they put me in one.

84

I will never take any of this for granted. How on earth could I, if I am still conscious? From the very deepest, fundamental viewpoint to the seemingly superficial, it's all an incredible story of highly unlikely events, that all melded perfectly together to create…this. The physical is incredible enough, but when you add in consciousness and spirit, it all becomes magical. But then, it seems you cannot have one without the other because, ultimately, they are all the same thing. That's where it gets a bit confusing for my tired and limited brain. I cannot even envisage an infinite space, and that, it would seem, is what we are suspended in, on this unlikely blue planet in an orbit that is perfectly designed to sustain us—if that's what we want. So, I wonder, when I look at the mayhem that we create on this planet, if the leaders, the visionaries, the architects of societies, the engineers of systems and the carers of people—if they ever stand back and just gawk in amazement at it all. I mean, you'd think that any conscious, sentient being would be in a constant state of awe, if they really stopped and simply looked at it all, what is really going on at the larger level, and what we are choosing to do with it all. I consider myself one of the extremely fortunate ones, to have been given the opportunity to glimpse this, and have some inkling of my part in it all, now and for ever.

85

It is so important to dream. When I met you, I had dreams that I did not even know were about meeting you. A fortune-teller had even told me, some months before, that I would be happily living with you. At the moment I met you, I was not aware of that story I had been told. And still my dream came true. It seems to me that you can consciously follow up on dreams, with actions, plans and focused intention. Or you can simply let them go. People who find success in life through action tend to think that is the only way to achieve dreams. You have to work at it, learn, mix with the right people, take the right actions. Sure, that will work, to some extent, and some have got where they think they want to go. In my experience, working at a dream distorts or even hides the dream from me, because I decide an outcome that I think I want, rather than letting the universe choose the perfect outcomes for me. Let's face it. I have not the slightest notion of how much abundance is there for me, or what form it may take. And I can only be true to me if I get out of the way so the dreams can take shape, rather than me attempting, without having a clue how to do it, to shape the dream. In the early hours of each day's dawning, dreams come and dreams evaporate within me. I have no control over them or the fantastic images, ideas, scenarios that unfold, perhaps just for milliseconds. So, why do I try to control these things in my waking hours, when the perfect example of how to achieve my dreams is standing right in front of me.

86

I cannot imagine how I was ever able to live anywhere else, if I am honest. I don't think I ever did truly live anywhere else. It makes me wonder, then, what is truly living? I used to find I had to battle inside, to make a huge effort, to be truly present. It seems to be so much easier to do that, here, these days. There was a time, for instance, when your presence would have such a force of distraction, that I would not be present to me at all. I could feel little strands of energy jumping out of me towards you, focusing on the slightest noise, the slightest movement, just the energy that surrounds you. It was lovely, in so many ways, to be so hyper-aware of your presence in all its aspects, but now I know I can have that and be present to myself as well. It doesn't have to be one or the other. And that's the great part about this realization—that if I am truly present to me, I am therefore also truly present to you. It may sound like trying to be in two places at once but, in fact, it is a unity in universality that is better than the flip-flopping and trying and confusion that caused so much tension in my life—and yours, because of any uncertainty. Now, the drama is in its right place: on the canvas, in the books, in the exercise and elsewhere, where it is not contained and controlled, but free to play its proper part in my life. I watch you constantly, inside and out, and I know that, in everything, we are truly living the vision we always wanted.

87

As we moved further from society and more into our own world where we choose, when we want to be, and to invite others in, I see we have taken on, more and more, classic male and female roles. It had never been a conscious intention at the outset, to do that, but I am happy that it has happened. There must be something in our DNA, right at the very core of what we are, that makes that the natural way to be. I guess that is obvious in so many ways—our different physical make up and functions being the most visible. It just goes to show, as well, how far humanity has strayed when civilization brings about a desire and even an imperative for sexual equality in ways that we are not designed for. I'm not talking about injustices, but the skewing of the natural order through 'politically correct' imposed behaviours and other head-based ideas that have been layered on top of the balance that was originally there. There was a time when the feminine was sacred, before the male became fearful of it. I am so grateful to see the sacred in the feminine and to admire, respect and love it. For without that sacred aspect, that all-powerful, creative, nurturing, wise and beautiful aspect, we men would surely be no more than animals. One can see, when that recognition wanes in, perhaps, old and battered relationships, or high-pressure work situations, or whatever, the spark of life leaves. So, my love, stay powerful, celebrate who you are, always, as I do.

88

It's been gratifying to see, having stuck to our guns and kept our vision to the forefront, how art and writing have taken on a deeper significance in our visitors' lives. They are, to my mind, the lucky ones. At least, that's how I feel about us. So many have lost the art of communication, and of making things with their hands. A whole generation has grown up with the technology of communication, but with none of its beauty, subtlety, art. They live in a world of auto-correct, auto-translate, emojis, acronyms, bad grammar and very limited vocabularies—never to explore the poetry of language, the beauty of well-crafted expression, the richness of feeling and breadth of meaning that it can imbue life with. Those who value it have, for the most part, been sidelined and marginalized like elders of a tribe that suffocates as it is driven out of existence by the gauche, the loud, the crude and the clever. And the thumbs of the masses twitch as they watch others with detached, bemused admiration, as they employ all their digits in creative activity, music, art, making things that their own addled brains could no more concentrate on for more than three minutes, let alone devote days, months or years perfecting. What an incredible thing we are doing in our home, nurturing whole human beings to be the kind of people who will truly enjoy life to the full, and thereby contribute qualities to the world that are being lost every day, but that truly define our humanity.

89

To keep moving forward, against the tide, can be a lonely activity. When one is creative, not following trends, how do we even know where 'forward' is? All we have is our own certainty, our own sense of adventure, our own uniqueness to guide us. I love oil paints in a world that favours plastics and other artificial substances and media. Does that mean I am stuck in past idealism? Like a Teddy Boy in the 1990s? No. It means I have seen that there is no end to the creativity enclosed in a simple, natural, ancient tube of oil paint. The fear of becoming an irrelevant old fool, that I am sure many have, is removed by passion and making the effort, continuously, to stand alone, in one's own space, proud yet humble, clear yet knowing nothing, still yet searching voraciously. "Never stop," my trainer used to say at the gym, when he saw me resting after a set. "Use different muscles, but never stop." That makes so much sense to me now, as age brings with it the ever-present temptation to pause, just for a minute, but then longer and longer, and the spark of daring, the excitement of jumping off, fades into a false comfort of rest. The decline, where I would no longer contribute, no longer have the will or the temptation to find my way around another corner, step into another darkened room and find the elusive light switch, have the courage to make love to this unpredictable mistress called life, take the neatness and throw it off the cliff, be the incorrigible disrupter, be worthy of you.

90

Whatever your opinion of it, whatever form it takes, art is honest. What you see is what you get. And what you get from it is whatever it is. I cannot 'sell' art. That's why the practice is such a lottery. I cannot persuade someone that they have sufficient feeling for a piece that I can convince them to buy it. It's ironic, in a world where whole industries and governments spend all their efforts on selling—whether it's a paper clip or a space program—that the artist is sometimes seen as the rogue, the charlatan or the fake. That an artist who puts his heart and soul innocently (or otherwise) into creating that which inspires or stimulates thought on the state of our world, of people, of politics—whatever—can be the target of such criticism, is alarming. Yet it is also obvious. Because 'selling' is built on a lie in so many cases, because it is based on manufactured need or manipulation of perceived need—often on the part of both parties—the truth is unwelcome. And art is truth. Even bad art, if there is such a thing, is truth—a real reflection of a state of mind, an ability, a life's experience and understanding. Even highly structured and intellectually-based clever art is truth. It all fascinates and awakens something in us. So we must stop shooting the messenger, for he reveals the heart.

91

Sometimes I go too fast. Sometimes things happen too fast, people talk too fast. What is the pace at which we are truly designed to work, I wonder? Or is it that I have slowed down as I got older, my brain functions not able to process information so quickly? Or is it that I now have so much information in me that each new input from my senses has to somehow jostle for a place in the crowd and it takes more effort to make the right neural connections because of the multitude of routes that each new event could take? Why do some people's conversations feel like an onslaught that I want to escape from, while others can feel like the very lifeblood of my soul that keeps me alive and enjoying it? How much processing happens with one single light touch? I try to put these things out of my mind as I run a finger over the surface of your back. A touch so light that it is almost not a touch at all. And I try to move my finger smoothly, and as slowly as possible, because I know, from when you do the same to me, slow is still too fast. Forever is just about right. Yes. And to move my fingers over your back can take an eternity, if it is done right. You lie still. Half awake, half asleep, yet every pore of your skin under my finger is having a party. I watch its slow progress against the warm shadows on the balcony, under the gently flapping canopy. Past the plant pot, blurry in the background, along the bright-orange towel you lie on. Three seconds of heaven. A timeless universe for us.

92

Where am I? If I stop to think about that too much, I could easily panic, or get so confused it would disable me until you brought normality back; the familiar, the anchors that keep us all tethered to the ground, perhaps. A cup of tea, some homemade biscuits, something that needs to be done, a cuddle. All signs that there is some sort of order to all of this. Why is place and a sense of it so important, anyway? I think of it less, now, but when it comes, I scramble to get myself back to the seemingly familiar. I wonder if all artists have that same fear of flying, fear of floating away with no controls. Cutting the cord. I wonder if they hang on through complexity, realism, process or whatever their drug of choice, just in case they lose it. Making your technique the rock, keeping it and developing it to ever loftier heights, is a mark of safety. And it can be so time-consuming and demands so much attention that it removes whole chunks of time and attention so that other thoughts cannot impinge. The devil is in the detail. Absorbed by it, it keeps you in the illusion of safety. In that case, why constantly seek creativity? Most stop at the point where sales are solid and the wine flows with reviews, and agents feel safe with repeatable products for clients who demand the same but different but the same. Where am I, in all of this? Untalented? Clumsy? Problematic? Insignificant? Alone, yet gloriously connected to everything.

93

I'm reading a book, holding it with my left hand, not wanting to reach the bottom of the page, because that would mean moving my right hand, which is resting on your left ear as you snooze with your head resting on my lap. Trying to stay with the story, but more concerned not to disturb you. I glance down. Your hair spreads out across my legs. Your bare shoulder moves, almost imperceptibly, with your breathing. I feel the contours of your ear beneath the palm of my hand, and the softness of your cheek beneath my fingers. I cannot hear you breathe, but I feel the warmth of your breath on my leg. All is well. All is quiet. I am grateful. This ear, and what lies beneath it, has played such a huge part in both our lives. Our meeting of souls has been strengthened by it in ways that may never have happened, had you not gone through years of pain and anguish, discomfort and sleepless nights. I am not happy about any of that. It grieves me every day, and part of me wishes with all my heart that I could have somehow taken all that dreadful experience away from you. But it is what it is. The past has happened and we cannot change that. But we did choose a wonderful present, much of the time when we were present. And we chose a wonderful future all the time. So, naturally, that has happened. So, I'll stay on this page, this perfect page, for as long as I can.

94

I take three random words. I find myself staring blankly at the outside wall of the studio, having gone out to pick some beans for dinner. Three words that mean nothing to each other and would most likely never be seen in the same context, let alone the same sentence. I contemplate them, absorb them and slowly an image starts to form in my mind. Initially, it is a cliché, something obvious and literal. And I know that if I work with them, they will evolve into something else. I take the beans back to the kitchen and put them on the counter. You are not there, so I don't break the flow. I head for the studio. No, I won't say or write these words. That would bring them back down to where I don't want them. As I walk, I contemplate the meaning of subject matter and abstraction—both words that start to lose their meaning, as I have conventionally thought of them. Subject matter dissolves into a deeper process as I start to lay down some thoughts or images, or non-thoughts and random (can they really be random?) musings. And so the process starts to take those first three words and re-connect them through me to some greater whole where, in fact, all is connected. So the words are simply a starting point. They have no meaning or context in and of themselves, except that they are a doorway I can choose to find a deeper truth.

95

I cut the engine on the van. It's been a productive morning. I'm glad I took the trouble to load up the stuff from the studio and get set up in the early morning on a cliff further down the coast. Sometimes, I have to disrupt myself in order to be disruptive. Escape the safety and comfort of the studio. Challenge myself with the unfamiliar, risk being discovered and talked to as I grapple with the beginnings of a new idea. I never get bored with my work, but sometimes I know I need some sort of considerable discomfort in order to make a breakthrough. I don't think I have to go through the 'struggling artist' cliché, and I don't intend to, but external disruption inevitably causes internal disruption that, in turn, leads to creativity. And having someone see the emergence from a detached point of view—a stranger who leads a very different life—can reveal all sorts of possibilities, as long as I can get my agonized ego out of the way. When the noisy engine is stopped, the silence of the hillside hits me. I get out and lean against the side of the van. In the distance, I see my oasis. A dark green cluster, held in place by a white wandering wall, topped by burnt-orange tiles, glinting solar panels to one side, a static wind turbine. I smell the baked soil around me, and feel like a soldier, returning from a long engagement, changed in some way by the morning's events. A deep peace in my heart, accompanied by an equally deep yearning to be steeped in your love again.

96

Those who end up influencing situations seem to be the ones who can gather, assimilate and take action on information in ways that supersede those abilities in those around them. That's the society that has been born out of centuries of relationships and a universal survival instinct. We are still scrapping in the schoolyard and trying to take advantage of weaknesses in others and in the environment. We're still hell-bent on amassing stuff and comfort at the expense of others. Art and organic farming are two ways we can reverse that trend and give back, exchanging energies in healthy, sustainable ways. Providing food that is wholesome and healthy while at the same time protecting the source of it all—for our bodies and our ecosystem. Providing visual, spiritual and physical experiences that touch our souls and senses, enriching our consciousness and developing our minds and humanity, are the gifts that art brings. We can be expansive, sustainable, highly evolved and therefore peaceful, healthy and super-conscious if we choose to be. If I ruled the world (which I would obviously never want to do) it would be as a servant to these ideals. But, for the time being, maybe I can influence my own small space on this planet, through my art and welcoming those who see.

97

I find I learn a lot from my models. About me, about them, about acceptance, trust, engagement, sensuality and more. So often, it's an unspoken dialogue, a visual and personal one. Just as poetry is, when done best, a beautiful exploration beyond base language, so is the relationship between artist and model. Or it can be an exploration beyond form. I find it fascinating to feel the differences between models and how I react to them. The most classically beautiful can be the worst, and vice versa. The best are those who work beyond a brief, don't need constant arranging, fully accept and are comfortable with their bodies, yet retain an edginess, an awareness of their own qualities, a spark. They are the ones who truly engage, bring an extra quality to the work, who can also discuss and enjoy the fruits of their labour. They are the dancers, the fitness freaks, the healthy lifers. With them, I can expand my work to new heights, and enjoy exploring the body's infinite mysteries. Its shape, structure, colour, consciousness, energy all fascinate me, and I can constantly strive to somehow go further with it. To where, I am not sure and, as a happily married man, I am always battling the tendency to edit, limit and otherwise keep within stupid 'safe' boundaries that threaten to curb the journey. Yet I also know that you would not wish that for me, and that the art must flourish however it will, or it is nothing at all.

98

I have spent most of my life trying to figure it all out, feeling less than and inadequate a lot of the time, because I simply cannot. In a way, I feel sorry for those who may think they have it all figured out, because they are surely missing the bigger picture, or satisfying themselves with a small fraction of the whole, or they have given up and simply want to manage their existence in a way that is acceptable to them and their peers. Now I know that I actually don't want to figure it all out. There is no point in trying and, anyway, that is not the point of it all. If it ever had been the point, I'm sure we would have developed the internal resources to do just that. Otherwise, what is the point of everything that has happened on this earth and beyond for all these millennia? Living here, and having been blessed with you, this life, this place, I can see clearly that it's all about love and nothing else. And that is definitely something I don't want to figure out, and I know many have died trying to. No, there's something going on here that is far bigger than us, far more important than what our left brain would have us believe, and far more incredible than credibility could ever give credence to. So, I just sit back, enjoy, observe, don't judge, be still, somehow get my mind out of the way so I am not thinking about it. Just move with it in gratitude, be real and present—no icons, woosey behaviour, rituals or anything like that – and surrender to the magic surrounding me.

99

I turn another page. It's quite a good novel, yet my own reality is so much better. Raising my eyes just a little, over the top of the pages, opens a perfect vista. Through our glass doors beyond the balcony to the quiet sea, softly bathed in the warm glow of the set sun that slowly sinks beyond the horizon. Sea birds settle, contemplating this view as they do every single day of their lives with their knowing eyes, as they calmly rearrange feathers and shuffle their feet into a comfortable position for the night. Much as I am doing right now. Your leg over mine, gently holding me in place – in the bed, yes, but also in so many other ways. Nobody could write such a perfect novel. It can only be written in the moment, in the ethers, in the feelings, the light, the cooling air, the surge of a grateful breath. It cannot be written down, and that is what makes it so amazing, so true. Man has spent lifetimes trying to pass on intangible, amazing experiences, rich tastes, majestic emotions, the elusive qualities of the heartbeats that power our lives. Just as painters, in their own ways, have endeavoured against the odds, scratching pigment from the earth and trying, with all their passion, to produce a faint approximation that speaks to others with the same intensity they feel in its execution, have also failed. We are so dumb, and our actions so crude, when it comes to expressing the magnificence of a single moment like this, the novel unwritten, as the truly best story unfolds.

100

As daylight starts to flood the studio with muted cool tones, I am fiddling with this and that, tidying up a dead space to refresh it, looking for a tool I put somewhere, months ago, and that I want to use today. All the time, the canvas is emerging from the shadows on the stand in the centre of the room. I glance at it, asking permission to observe the previous day's gestures, willing the paint to be dry enough to add more layers today. It's messy. It's been on the go for a few days now. Absorbing each day's fresh energy, mood, mind, heart—through paint, actions, considerations, meditation, anger, frustration, happiness. What is it? I don't even stop to think. I have to let it flow. Otherwise, I let my mind get in the way and the deeper work is subsumed by clumsy logic. The kind of logic that tells you how to construct, build layers, choose a palette, dark over light or otherwise, create contrasts, draw a line from here to there, mix particular media. I know I can wear all of that in background, automatically. I don't need to be involved. I need to be immersed in some other way that somehow magically arrives and does the work for me, so that what emerges is somehow energized, powerful, moving and has depth that emanates from a different kind of struggle. No, messy abstracts like this do not emerge from frantic, messy energy, but from days of going inside, opening doors, being still, loving light, presence and inspired action.

101

We all need renewal in our lives. For me, in my latter years, it's a kind of reassurance that I AM still alive, that I count, that what I am matters in some unfathomable way. Manuel and I are digging next to the wall. It's a long project. I'm probably holding him up but I want to do it. It's a mark of the time we have lived here that creepers have established themselves here and there, threatening to dig into the wall. They leave ragged, dark marks when we pull them away, their tendrils objecting ungraciously. It satisfies me to do this, and to be in this process of renewal, establishing us, yet again, in our space, as WE want it. We expose the ragged line of paint at the base of the wall, wire-brushing below its boundary and into the bare concrete. We will not only renew, we will go deeper when we re-paint it. My mood lifts with each freshly exposed length of concrete, with each new pile of removed old growth sitting on the pathway. I wipe away beads of sweat that threaten my eyelids. I catch Manuel's eye, we smile and continue in silence. This work feels ancient, constant, like service. Part of the process for every living organism—growth, decay, renewal—in doing this we admit to the beautiful reality, take part in the inevitable cycle that man is intrinsically part of. Cleaning boundaries and respecting them, yet merging with a universal truth. I am grateful for his strength, honesty and our connection, built through the years, with strong boundaries in constant renewal.

102

What is inspiration? I still get confused about that. I produce paintings that feel as if they mean so much each time I do one, yet I don't know where it comes from. You say my paintings are inspired. I feel that as well, some of the time. At other times, they can be a struggle, sometimes my mind goes blank, sometimes I just don't know how to continue, and I freeze. Yet, still, by the time I feel I have gone through enough of a process to declare a painting finished, there is inspiration there. Maybe I think too much. Maybe it's all about play—that activity I dismissed so often as being trivial and unworthy. Maybe the boundary between play and discovery is so blurred that the two merge into one as I work. So much of the time, though, I am scared by time itself. The need to get things done, get a result, have something to show for the investment, can take over if I am not careful. So I have to find that timeless place inside me, where I decide that I am in charge yet flowing within the universal abundant flow that determines, without my paranoid interjection, the marks that appear, the meaning or otherwise that is instilled in a work, the emotion that enshrines the cloth, its surroundings and those who lay eyes on it, and what it gives them or what they bring to it. Far too complicated for me to process, so I might as well not try, but surrender to whatever inspiration itself decides it will be today.

103

If a day goes by and I miss it, that's a tragedy—but not one to hold on to. It doesn't happen often, thank goodness. But, when it does, I resolve to never let it happen again. Clearly, that doesn't really work, as it does occasionally happen, despite my resolutions. Days can be lost in grief, in tiredness, in forgetfulness or argument. The latter is the real killer of days. Anger born out of lack of connection to myself, which leads to unworthiness. After all, if there is no connection to all that is, all that is beautiful, important and real, the corollary to that experience must be unworthiness. How can it be anything but that? These days, I am better at quietly returning to the reality; supplanting what I see in delusory moments as reality, with true reality. And I am astounded, every time, at the limitless, infinite potential of positive experience that there is on the other side of that infinitesimally thin barrier that seems so impermeable when I am on the wrong side of it. Our days are only there to be filled with amazing, beautiful and fulfilling experiences. Why else would all this incredible creation exist? Why would it have come into existence? For us to destroy it? For us to find conflict, unhappiness, pain and suffering? Think about it. That's nuts. So, I have to remind myself every minute, by being present every moment, that each day is a precious gift to welcome with all my heart.

104

It was interesting to see how much of our lives was held hostage by computers and the internet. We are so fortunate, now, to be in a position where these things have been put firmly back in their place. Tools to serve us, not the other way around. It had all got just too personal, too integrated into us, and far too invasive—even hard-wired. It's been a strange re-revelation to discover again things about us that would have been taken for granted in days gone by, before man made himself a slave, a commodity in his own machine. It was not only interesting; it was shocking to see just how far we have slipped back from the massive human and spiritual beings that we can be, to anonymous uncertain pawns in a game that was definitely not of our choosing —although, of course, we succumbed to it by choice. I know that I could no longer see, I had lost hope and, with that, there were days when nothing mattered. Life, death and everything in between became an abstraction. And, with that, it lost value, meaning and importance. My disease was cured by keeping alive a vision so clearly in my heart and mind that it became our reality. At the time, it was a challenge to even believe in it, but the result is plain to see. Thoughts do become things. It's the ultimate logic that is so easy to miss if we set our focus outside. Yes, I check e-mails, but I also hand-write letters and, now, instead of trawling the internet for inspiration, I find it inside, and play with the outside, and I love my life.

105

I am not sure when the turning point came in my art, but it certainly did. Maybe it happened over time. Maybe it was simply consistent effort and application. I don't know and I don't really care. Now I am just so grateful that I seem to have mastered some parts of the process. A drawn line seems to go where it is meant to go, textures that no computer could draw emerge from the layers of physicality that I am putting down—more and more. I no longer have to work through poor ideas, bad renderings or wrong choices. So, the work comes quicker, cleaner in its imagery, bolder in its rendition. That feels good. And it also feels good that there are things I will never master. Just like my ever-emerging relationship with you, my relationship with my art is also changing, constantly upgrading, diving off in different directions as I stay present to it and to the ever-changing world that feeds it. It is so subtle. What, then, have I mastered? I cannot really define it. Are we ever truly masters, or are we mergers—with reality, the present, the now? Is it just our egos that want us to say "I have mastered this", when, in fact, we are truly innocent, know nothing, and cannot even figure out what keeps our heart beating? Truly, if I am a master of anything, I am a master of not knowing. Every blank canvas shows me that, and every morning that I wake up and see the love in your eyes confirms it beyond a doubt.

106

Suck it up is a phrase that comes to mind. I am thinking about lift, and how the human spirit can be taken from its base condition where, inevitably, it descends into fear and confusion, to a higher place. So, bear with me. Suck it up is usually not a nice way to say 'deal with it' in a completely unsympathetic way. But I am thinking of it another way. The way that airplane wings create lift. There is a tendency to think that, in order to take off, the wings press more and more air downwards and then ride on that cushion of compressed air to lift off. Much as we see the oppressive nature of governments and industries pressing restrictive measures, agendas and control onto entire populations. The pressure of conflicting information, regulation and aggression pushing humanity down into submission under the weight of it all, where people are powerless to press back. But that is not how the airplane's wing works. The power of lift is above the wing, where the pressure differential creates a partial vacuum, and the wing has to move into that vacuum. It has no choice. So, it is interesting that a vacuum is more powerful than pressure, and the best place to be is above the wing. That is where we must be, in all the madness. Not engaging in the burgeoning pressure, the designed confusion and mis-informed action. We must be in silence, in the lift, in connection with our higher selves.

107

I look at politicians coming to power (so-called) and it makes me laugh. They are kids. They could be my children or even my grandchildren. What do they know? I see the hard-suited enthusiasm, like a drug, pushing them to make confident speeches that hide their panic and uncertainty, and taking actions based on their own cognitive bias urged on by the interests of others who, frothing at the mouth, feed them with arguments, reasons, imperatives that they have no way of assessing on a broader scale than a four- or five-year re-election cycle. A beauty contest wielded at a public who know even less than they do, as they plan their escape from the electoral tiger simply by finding ways to run faster than their closest opponent. How ridiculous is that? How is this any sort of democracy? How can this be a way to sustain an economy, let alone a society? It is incredible to me that we have not found a better way, that the lessons of history have had no impact other than to change strategies. Physical war to economic, economic to psychological, and so on. We are better than all of this, if we want to be, and if we choose to be. How can we return to our basic and best human qualities, so we can turn this monster around? My mind is at a loss, yet my heart knows full well the true potential of our miraculous existence.

108

Sometimes, you just have to dive in—take a bit of a risk. The waves look ominous today. Powerful. A cloudy sky turns each surging breaker into a dark-blue-grey mass, rising like a wall, cresting and falling into the tumult of crashing water, rushing the beach—then sucking back, hissing into the deep. It looks like Armageddon. It's daunting, dramatic, haunting, loud. I approach slowly, fighting the pull in my shins to hurry me into the vortex. Salt on my lips as I carefully place my feet, one step at a time, peering through the briney spray. This is too strong for me. I know that, of course. There will be surrender, sometime soon. An ogre of a wave rises before me, above me, darker than the rest. The pull on my thighs starts to release, and I dive headline into the dark, muffled world of waving stillness. Dancing shafts of light beckon me peacefully back to the surface. I feel good, taken care of, rewarded for my moment of bravery. This amazing power that I joined with has no malicious intent. It simply is what it is—to be enjoyed and respected. I position myself for the next big one. It lifts me up and laughs with me as it rushes me back to the shore and reminds me that, together, we are powerful, the risks we take are as small as we are insignificant in all of this, and all we need to concentrate on is flowing with it and enjoying the ride.

109

Wouldn't it be great to be able to fly like a humming bird? To choose a position in space and stay there, completely still, for as long as you like. I could do with that ability, right now. When the big canvases are against the wall, climbing up and down, re-positioning ladders, carrying paint and brushes, all brings too much mechanical challenge to the process. If I lay the canvas on the floor, I need tool extensions and, to see the work, I need a hoist so I can winch myself up to the ceiling now and then for a better view. Maybe I need one of those extending electric platforms they use in building, or to create a deep slot in the ground below one wall, as Dali did, so I can raise and lower the work and always have it at a convenient height. Or, maybe, the physical challenge of making my way around the canvas is all part of what makes the work what it is. Perhaps I should crawl over wet paint, or let the ladder make marks where I rest it. After all, I am not creating hyper-realist 'gosh-isn't-that-clever' paintings to impress people on social media. So often, in the past, at least, the marks of struggle, of changes, alterations and such, were important parts, integral to the final work. Yes, show the process, be proud of it, leave the heart and blood on the canvas. Don't forever be checking for tidiness and acceptability. Make the focus and intent of the work its prime mover. Never lose the passion.

110

They say that, as you get older, you become more childlike. I'm looking forward to that. I find I can remember a certain period at grammar school, whereas after that and before you came into my life, very little. I wonder if they were good years—developmental, educational, productive—or were they just wasted in confusion? At school, I felt much more on top of things. Afterwards, I started doubting myself. And it was only when I met you that I started to re-build, but in a better way. I cannot even describe how, but I know that the intervening years were the ones where I was particularly unconscious and drifting reactively, much of the time. So, it is with huge relief and gratitude that I have arrived at this point of happiness and clarity about life. I estimate that half of my total life, at least, will be in this enlightened and contented state. So, I intend to put my life to good use. Not under pressure in any way, but productive, contributive and constructive in ways that I know and value as true. It always comes back to the art. That vast unknown, unexplored territory that is filled with nothing but possibility, excitement, peace, realizations, unity, colour, fulfillment and yes, some frustration that I must manage so my mind is kept in its place while the other qualities dominate and take me and you on the best ride of our lives. I have time, I have ability and I have what I need. Let's go!

111

These flowers are special—to me, at least, but also in and of themselves. The lady who sells them at the market is very patient with me. I appreciate that. We don't actually need to buy flowers as we have an abundance of them in the courtyard and in the back garden. But these flowers are special. I search the array, checking each individual one for blemishes, healthy leaves, arrangement of petals, colour and scent. Each one is unique. Studying them like this, detached from my own environment, where we nurture our own flowers, somehow gives me more focus. They are incredible things. The designs of nature are superb, unique and so creative, as well as being practical and functional in ways that have evolved over centuries. I am not necessarily looking for my idea of perfection in each stem. Just some sort of quality that draws my attention in a good way. I know that I am too judgemental, so I fight that and try to look with an open heart. Each one is, after all, far beyond anything I could have created with my own hands. Sometimes I do pick what may be considered to be blemished plants, purely for their courage, love and the sheer unlikeliness that, despite whatever they have been through, they are still here. Beings that are simply there to bring pleasure, their whole lives devoted to just a few weeks of radiance and exquisite scents and life-giving pollen. I really hope you like them.

112

I must stop looking at the efforts of artists on Facebook and the rest of the web, and find my own way. I see now that I have my own path and that, even now, it has yet to be defined. Abstraction is not collage in paint, it is not driven by technique and the collection of colours and shapes purely for the sake of an aesthetic. It is deeper than that. It is an abstraction of an idea, a taking of that idea beyond the obvious, a generator of thoughts and a creator of mystery for the mind that must stretch beyond its cage when it is shown a form that has little reference to the base actuality. Richter[12] comes to mind, with is dark, angst-ridden form in the Birkenau[13] series and, later, the tumultuous, explosive imagery based on the 911 event[14]. The work clearly comes from somewhere other than an appealing arrangement of things that get 'likes'. We are so visually ignorant, I think. The education system of my day never took art seriously, except in a rather stuffy academic way. It never held high the passionate feelings of the individual, bringing them to the fore and celebrating them, rather than boxing and judging whatever they produced. Yet I still see abstraction as a high form of story and revelation that, given some nurturing, belief and self-worth, will generate the art that will be my legacy.

113

Just like any normal, ordinary day; like all the days of my life and all the days of those who have gone before, today is miraculous, marvellous, unique and extraordinary. I'd missed those facts for so much of my life, but it doesn't make them any less true. A grain of sand, just like a universe with all that it contains, is just as extraordinary. And how unlikely is each single element that makes up a universe? What are the chances that each molecule, every atom, every elemental part of every atom, would come into being and have a place that was perfectly manifested through energy and consciousness into a part of this magnificence? And look at us. What the heck are we, when you think in such terms? Scientists would tell us that we are largely water. Others assure us that we are spiritual beings manifest in physical form. I'm not sure what all that means. But there are times when it is all so mind-boggling that I cannot move, or think—knowing that, in doing so, I cause a shift, the consequences of which I may never know or understand in any meaningful, practical or useful way. So, I stand on the terrace, coffee in hand, my other arm wrapped lovingly and longingly round your waist that feels like another part of heaven to me. And we gaze in silence as the world silently tilts towards the sun on its unfathomable axis as it continues to roll on its infinite journey giving us days like this.

114

I never tire of watching you. You're captivating. Now, more than ever, I watch you. So-called entertainment was never as good as this. Never so exquisite, gorgeous, exciting, mysterious or fulfilling. Right now, you are making another loaf. But it could be anything. It's those hands. Delicate, swift, tender, compelling. Shaping the dough, kneading it, aerating it, scattering flour over it so deftly in the glancing sunlight on the counter top. As usual, you are completely unconscious of the power you have, your casual, take-it-or-leave-it silky movements. Somehow, you are able to function at this incredible level and still talk about something else. You think I am losing my hearing, but my male brain is transfixed and filled with your hands, blocking out casual conversation. The same hands that hold the scissors and massage my scalp when you cut my hair, that tap at lightning speed over the keys to transfer mind to matter, that touch me in heavenly ways, that expertly sweep the water so gracefully as you breaststroke in the sea. You look annoyed for a moment. Oh, yes, I did put the rubbish out. Yes, I will fix the curtain rail. I promise. But right now I am busy and this cannot wait. It will pass in the next few moments and it's my desire, my will, my job as an artist, my duty and my obsession as a lover, to see you, to be truly with you, to be smothered in your grace, to be everything that I can be for you, and to love you.

115

I am so glad to have questioned everything and not bought in to things that didn't resonate with my gut. I have seen how easy it is to manipulate people into some sort of distorted perception of how things are supposed to be. After all, it happens from Day 1. The day we are born, the machine grinds into action, taking us away from ourselves into someone else's distorted reality. I followed it for a while. We all do, until our frame of reference expands—if it ever does—so we can start to make our first faltering, daring steps into reasoning and awareness. Even then, the road is pitted with alternatives to our initial perceptions that are just as nutty, just as damaging, however seemingly attractive. In a sense, we have to find ourselves first, before we even consider how to proceed. I guess that's the gut feeling part of it, the outrageous notion that we know something else, more than our peers or teachers or leaders, that is begging to breathe and be seen. Trust in ourselves has to somehow come first, breaking through the heavy burden of received knowledge. So, how does that even start? For me, it was simply acknowledging my doubts about the stories I was being told, and acting on those doubts, often at my own cost, to find out what that still, small voice was saying, in the calm beyond logic and fear. And the journey has been and continues to be magical, because that's what it all is, when you climb down from the illusion of invincibility and domination of life, and ego. Rebirth is a continuous state.

116

The rhythm is established. This painting, like a good story wanting to be written, is painting itself. And it could be anything. Anything that I allow myself to step into, without question or, having dismissed or dealt with the questions along the way, without assigning them too much importance. The questions, after all, are my mind's way of persisting with complications and introducing doubt to a seed planted through the mysterious, perfect mechanism that is beyond mind, called a creative spark, or intuition, or inspiration or magic. The mind doesn't like to lose control to a greater force, but when I can quieten it down, when the physical process takes over and time disappears and the world focuses on this square of canvas to the exclusion of all else, the muse flows. That's when it all happens. That's when I remove me from the picture, literally, and allow the painting to be painted, flowing with its own energy, showing me new angles, colour combinations, forms, shapes; and bringing forth new worlds that I must be careful not to assess or judge or try to interpret for fear of stepping out of this tsunami that I have to acknowledge, that I crave to acknowledge and be subsumed by, and that is so much greater than me anyway. Although I can extinguish my connection with it in one breath, one thought, a change of focus or pace. As infinitely delicate as it is, once the rhythm is established, I have another rare opportunity to be so much more.

117

There are only beginnings. No endings. That's what I am noticing, these days. Everything is new. Every experience I have is for the first time. Why is that? Nothing has changed materially. Maybe it's just a change in perspective, but I find it exciting, humbling, intriguing. Every single thing is new. It's as if I have lost my memory, although it is still intact. It is as though I have just been born, yet I have years behind me. It's true that my memory is selective, to some degree, but this is crazy. Is it what's known as being in the moment, I wonder? Fascinating. I start my day in the kitchen—after my five rites[2]. You come downstairs and you are new. I feel an adolescent surge in my heart and body. I cannot help but walk over and hug you, kiss you, feel the bed-warm contours of your beautiful body under my hands, bathe in the tones of your voice, dive into your infinite eyes. It's all new. I know, intellectually, that I have done this nearly every single day for many years, but this is different. This is now. And it's incredible, powerful, soul-filling, heart-pumping, fresh. Just like the morning. Just like the water in my glass and the froth that rims my coffee. Just like this individual, unique and ever-changing cloud that rests quietly over a sparkling sea. Just like each momentary sparkle on the water. Everything. Brand new. And I cannot be other than amazed, and so grateful, and in love.

118

There is so much to do, yet I know that the doing of it must come from a place of stillness. Otherwise, I am merely expending energy wastefully. Each day brings its own list of mundane and not so mundane, important, pressing—urgent, even. All crowding into the 24 hours available, demanding priority. Sometimes I simply give in to doing the mundane as an escape from having to deal with the important or the creative. Creativity is never mundane and, however many times I approach it, it always has challenges that never seem to diminish. I've never been a team player. I am not really sure I know what the term means. Is it acceptance of compromise or subtle manipulation? Knowing how to play people, identifying weaknesses and strengths, assessing egos—all to drive through a result. And, because of that, can a team ever truly achieve excellence—or just a pre-ordained result to a better or worse degree than the individual? No, I truly don't understand it, which is the reason I suppose I feel I have to do it all myself. Condemned by my own ego, perhaps, never to allow collaboration into my work. So, I always have too much to do. My only true partner in life is the only one who sees through all this and helps me find space, to put things in perspective, show me priorities despite my raging mind's interpretations, and helps me find the peace, the silence, the space in me where great achievements can be nurtured and can unfold.

119

To be successful in life is to be a storyteller. It seems to be one of the main qualifications, these days. Social media and the crazy celebrity culture that invade our lives at every turn demand performance and a never-ending supply of energy so you can tell and re-tell your story infinitely in order to trawl the net. It's frenetic out there. I tried it, and it gave me little satisfaction, because there was always a yearning in me to simply be, and for that to be good enough. As I carefully add a stunning indigo-blue area to my new abstract, I realize how far I have travelled in the opposite direction. Yet, like Alice in the looking glass, it was exactly the opposite of what my mind would have me believe, that brought me my success. Yet I am a storyteller—so my original premise is correct—but the stories I tell and the way I tell them are different. Ironically, I see now that being opposite to the world's opinion of how things work is actually far better and more successful in every way. And I am not talking about the money. It's the depth, the nuanced messages, the creative twists, the visual surprises that are free to dance once I drop the second-hand expectations. I am able to draw on a different part of life that is somehow ancient and somehow new, somehow still yet full of energy and glorious movement, somehow of a universal knowing, if that doesn't sound too presumptuous, that touches and points to something urgent, important, fundamental and attractive, in all who experience it.

120

I live my life like a hermit crab standing at the door of my shell, ready to scurry back and close my eyes to the outer world. That's my default position. Looking out yet wanting to feel safe. Ready to avoid predators but always hoping for contact of a gentler kind. Not one that will tear my soft flesh from my delicate limbs, but one that will intrigue, fascinate, excite, fulfill. Am I getting more sensitive to the world or am I just tired of sorting through superficial contacts, disingenuous inquiry, manipulation and hopeful exploitation? Maybe I am more sensitive—to what is going to work and what is not, and to the value of time and good experiences. Yes, my door is well oiled, fast-action, secure-locking. That's kind of satisfying in itself. A good, firm, authoritative clunk. Protection guaranteed in a shell of steel. Since I have lived in this wonderful home, I have come to understand the value of silence, the clarity of the moment, the careful consideration and flow of actions. Each one is a miracle in itself, and filled with so much more than the fleeting, raging, confusing, fast, crazy externalities that I have spent so much of my life focusing on, trying to catch, expending my passions and yearnings on. Maybe we all need to learn a bit more from the humble hermit crab. Most of us spend our lives walking sideways anyway, with our eyes fixed on the wrong horizon that we never approach, missing our true destination as we run for safety.

121

Whether we like it or not, we are social beings. I have long had the idea that being an artist or an author is a completely isolated and solitary existence. But now I know better. Yes, for sure, there are long periods when I need nothing more than my own company and a clear thinking process, a chance to work through ideas, clean out the dross, shape things in my mind, my heart and my hands. However, this only happens as a result of my interactions with the world, and I have to be mindful of that as well. I even have to be mindful of time spent with you. Too little and my heart closes; too much and I have little to bring to you, other than routine, some pleasures, worries and concerns. My challenge is that so few people fire me up in the ways that you do, so I have to go out scouting and picking up what pieces of others appeal. I wish, sometimes, that I was more of a people person. Usually they disappoint me. You never do. Today, I am at a phase in a painting where I am not yet clear about my next move. The temptation is to drive, walk, bike, drink a coffee, chat, read the papers. Is that escape, or am I feeding the process with these things? I guess I won't know unless I do them. Sometimes, the studio feels expansive; at other times, it feels suffocating and restrictive. It doesn't change, so it must be me. Am I just complicating a simple situation? The answers all reveal themselves in the journey, but they are a secret, for now.

122

How does it work? I wonder. As we grow older, do we become better, greater in some way, or do we fade into obscurity, losing our higher faculties and becoming dumb husks with only hints of our former selves? They say that, as you get older, you get wiser. I guess there is a peak somewhere, that's different for everyone, where the cogs slow down and dependence on others increases—physically and mentally, perhaps—until at some point it is deemed that enough is enough. In a way, it is ironic that, as we become slowly aware of the hollow promises we have chased all our lives, we are physically forced to slow down. Is that not a very subtle clue that our body is urging us to notice, to finally tell us that the answers are not out there, but in here, in the stillness, where we came from? We are not, until we are, and that knowing is forced upon us at a time of life when we can do little else other than take notice—or, if we choose, we can simply carry on resisting until we get eaten up by whatever ill or circumstance that we may be susceptible to. Yes, we can become better. We can distribute what we have learned along the way—however small or humble that may appear to us—because we cannot know the impact even the smallest thing can have on the life of another, and we may never see its effect. But we can know we are magnificent, loving, giving beings.

123

It's amazing how our thoughts, feelings, attitudes, beliefs and conditioning manifest in reality. It was obvious to me for a long time that what I ate and how much exercise I got manifested changes in my body, but it took quite a lot longer to grasp the rest of it. When I think about it, it's funny. After all, it wasn't as if I needed proof beforehand, that if I ate fast food all the time, or drank beer every night, there would be changes. Obvious. As I walk around our property, I touch the framework that holds the solar panels in place, I run my hands over the concrete base that keeps the wind turbine standing erect against whatever nature throws at it. I lean on our boundary wall, solid as the rock it stands on, casting my eyes along its length either side of me, feeling its reassurance. The house itself, with its sturdy walls, strong doors, storm-proof roof. The windows—large and open to the good, sealed with strong shutters in challenging conditions. And so much pure white all around me, mingled with terracotta, green and bright sprays of riotous colour. All of it a metaphor, a reflection of what we have become, and therefore why it is. We attracted it. More than that, we became it. Solid, rich, colourful, pure in heart, strong and resilient. We built the foundations, over the years, with faith and understanding. And the funny part about it is that we had no idea that the outcome, even if it happened, could be so perfect and so far beyond our limited imagination.

124

As a race, we have lost far more than we have gained. We've sold our souls and enslaved ourselves to the machine, substituted our humanity for bytes at the tech cherry. It's a devastating progress, an ignorant misconception of what we are and what we can be. Yes, I speak from my comfortable isolation from all the madness but, remember, we put ourselves here by following another path that most dismiss as being the ravings of impractical, unrealistic minds, seduced by the hype of some who carry the message through that very same machine. There is no justification to be made, as far as I am concerned. Those who visit us here take a chance and have an opportunity to listen to that smothered tiny voice inside that knows their truth. It's challenging, we know, to stand beneath that big black wave that carries all things, all minds, all dreams—and say "No, I am me! I am worth more than this." And then to let it grow, realize it and truly know it. Until you are unbreakable, true and real again. Just like you were when you emerged from the womb, before your soul began to cry. And so, yes, I can stand here now, with you at my side, isolated from the world but for a few threads of our choosing, different in ways that people notice but few can really grasp, disturbing those who have the spark of recognition of their own being. And I am so, so proud, humbled, loved and clear. I can do nothing but celebrate.

125

Just as a wonderful meal is exquisite, or as a well resolved painting is satisfyingly powerful, every part of our house has compellingly attractive spaces. I can stand or sit or lie anywhere and it is always a sublime experience. Sometimes I do that. Simply find a space and enjoy it. Sometimes it takes a while to settle in and relax as I have to choose one aspect rather than be tempted to try and fit them all in at once. Then I get excited, or anxious. But if I simply stop and relax, there is always plenty there to absorb. It changes constantly with the light, my moods, your presence, the daily stuff of living being introduced, moved around etc. I sit at the end of the dining table, facing the tall wall with its huge abstract. To the right, three stone steps and the archway to the hall and stairs radiate softly from the tower. In my peripheral vision to the right, a discreet group of sculptures throw musical shadows on the floor and wall. To my left, light floods in through the open windows, the edges of shadows, cast across the painting, softened by foliage and adding fresh dimensions and movement to the abstract. Specks of dust in the air define the light's path obliquely down to the table and onward to the smooth marble floor, colliding with bowls, condiment set, chairbacks, as it designs its image of evidence, almost imperceptibly, crawling towards me to meet my eyes in the mid-afternoon. One moment, one of infinite meditation in incredible abundance.

126

I stand at the door of your office. It's a different version of all the offices I imagine you have ever occupied. There's a comfort in continuity, I think, that allows processes to work and give free rein to creativity by virtue of their transparency. This office has a nicer wooden desk, a very comfortable chair, a bigger screen so there is more space to leave folders where they shouldn't be (but I have that covered), a treatment table, neat cabinets, two comfortable chairs, a rolled-up yoga mat—orange—a humidifier, a small fridge with a water cooler on top, various supplement bottles, a clipboard, a printer. And you. Sitting bolt upright, shoulders back, pounding the keyboard with a methodic, comforting, fast rumble that tells me that, behind studious-looking glasses, your eyes are locked on the emerging tome, brain processing faster than the computer can keep up. I feel sure that, if I had x-ray vision, I would see cogs interlocking, wheels spinning, pistons lurching to and fro, steam rising. Yet there is a peacefulness here as well, mixed in with your sexiness, and a sense that you are completely at home, in your space, in command and loving every moment. I walk in, brush a lock of your hair off your neck, bend down and kiss it, ever so gently, loving the warm skin. You murmur a smile. I walk back out the door and await whatever it is you will be dying to tell me when you have finished. I love your energy and the riches you always bring.

127

This day, so many years ago, I was preparing. Well, preparing is probably too strong a word. Yes, I was preparing clothes and other stuff but, otherwise, how could I possibly prepare for what was about to happen and what was going to continue into the future? What an incredible journey, bonded by love and launched through scenarios, places, feelings, experiences that I could never have imagined I would have the privilege of knowing. And we got better, and closer, along the way. Things that have split apart other relationships only made us stronger. And I am so grateful for your wisdom and guidance through dark places that I never dared visit before. Now, look! We did it! And we are still doing it, probably more than ever. We are more focused, less wasteful of our resources and energy, no longer searching in so many ways—just in the ways that matter. I am your king and you are my queen. I think all this in a flash, as you come to our table, two plates in hand, with a delicious lunch perfectly arranged on them. All from our garden, freshly picked today, by your loving hands. You smile and sit opposite me. I feel your legs and feet searching for mine and coming to rest on my lap. I am both wanting to eat, but also take you in with all my heart. Life is just so good, such a beautiful thing. I feel young, just starting again, in perfection.

128

I find authoritarianism a distressing and somewhat confusing thing. Firstly, that elected leaders—elected to serve—can take authoritarianism on as a tool of their trade, to get things done that they may or may not believe are in the interests of those they supposedly serve, is a sad failing of finer human qualities that they choose not to develop or utilize. Secondly, that in becoming an authority, there is no heart or soul in their philosophy—only backroom deals and popularism. Yet I also feel sad for those poor souls whose egos drive them to dysfunctional leadership, leaving them hollow, despised and worn out at the end of it. It's so sad that the world has evolved (or devolved) to a point where this seems to be the de facto modus operandi of leaders everywhere. So, we are left to pick our way through darkened streets with burning eyes at every corner and blackmailed compliance in an ever-tightening grip on the world. I will not be sad to leave. I don't fear death. But, while I am alive, I will remain the creative, the disrupter, a spiritual being, a lover and an artist. For that is what I am. And the thing about authoritarian leadership is that it is weak, because it cannot change that, whatever they may do to me. So, again I say, to me, find your way to your art and let it shine. Write your story in your own words, and totally love your life!

129

It's not as if we have to go looking for ideas for our next projects. There was a time, I seem to remember, that I felt I needed to go into the world to be stimulated and have ideas pop up out of random conversations, events and the like. But, now, I find them more and more inside. And on the beach, walking with you. The light on the shore is almost amber as the sun sets behind us. A diligent group of very business-like little birds busily race to and fro in the silver surf as it spreads its frothy film and pulls on pebbles as it recedes, insistently inviting them back to its protection in the deep. I watch your feet as we walk, gently sinking with each step in to a warm cushion of sand, leaving a momentary evidence of your presence as each foot lifts and the rushing water washes it clean for the next step. "Lewee." My heart warms in expectation. "I was thinking…" Here we go, I think. I smile and time stops as we are wrapped in the silent roar of the surf, providing us with our private space to dream, scheme and laugh as the idea takes shape, is weighed, coloured, given space without judgement. And it moves with us in the light, a presence being born that cannot be undone but can only move forward, should we want to give it energy. In that moment, I know this walk will never end, because they never do. There is always a part that remains, stays with me and becomes a beautiful part of our life journey. You smile. You know that too.

130

The work is becoming more and more abstract, strange and mysterious. As I change, so does it. Maybe it's becoming clearer and closer to the reality of me. That it should be more strange and mysterious as time goes on is kind of interesting. What does that say about me? Or does it simply get closer to a truth that I cannot comprehend with my mind? As soon as I stop to think about it, the work changes. Thoughts become things, quantum physics manifested. Where we place our attention changes whatever reality is. However, another part of me in this complex mesh of awareness or whatever it is, wants to think that the positive energy (whatever that is!) transmits to the observer of the work. That, logically, seems a bit of a stretch, but I live in hope that, somehow, whatever is going on in me or the world can be represented—or at least my positive reaction to it, or my interpretation of it—in a way that uplifts, inspires, amuses, intrigues, enlightens or otherwise trips a switch that says yes, we are human and we are better than all this nonsense, all this pain, all this frivolous invention that has seduced us away from real life and what really matters, that has meaning. And then I am stumped again, because all of these worthy thoughts of mine seem so preposterous, founded on what, going where? Something inside just says STOP! Nothing is anything. A vacuum is all that doesn't remain. And the only way I can get back and function at all is to turn inside, switch on, and love.

131

It's always a surprise when the entry phone buzzes. We are so wrapped up in our own world here, and the natural peace of our surroundings, that the buzz can feel like a rude intrusion. We are often curious, though, like prehistoric animals seeing a new species for the first time, we peer at the screen. Is it friendly? The poor postman leafs through letters and parcels nesting in the crook of his arm and looks around aimlessly, the door of his idling van hanging open so when these strange foreigners actually deign to receive their mail, he can shoot off and get on with his life. Satisfied that this animal is not going to attack us, we carefully press the buzzer for long enough for him to register that the gate is slowing opening, and we make our way to the front door. Eyes squinting in the soft morning heat, we smile at him—as much to cool his impatience as he walks through the courtyard as to greet him as he delivers unknown goodies from god only knows where, into our hands. He's actually one of our favourite visitors. It's simple with him. He brings us nice stuff, we sign, he sighs and leaves. It's like Christmas every time, for us. And, at Christmas, we make sure he is looked after—a nice bottle of festive juice, some home-made choices and flowers for his adoring wife. Well, I assume she is, based purely on personal experience. We always celebrate his arrival—the channel whereby much of what we put out comes back to us in kind.

132

On days like this, it can get a bit frantic. The idea hasn't come yet, or it is twisted and misshapen in my mind, or there is unease in my chest. So I walk around the studio, dabbling, re-arranging stuff. At the same time, I am marvelling at the two-dimensional plane before me, taunting me, dominating me. When I think of all the work I have seen in my life, the images of infinite variety that have passed in front of my eyes, the fascination and the feelings I have felt, it's amazing. That humans are infinitely capable of fantastic things. Our big differentiation from animals—creativity and the ability to think into existence that which has not existed before. And so, to feel so helpless at this moment is also daunting. The best thing to do is simply start, without intellectual or emotional investment in an outcome, knowing that everything can be changed, destroyed, re-built with a little time and self-forgiveness. It's not important, yet it is important. It's trivial yet central to my existence, my identity. And I cannot even define any of it without it coming out wrong. I suppose that is where art surpasses everything else, when it works. I open the studio door wide to relieve the pressure, freshen the air, introduce new light. The breeze dislodges paper on the table and it drifts down to the floor. It's nature's way of saying, "Here, let me help you arrange this. Here's a fresh way of seeing things." And immediately I know, and start again.

133

I touch another world when I get into the Aston Martin. Even opening the door, feeling the smooth mechanism working, the balance of the door itself. Then sliding into the seat. Aromatic yellow leather, hand-stitched and shaped perfectly to my form. Then there's simply looking at the dashboard. That takes a minute or two. I always leave the roof down when it's in the garage so that, when I press the start button, I get the full experience of the engine launching itself with impatient energy. The salesman had talked too much. I had to shut him up. I could build my own relationship with this beast. He was speaking of things that may have impressed those who knew about the technology or who cared for comparisons. For me, this encounter was a quiet, spiritual, moment. Now, as I drive it out of the garage and the boom adjusts to outdoor acoustics, I don't want to see another car or even talk about this one to anyone on my journey. I stop by the front door. You emerge, all smiles and light. I open your door and you join me. Belt up, open the gate. Enter The World. Much as I love driving it, I still just love it when we are safe in our own world. Traffic, other people, even the glances of admiration impinge on our experience. But I have learned to be magnanimous, wave back, smile as we tour the back roads, loving the power and the handling. I never want to stop, but we have to, now and then, usually hidden, pre-arranged with friends. After all, we have to eat, and shopping was never this much fun before.

134

What are the chances, do you think? That we somehow came into this world, this little blue planet floating in trillions of light years of nothingness, that is set up with everything we need, not only for survival but also for us to thrive and enjoy? That we take on a form that gives us mobility, thought, conscience, creativity, consciousness. That the sky is blue and it sits all around the globe, protecting us and giving us life. That there are weather systems that nurture life, seasons that follow rhythms of life, death and rebirth. That we have learned to communicate with each other in languages, sounds, written words, electronic devices. That our bodies function for tens of years without us having to really figure much out. That we are a miracle of evolution that can adapt to the seasons, our environment, social conditions. That we can sing and act and paint in stories that explore and celebrate all of this miraculous stuff. That we breathe and that blood courses through our veins and that in all our human complexity we have simple yet powerful urges, wants and desires. And that, in all of this, in a café, in a village, in a country, on a continent, on this tiny, tiny globe floating around a life-giving sun set at the perfect distance to ensure that we don't bake or freeze, I met you? What were the chances, do you think? Wow! Too much! Better to just roll over, put my arm around you, watch you as you sleep, and love every single minute.

135

"Let me help you with that." As I walk into the living area, you're struggling to push the sofa into a new position. I put my shoulder behind it and the heavy sofa grinds into place, leaving behind a few dust eddies and dead insects. I get the dust pan and brush it all away. A newly exposed corner demands other changes. Simply moving the sofa a few feet creates a ripple effect. It feels uncomfortable. We've been sitting, lying, cuddling in that position, with its accompanying view, for months now. We've looked forward to relaxing there just before bed. Now we have a DFA[15]. You own that decision. I support you in it. Now I have to own it. Newness demands adjustment. Slight annoyance gives way to fresh enthusiasm. Yet I must not take over. This was your initiative, your action that disturbed my immediate plans of a drink and nibbles overlooking the sea. I suggest we try different things. I take down three paintings and replace them with two new ones. More spacious. Less clutter. You move the tall vase and change the cushions on the sofa. The feng shui moves, the space offers new perspectives and new feelings. We stand back, move around to get the full impact, search our feelings. Do we like it? I watch your mind working out the finishing touches that I know will happen. When I'm not there. We are still so young, still moving, still creating, still alive.

136

I wonder why I always seem to be dealing with similar challenges every time I start a painting. A lot of art is very clearly cerebral. Fascinating, clever, impressive, celebrated and loved by the media and the industry. Yet somehow I know it will pass into oblivion. It is limited in some way. 'Art fashion' changes ever faster, so impact can be short-lived. Now more than ever. I don't feel anything for such work other than an initial rush of fascination. So, my challenge is to find the subtle interchange of heart and mind and play with that, translating feelings into structures, colour and shape, in ways that speak to deeper parts of the human psyche. After all, it is only when the work disturbs—that and changes the viewer in some way—that it has value beyond the art industry circus. I am not trying to manipulate, either, or work out a subversive approach that seduces for sales. No, the only person I have to impress is me. I want each piece to be remarkable, astounding, in some way that goes far beyond my limited mind. It may be very quiet, it may be nice—or not. But unless it does something, what is it for? And the only way it can impress me is if it truly comes from the heart and successfully shows whatever it is there to show. I cannot account for the reactions of others. There is nothing to know, here. And so the challenge remains. Where to start? What to do? How can I best spend my time? The answer is not to waste my time and energy on all these thoughts, to have courage, let go and simply get started.

137

The future, ultimately, merges with the past and becomes the present. As I write, I sometimes no longer think of this as a future now. It's a now, now. Because I know that thoughts become things and that everything is connected in time and space; with time, I believe, tending towards an illusion, the very idea of projecting into the future becomes a nonsense. Maybe thoughts are things. After all, if the basis of everything is light and sound born out of a universal consciousness, then thoughts must be a tad more solid than I imagine them to be, and the solid is a lot less tangible than it appears to be. We have been so easily convinced and brainwashed into this grand illusion that, even now, I find it hard to break free of its bonds. They are just so strong. Yet, if I were to, if I was able, I wonder what kind of existence, what kind of relevance I would have. Would the 'I' that I have guarded, protected, grappled with all these years, simply merge into some other state—or something—or nothing? Even thinking these thoughts is somewhat destabilizing. They make me question the mundane things that keep me anchored here, in this beautiful place, with you, in my body, in my studio, on our beach, in our kitchen, in our bed. All the things that I value and love, by attachment and my own limitations, are so much more appealing than some vague, imagined ether—or what? Yet I do know the love—the perfect anchor and connection to both.

138

Bugs and birds are on my mind today as I repair one of the nets over the vegetables that protect them from the hottest parts of the day. We spend so much energy protecting ourselves and our food source from all the elements and bugs and birds that live with us here, that I begin to wonder if there is a more natural way to exist. After all, I don't know how much damage I am doing, how much of the natural ecological balance I am disturbing, or even what benefits I am missing out on, by my actions. I came into this way of living relatively late in life and without a culture that carried the wisdom of ages about our natural balance and the parts played by its various constituents. So, is a bug that eats a few young leaves a bad thing? Should I try to kill it or otherwise discourage it? A bird caught in a net is a more emotional thing. It's appealing, delicate, fluffy and makes a nice sound. Never mind that it was trying to steal my food. I am already allowing for that by providing food for the birds in a nearby location, so that my human logic hopefully influences bird logic and they choose the easier option. I know nothing of bird psychology. I don't think they have very sophisticated brains. So, while I can alleviate my guilt with the birds, the bugs are more challenging. When I think about it, even without much of a brain, they actually have the better of me. They just do what they do. Eat, shit and survive. Maybe they have a lesson for me to learn. Problem is, I have a brain.

139

I'm tempted to look at colour theory. I've resisted it all my life, so far, as a cold, calculating methodology that somehow takes away from the spontaneity that I hope to achieve by intuitively choosing and mixing colours, sometimes with less than stellar effect. It's amazing, though, just how much we are influenced by colour and colour combinations. I have known this from my marketing days, of course, but somehow it has never really transferred to my art works. With colour, form can become secondary, as I have seen in so many simple abstracts. It's the colour that grabs the attention, and the emotion, first, and then the form intrigues or draws you further in. I wonder if there is some sort of delineation and relationship. Colour, emotion, feeling, right brain; form, intellect, rationale, left brain. I hope I am not having a realization that teenagers become aware of in their first year of art school. Yet maybe that wouldn't be such a bad thing. Maybe, sometimes, it takes a lifetime of experiences to truly grasp some things that really don't sink in until the right time arrives. Maybe that's why so few artists really make it. Most fall away and choose another path, some revert to becoming technique machines for specific markets, the few break through, often becoming investment pawns in a bigger financial game. (I still don't understand money). There is something pure in each discovery. Innocent, fresh and inspiring. Another stage on my unique, magical journey.

140

I am not used to it, any more. I cannot imagine living a busy city life. I am in the café with its noise, the people, the waitress invading my space, posters, music, tables, chairs, open cupboard doors. Conversations, radio, cutlery, talking, walking, arranging, thinking loudly. I never used to notice it all. It just formed a constant backdrop to life, but it feels different now. What surprises me is that this happens every day. The same people go through the same motions, day in, day out. White noise in my life. None of it makes any sense any more. It changes when a conversation happens. Even just a simple "hello" gives it some sort of context in the random exchanges of energy, activity, feelings, avoidance. People are generally closed, in their own impossibly complex set of circumstances and experiences. No wonder we connect on such rare occasions. No wonder that, when we do, our whole world lights up and the channels sing, because surely that is how we are meant to be—connected within and without. The girl playing the piano has a connection that rolls and twinkles through the keys into her body. Unless we have a focus like that, we tend to drift, looking outwardly for stimulation or peace. And, at times like this, when I am an island in a weird world, I am so grateful to know that I can come back to a real place where I can connect, and do connect, inwardly to my soul and outwardly with the most incredible person I know.

141

Technology has stolen our dreams, our foresight, our sight. I am in my studio taking a break, surfing the internet. Yet another highly over-processed image comes up. A photo designed to have impact. Colours distorted, shapes over-defined, bits carefully added here and there—a stormy sky of a kind no one has ever seen, looks artificially dark over the scene. And, somehow, in all its brilliance and hyper-realism, the whole thing is just boring. We see this all the time and then, when we look with our own eyes at what is around us, we may see it as comparatively dull and uninteresting. The photo acts like a quick fix in an otherwise unsatisfying world. What have we done? Can we no longer see? Can we no longer look at the beauty around us and dream? The days when photography was not so certain, with its chemical processing, mechanical focus, assessment of light and manual measurements, somehow yielded more beauty, more surprises, more happy accidents that were often beautiful and mysterious. Rather than gauche cleverness, they offered insights into the unseen and the subconscious. Sometimes, a blurred form could evoke so much more than the enhanced literal. I want to move forward with my vision, not get weighed down with technology's crude popularism. People deserve so much more than the sharp focus of realism. Because we are more than that. True realism goes way beyond the reflection, deep into the psyche.

142

We're sitting on the beach, each cradling a glass of your home-made dandelion wine, enjoying a cooling breeze that ripples under our T-shirts and brushes the hairs on my legs. Behind us, the warm glow of the evening home. The faint sound of Clara putting the dishes away after our special meal. Special? Yes. Every now and then, we choose a time or a day to celebrate… anything. Because, in truth, it's all there to celebrate all the time, but we have to ration ourselves or we'd never get anything done. And we love getting things done—but it's important to remember to celebrate and give thanks. Like now, we sometimes celebrate in silence. Being swathed in such beautiful surroundings, sounds of the sea, the wind and the birds, the scents of the herbs in our garden, wild flowers, the sea air, are all the enticement we need—or want—on occasions such as this. And, of course, to feel our deep connection that we see as part of all of this. Seamlessly and deeply interwoven through time and space, it pervades every aspect, every cell and molecule, caressing each thought, enlivening each feeling, delicately nudging at our awareness, carefully and exquisitely reminding us of the illusion and how to be in it but, more importantly, showing us that we are infinite. Of course everything is connected. It could not be any other way. I take another sip of wine—your wine—and catch your eye. And I see it in that instant. Everything, everywhere, always.

143

I take my bowl of granola onto the balcony and settle down to absorb the new day, as grey quietly gives way to blue and the gentle surf caresses the sand, massaging it smooth. I am at one until a fly lands on my bowl. I flick it away and return to my spiritual state. The fly buzzes in my ear. Fuck it. I swat it away and it immediately chooses to explore my ankle. Damn. This isn't going to happen. I retreat indoors and close the sliding door. Inside feels a bit stuffy, but I'll deal with that. I sit at the dining room table where my new companion has followed me, it seems, and is now walking jerky paths across the table in my general direction. Stay cool. It stops and rubs its front legs together, then cleans its proboscis (is that what it is?) while weaving its head to and fro. Then the middle legs set to work cleaning the wings, followed by the back legs completing the morning's ablutions. There are a few moments of quiet observation as we stare each other out. He has the advantage here. I only have two eyes. I wonder if he (or she) has a sense of humour, or just a vicious streak that loves to torment humans. But, I have to admit, he has incredible reflexes and flying skills that I can only dream of. And those eyes—reflecting all the colours of the rainbow in their incredible construction. Magnificent natural evolution. But…smash! Dead. Off the table. I'm having breakfast.

144

Each and every day, we stand at the crossroads. More than that, each and every moment in every day. We have choices, we make choices. There is no room for regret or other wasteful emotions, because each moment passes, and we can and do make a fresh choice. Constantly moving. Stand up, sit down; take a mouthful of food, take a sip of water; say something uplifting, be lazy and careless with our words; choose inside or outside; move up or move down. Whatever state we are at in our lives, whatever we are doing, that dynamic is always there, shaping our course, building us up or breaking us down. Already, before I get to the studio, I have been through this process, over and over again. From the minute I opened my eyes, kissed you gently as you slept, got up, washed, ate breakfast, opened the shutters, I have partly followed a routine, partly made fresh choices, but always consciously. I mix a colour. I attempt to be aware of its purpose, yet I don't want to clumsily influence the outcome of its application if, somehow, by my standing apart from too high a degree of intention, some unexpected magic can be set free on the canvas, and I will stand in awe of what has been given to me. Is it possible to proactively choose to let this happen? Another crossroads, perhaps. Or is it simply that, by making choices with some sort of humility, as innocents who really don't know how this all works, everything is shaped for us anyway, in our best interests?

145

I seem to spend my life trying to break out of habits. They say we are creatures of habit. Maybe that is so, but some habits surely have to be discarded along the way. I have noticed that, having lived in this house for some time, I am almost wearing paths through it. I can count the paces from one position to another, and I see spaces where dust gathers because I so rarely go there. Sometimes I make purposeful detours into different areas to see things from a different perspective for a moment or two, or for fear that I wear a goat path in the flow where I usually go. Then, of course, I feel a bit silly for even going there in my head. Yet there is a relevance to all this, in my art. I have to keep breaking away from the well-trodden path. There is too much comfort in reverting to the path I have already walked, although another part of me knows that, having walked it once or twice, the viewpoints remain the same. So, even if I am working on a series, or another painting that has similarities to or echoes of a previous one, in my mind I have to be on a new path. Why this obsession? I want to live. I have never before had such a passion for life, because each day brings new life, new scenarios, new feelings, new juxtapositions, new conversations with my love. So, why would I waste my time going over old ground when there is so much infinite new stuff to fill my day, my heart, my intellect, my actions?

146

I believe there's a balance to be struck between envisioning and doing. Too much envisioning becomes dreaming that stays in fantasy. But when it is balanced with intention and doing, it develops in more healthy, concrete ways. I particularly notice that with the art. Ideas only move forward with action, and action sparks more creativity. All too often, though, I have to be careful not to let the action disappoint. Dreams can be perfect, whereas actions must be learned, repeated and practiced to achieve any level of competence. And I also have to be careful not to hold up the vision as an unachievable perfection, thereby preventing me from even getting started on the actions I need to perform to achieve it. Another weird thing is that, once I have achieved something or once I had nudged the energies or universe or whatever, into motion to support me, I forget the initial angst and intention and simply let myself go for the ride. This is a pattern that has repeated often enough, surely, for me to recognize it and trust that it will happen when I truly and sincerely ask for it. Am I stubborn? Why is it so hard to trust, each and every time, especially when I feel it is important or urgent? Our home, our life, us. Surely, that is enough? Yet I don't beat myself up over it. That is not its purpose. And I am grateful that I am still the student at the start of my journey, every single time it happens.

147

The studio tests me every time I go in. Always dilemmas. Always questions. Do I paint towards a goal or do I let go and see what comes? Is my intention clear enough to allow me to construct and manipulate, think through and shape the result, without it becoming stiff, meaningless, static, crude or crass? Will my physical actions of mixing paint, choosing a brush, applying marks, take me away from any connection or clarity that I may have? Will I even be capable of putting the marks down in ways that work? And what about building layers? Is it possible, even, with my pseudo-intuitive approach, to plan anything and allow for dimension and depth to build, for luminosity to grow, for crude marks to be anything but that? I know, from experience, that there is a rhythm to every piece. A beginning, a process, uncertainty moving towards clarity as forms take their place. It's still a messy process. The works I do with forethought and careful planning tend to be the best resolved, yet are often the most empty, the most disappointing. I think the answer is in drawing all the time. Getting fluid so the brain-hand barrier weakens and becomes more transparent, more natural. Only then can shapes flow without the worry of correctness in my seemingly desperate efforts to simply see and bring that sight to life on the surface. Yet, through all this masochism, I still love what I do.

148

A group of teenagers sit at a table near me. Pure theatre. I can watch because they don't see me. I am there, but their world is what consumes them. They talk loudly and laugh a collective laugh whenever a comment or a look or an action deems it a cue for another collective laugh. This group's uniform is jagged, precise haircuts and torn jeans, a certain type of hoodie and the ubiquitous cellphone. Cracked screens appear to be *de rigueur*. The subgroups of the sexes have stronger ties than the main group; the boys with louder energy, displayed like cockerels, the girls the recipients, the vessels of measure of progress in the pretence of casual seduction. They look clean and well looked-after. I imagine they have good relationships with parents they are managing as they strike out towards independence, while keeping one hand in the money pot. For moments like this. The energy rises and swirls and dips across the group as leaders prance and followers pay their dues, preening on the fringes with their private thoughts and unfulfilled desires that hold them in tense admiration. A hormonal tsunami in role-play. And I am invisible now. Even if I spoke, I would still be invisible, or a curio, or a device for expression of wit. It would only have a chance of working one on one. For now, though, they are my unwitting entertainment, and I love them all.

149

I walk out of our gate and cross the road. Even now, I feel a need to get out occasionally, from the comforts, the organization, the warm feelings that occasionally need a contrast for me to truly appreciate them. And I do. Yet occasionally something nags at me. The ground is uneven beneath my feet. Stones and rocks threaten to pierce my shoes as I clamber over them. Sharp gorse cuts my shins. And all around there are the aromas, ancient aromas that don't acknowledge my presence, but that speak of life before. Plants, baked earth, wild flowers, gnarled old trees that demand nothing and simply survive. A humble yet proud courage in an unforgiving environment where only the strong survive. Insects, crickets and the occasional bird ignore me as I trudge up the slight incline. Four hundred sweaty yards are enough for me to find another vista, inland. It spreads out flat in front of me, into the shimmering haze. To the left, more of the same for miles. To the right, the hills rise up, giving protection to the village unseen from here, and a gateway to the farmland beyond. I feel alive, alone and at one with the land and the sky and the hot breeze that carries so much life; evidence of a living planet. I find comfort in that, and being able to be alone with it for just long enough to re-connect. At that point, I need nothing. Maybe water. And then I can return, a small part of me changed, my compass re-set. I am at peace.

150

I can understand why successful people become isolated. When you take anything to the extreme, something inside you changes and you have little room for the mundanity of life and the effort it takes to integrate other people, even for a short time, into your presence. Howard Hughes, Michael Jackson, Salvador Dalí, Stanley Kubrick and so many more. I get it. Having lived for a while in our secret place, working as we do, seeking beyond what many never or rarely become aware of, pushing into unknown territory and breaking the rules—no wonder the interface between our home and the world can become a little strained. In a way, it's a lonely existence, with few close friends and only a handful of others we can trust enough to open our hearts and minds to. I don't want to think of it as a price to pay for what we have and what we are, because it is our wholehearted choice. It's our choice to live life to 150% and be everything we can be. There is so much to discover, learn, love and enjoy. Maybe those who toe the line are paying a bigger price—that of never truly being fully alive. Maybe they are happy as they are. I will never know. I suppose we all have different triggers and paths. One second with you confirms that I have chosen a good one—the best one for me and, hopefully, you feel the same. I may never truly know that, either. What I do know is that, in allowing our uniqueness to flourish, we have an incredible, extreme connection.

151

As life speeds up all around us, I have less and less interest in the things that still captivate 'normal' people. I have opted in, but most of them think the opposite. It's an ancient story. It seems to be a fundamental part of our nature and our existence. Left, right, good, bad, inside, outside. All the dualities that I have visited so many times along the way. I am even tired of talking about them. It all becomes pointless and a depressing repetition. Especially when I have opted in. There is no point in dipping my toe, every now and then, into that world, when I live and love in this one. I used to think I had to do that for the sake of having something recognizable or relevant to say in my art, so I could stimulate thought and others would attach value to what I do, validate me and give me some meaning. But that is all a delusion. I can only appeal to those who see and experience, even just a little, the world that I am in. And there is no intellectual bridge that can be crossed to get there. So, it all remains a mystery, an instinctive knowing, both in what I do and in the connection it makes with others. I realize now that when I lived in that other world, that blindingly fast carousel of information overload, when something caught my eye, when a piece of art stopped me in that rabid flow, it was because I felt that still small voice beckoning me to leave it all behind and truly be myself.

152

I think I am getting better at it. Simply being aware of where I am. It's important because that's the only place I am. I am nowhere else, in fact. As a child, I can recall being that present. Days were interminable, back then. Exploring my world took up most of my time when I wasn't being force-fed at school. That and drawing and inventing. Whole books chock-full of ideas, thoughts, images. Then there were days of climbing the chestnut tree. Every branch a new feeling, every step a new discovery, every new height a greater achievement, and a different perspective. To be high up when life was low down was exciting. The smell of freshly cut grass. The taste of hawthorn leaves, the challenge of a new relationship, learning to ride a bike, the raging turmoil of a growing body. Having squeezed through life's rush, immersed in cold confusion, ravaged by externalities, I feel I am approaching some sort of sanity, some sort of presence, an 'I am', at last. It's so subtle, missable, instantaneous, forgettable, still. Yet it is there and, like that child, I get excited when I touch it. It's not about control or mastery as the 'gurus' would have you believe from their limited experience. After all, they are just children as well, seduced by the sparkle of a magical experience, speaking it too soon and losing it in that communication. No, this 'I am' is only mine. It can hint to others through my actions and my work but, despite these words, I cannot speak it. Only be it. I am.

153

I have stepped outside of society. I no longer feel the things I used to feel that kept me tethered. The denial of spoken language has taken me further into my own world. Yes, there is fear there, and confrontation of the most basic kind. A man and his demons. Yet there is also a man and his freedom. I sometimes wonder if I retracted out of the world for less than worthy reasons. Was I a coward? Did I not want to risk? Was I simply a private person who didn't feel that my own simple feelings would be worthy of a greater part to play? Others have succeeded with very little. You have succeeded through huge wisdom and talent and now it comes easily to you. You are successfully bridging the gap that I have found so hard to bridge. So, I am left in a strange world. Working from the inside out, selling from the outside to people I cannot relate to, but who seem ever more needy for what I produce. It's a mystery to me. Magic. Each day is a celebration of survival played out through non-logical, non-linear creative inspiration. And, when I play, it is not so much easy as something I recognize as who I am. Sometimes, it is complex, sometimes, searching, confused. Sometimes, it is inspired and flowing. I run the whole gamut, from day to day. In between, I try my best to be here and to love you, never knowing, in this little corner of paradise, if I am truly succeeding. But that's the play, the game, the life.

154

Finding my way as an independent, creative being has been one of the greatest achievements of my life. And it's not about skill or influence or sparks of genius exploited. It is, and always has been, about love. Love of life, love of what I am doing, love of what I produce. The clues were all around me, all the time, but it was only when I actually started doing it that I stopped preventing it from happening. There it is, the double negative that should turn into a positive—but it didn't, for such a long time. When I was not in love, I could not see it, imagine it or even see myself deserving it. When I was in love, everything was there, like I had gone through some peculiar time warp and come out in a different dimension. I guess it was a parallel dimension because, on the outside, everything else looked much the same. But I was different. I now had a solid, unflinchable core, a foundation in rock from which I launched myself—without fanfare or a massive explosion—into…myself! Strange, now that I think about it, that I was not able to make the shift so much earlier, when I can see now, looking back, how the universe was supporting me all the way. After all, it sent me you. And, before that, I survived long periods of desert as small graces were dropped in my path, as stepping stones and indicators of the life I now live, and am so grateful for.

155

What does it take? Sometimes it's hard to know. What must I pull from the core of me, to shine and let the world know? What will it take to be seen or heard? How will the art manifest and move from my heart to others? What do I know? I come to the inevitable conclusion that I know none of this. However long I have lived, there are things that I cannot know. And it is only by celebrating that not knowing that I can create. Creativity is an acknowledgement—the acknowledgement of that not knowing made manifest through extraordinary things being brought into being. We cannot know, and we should give up trying to know, because when we think we know, there is no discovery, no miracle, no connection to that infinite source, no newness, no surprise, no awe and no happiness brought by fresh observation, knowledge, manifestations, creations. What does it take? It simply takes surrender, and gratitude for the ability and space and breath to function, to be a vessel for whatever gifts come through. It takes dedication, commitment, intention and action, but the rest is out of our hands, because if we embrace not knowing, we are actively allowing—with these four things—the universe to bring us what we cannot know, fresh and perfectly delivered in the now.

156

Our days are full. The rhythm of our lives is healthy, relaxed yet energetic. We have nothing but time and no time at all. That is not a complaint. It is filled with gratitude. We are enjoying constant renewal. What could be more satisfying than that? Our bodies may get older (although I don't see it in you), but our minds get younger. I often think we are younger and more full of fun than the people less than half our age who are still embroiled in finding their way, making brand new discoveries about life that we discovered at their age, too. We are healthily cynical but kind and enthusiastic for them when they make their revelations. The arrogance of youth, born out of innocence, so often turned to humility later for those who choose to take things further, to grow more. I feel sad for those who don't. Those who take on the mantle of their own limited knowing and wield it either defensively or offensively to bludgeon their way through life, they are the ones who get lost in eternal duality. Living here, we are mostly cocooned and apart from them. They have no interest in exploring the fringe that we represent and they have long since accepted our lack of interest in their interests. Yet in all their limited knowing, they miss a simple marketing ploy that we accidentally benefit from—a small band of highly motivated hearts and minds who are drawn like magnets to the possibility that what we have here will help to bring them to life.

157

I love it when we speak the truth. No subtexts. It's truly uplifting. It's something I instinctively search for in every interaction, be it with you or anyone else. When I find it, I know it. I think it defines friendships that can blossom in an instant with a stranger, or grow steadily over years to forge an impenetrable bond. In the early years of our lives, we speak the truth. Then we cover it up with compromises, manoeuvres, wants, needs and lies. Unless we develop Tourettes, in which case we are alone in our truth that haunts us. As we grow, our truth grows with us. When we meet a stranger, two mountains collide in a simple 'hello'. All those experiences, all those years, thoughts, actions, feelings and so much more, bumping up against each other in uncertainty, looking for a hidden gem. No wonder relationships are complicated. Maybe we are heavily laden ships, rather than mountains. Piled high with goods from other lands, or barges full of junk obediently following the canal. Fitting carefully through the locks, keeping our cargo under wraps as we nod to passersby. In my studio, I am deep in the hold of my ship, searching through the familiar and the unfamiliar, praying that no one will collide with my delicate rigging while I am out of sight, searching for my own truth. Thank goodness I have a little red telephone in my cabin, that is directly connected to you, so that amidst the swirling seas of uncertainty, I always can speak and receive the truth.

158

A wise man once said... nothing. And that was the best, most inspiring, life-changing event for me. It was the turning point. I had spent my life listening to others, searching for some magical connection, a flash of enlightenment that would somehow flow from their words and lift up the obstinate, dormant, cynical, empty part of me. I was waiting for that magical, tangible, physical event that would be the proof, the final revelation, the throw-your-arms-open-wide-on-the-top-of-a-mountain-sunrise moment of complete connection and understanding that I could then turn into a best-seller, get on the speaker circuit, trawl thousands of needy souls into my financial net and arrive, smiling with flashing teeth and shared sound bites as the world's savour. Perhaps not. But I suppose I was hoping for some of that, despite my self-image, which continually blocked the way. It didn't happen like that. Here I am, in paradise with you, living my best life because someone said... nothing. Perfect. And unexpected. And easy. Sooo easy. The switch turned. Slowly, at first, but with a definite, solid movement. And, once it started, it sped up, all on its own. And, before I knew it, it had flipped. And I looked back for just an instant and didn't recognize the sad child I had left behind. Facing forward again, I so appreciate everything in that nothing, for showing me the man I truly am.

159

Sometimes, to get completely out of touch with people and the ever-present buzz, we put a picnic in the cooler, load a couple of sunshades into the boat and head out to sea. On a typically windless day, the sea is calm as a millpond once we are half a mile from the shore and, because it is so calm, we only get the true peacefulness we are seeking once we shut off the motor and drift. By then, the land in the distance is no more than a blue wedge joining sea to sky, speckled with white dots and underlined in light yellow. Most of what we see is brilliant blue above, deep blue below. With no beginning and no end. The only sounds are the ripples of dolphin fins slicing the water occasionally, and their breath as they glance by and greet us. I take photos of you, against the clean lines of the boat and the divide of the horizon. I study your beautiful shape, your face, all angles. We eat together, gently rising and falling with the slight swell. We drink water in the sun. It all feels different out here. Why is that? Somehow clean and sharp in all its aspects. Taste changes in the open air. And we are so happily alone together. A few hours of bliss with only the lightest of tethers to the world—which, for us, is already pretty amazing. We are so thankful, yet keenly aware, after the third pull of the cord when the engine starts up, that we are attached to all this, we want to survive, to enjoy it all, so much more.

160

It's one of those all-too-rare moments of incredulity. I opened the front door of our home, and the tree that curves its way over the door's archway presented me with a leaf that hadn't been there yesterday. Conveniently placed, peeping into the opening at about my eye level, it smiled at me through glinting sun, waving and flickering to draw my attention. I see you. I go to meet the leaf and I am amazed. One leaf. A world all of its own. Amazingly complex networks of veins in perfect patterns, radiating from its stem. Semi-translucent green with yellow tints, they reach out to its very edges, where tiny crenellations decorate its edges, set into a hand, spread to the light. One leaf. A story repeated thousands of times on this one tree. Final destinations of water drawn by this silent, still being, from deep in the earth beneath us, over how much time and with what amazing skill I may never know, through solid wooden trunk and branches. To do what? To meet the sun and to give back to me and the rest of the world's creatures. The natural internet, where everything always was connected, well before any person knew it or spoke it. Well before we started to interfere, with arrogance and ignorance. And, despite our efforts to influence and corrupt the flow, this leaf still grows, and we still know nothing of its beauty. We are helpless, and incredulous.

161

How many times have I run to the water's edge? How many times have I sought out beaches, those places where life comes to a distinctive boundary, a completely different place, a living, breathing other entity where the rest of 'normal' life is cut out, simply by facing away from it, into this something else? How many times have I felt the freshness of entering this new world, this new paradigm with all its life and mysteries and colour and energy? Have I ever felt bored or down as I approach? No, I haven't. Always, every time, there is a sense of anticipation, of discovery. Whether it be the texture and feeling of sand beneath my feet, or rocks, or grasses that bend and quiver on the dunes, or boardwalks or cliffs or the ever-changing sea and sky. All of these things, the air in my lungs, the smell of salt in the air, seaweed and shells and bright wide vistas; somehow they feed me, renew me and give me another chance to get grounded in a reality that is so beautiful and awesome. And not a day passes that I am not grateful for all of this, even when I resist the urge to step into that world, or I simply watch it from the comfort of my home when nature reveals its full power to me. For as long as I live, I will always have that urge, that sense of wonder and fascination.

162

I have stopped wasting time. That we live a life at all is incredible. And that I have been blessed with you and this home of ours is doubly incredible. I feel as if I must be in the top 0.0001%. I have stopped wasting time on negative emotions, for that is really the only way we ever waste time. And that includes boredom. I don't ever want to go into all the whys and wherefores, all the guilt and pain, all the struggle and suffering. No; that only gives it airtime. It isn't even therapeutic, as some would have us believe. No. Focus higher, fresher energy, lightness of being, float on the lily pond. That is the way. We cannot measure our life by time alone. We can only measure it by feelings that only ever exist in the present. Otherwise, they are nothing—memories or projections. Why do people feel so reverent about the follies of the past when they cast reality aside and went to war? There is no sense in that. It will only truly never happen again if we never again let it poison our consciousness with mind games that start so small and innocent but, if we feed them, take hold and grow. Japanese knotweed[16]. Now, each breath, every word I speak, every stroke of the brush, every line I draw, every mouthful I take, is my total and magnificent reality right now. So, to me, that's pretty important. And it is my duty to me, and to you, and to the world, to make it a total blast!

163

The days are valuable. What is the best way to spend each of them? Spend! An interesting word. Do we spend our days like money? Do we deplete the bank account? Maybe with interest we re-stock and add back days. So it is important to be interested in each day. And I am. Very interested. In fact, my interest in each day is a bit of an obsession. Maybe, that way, I get to live for ever. As an artist, I hope that I invest lives with interest—after spending some money, but not necessarily—so maybe I am perpetuating that process of life elongation for others too. I am very fortunate that the accumulation of interest fills the days that I spend here. I don't know how the numbers stack up and when interest exceeds spend, but I do know that a full life of love and creativity creates a store of personal riches and, of course, interest is paid on the capital, so I may be winning there. No matter. Maybe I am irresponsible, but I do spend more and more days in reckless abandon, enjoying them for whatever they are and whatever they bring. And that fills my heart and mind with the best things in life, and the added interest is, to me, the cherry on the cake. But I was never cut out to be an accountant. Checks and balances were never my interest, ironically. For what is the point of waking each day, other than to live it to its fullest, as extraordinary as each one is.

164

Train journeys aren't what they used to be. Now, they are a reflection of how we have moved on. 'Faster' is the boast of all train services these days, with their rocket-ship features and silent rails. No more the clickety-click of a swaying carriage. No more deep conversations and rambling stories with co-travellers. Faster is good, of course, if your only purpose is to get from A to B and the humanity in between is to be ignored or even feared. There is no need for real, personal contact in a WiFi-enabled world. We have gained efficiency and lost each other in our race to survive and accumulate. So, I make the effort, whenever I am on a train, to be the unexpected voice beyond the cellphone, outside of social media or Hollywood or spreadsheets. It's not always wewlcome, at first, but there's a point to this, I feel, and it is inextricably linked to my art. For me, making the effort means rebuilding connections into the world from which we have been separated. For the recipient of my effort, sometimes there is relief and an opening up, a slightly uncomfortable recognition of their human communicative faculty that may need exercise with a stranger. For me, again, there is the chance of a fleeting friendship, insights and a glimpse at yet another aspect of someone's humanity—private thoughts and revelations that enrich us all.

165

Whatever it is that keep us alive, keeps all of this moving, growing, decaying, regenerating, seems at once so delicate and, on the other hand, so certain, solid and real. To touch the earth, to breathe, to feel. They are all so abstract and yet totally convincing as reality. And it can all change in an instant, although the underlying existence remains and continues because, in a sense, nothing is ever created or destroyed. Which makes the nature of it all the more mysterious. Especially when you ask why. A bird flew into a window today. That's what put me on this esoteric train of thought. Why create and nurture and grow this perfect little being that fills the air with its song, only to have it crash into my reinforced glass that it thought was another patch of clear sky? How do I reconcile my part in it? Where did the life go that was happily inhabiting this flitting creature? And those delicate little feathers and small body that lies almost weightless and warm in my hand—so perfectly put together and somehow grown from inside an egg. What happens to all this? All I can think is that somehow in this vast matrix of existence, it still has a place, where it transforms and re-emerges as something else. A constant engineering to an incomprehensible plan that weaves the energy through matter, time and space on a never-ending journey. And there is something I call me that stands in all this and can only wonder.

166

Wet on wet. It's the only way I can work today. There's an urgency that I cannot quite identify. The paint doesn't dry fast enough for my impatience. There's a price to pay for that, or an adjustment to be made in the way I am working. I keep the studio hot, move the stand to where it will catch the sun. It's early yet, so the heat isn't in it. Still, I want clean colours despite the speed that I feel compelled to maintain as the image develops. There's an upside, as well. I don't have time to dwell, think, stiffen up, so the image develops differently and goes beyond my tidying thoughts, takes me out of what I think I know and launches marks and compositions that are completely new to me. With each colour applied, I am hoping for something other than I get, because each action begins with it a thought, an assessment, a judgement, a qualification. Then there is the physical mixing, with its own set of parameters. Only after all that can the mark be applied. No wonder it cannot land with any sort of purity, much of the time, emerging as it does from a complete matrix of spiritual, physical mix, muscle, hot hair or fine plastic fibres, pigment, solvent, emotion, need, greed and so on. So, today, speed is of the essence, so less of that can impede movement, achievement, creation. I look at the world, and I feel it was created in the same way, so maybe, just maybe, what comes out of this frenzy will be just as amazing.

167

I close the door and leave the student to it. I know what she is going through because I have been there many times. I'm so grateful that we have the perfect situation here and that you are there to provide some support afterwards, if it is needed. When I left the studio, all was still. The best and worst place to be for her, sitting in front of a blank white canvas. Still and lonely as Switzerland on a Sunday; no distractions, no internet, nothing to say, no ideas, no thoughts. The temptation to simply destroy the oppressiveness of that white space with a mark—any mark—or a colour covering the whole space, roughly applied to reveal clues, shapes, allusions to something that could provide a starting point. The tightness in the chest. The conflicts of pain that should not be there and the supposition of joy at a finished work that somehow emerges over time and effort applied. The careful avoidance of cliché and the desire to be open to something unexpected, new, outside of experience and memory. Not wanting to copy the images thrown forward from living a life, but to somehow connect with a truth. Whatever this student does now will be a breakthrough for her. The key to her success is in being able to see that—whatever the outcome. I have learned that it is not for me to judge or assess my own work, nor is it the privilege of others—although they do, as that is the only way, sometimes, they can find their place in it—when there is something so much bigger going on.

168

I check on you in the bath. You have the window open so you can hear the birds and so the window doesn't steam up. The view outside is serene. The view, for me, inside, is magnificent. You, in the bath, framed by the view of the sea. I have plenty of time. You are well in to reading your latest novel-you-hope-will-never-end. Thank goodness the world of authors can keep up with you—just. You have hoovered up just about all the worthwhile novels in the world, yet still there is a trickle of new ones coming through that rise above the standard routine thrillers and that are not simply different combinations of intrigue, blood and gore and some sex thrown in on the side. Yes, I have time, and I don't want to leave this beautiful scene. I would much rather slip in beside you – but that would mean disturbing the story. Risky. I say something inane that you barely register, and close the door behind me. In the bedroom, I quietly set up the massage table, find some crisp white towels and then head downstairs to warm up the coconut oil and make some fine herbal tea. The kettle clicks off and the natural surround sound returns. Birds, sea, rustling leaves. A simple, relaxing symphony. Back upstairs, I lay things out as I hear water leaving the bath. I love this moment of anticipation. Towel round your head, towel round your still wet body, you open the door and smile. "Reeeally?" "Oh, yes!" I say.

169

I'm really too old for this, but I will still do it. The sea is a little rough, so the breakers are 'energetic', shall we say. I know that if I am patient and focused and observant, and I keep the boat pointing at 90 degrees to the waves, and I am decisive and firm in my actions when the right opportunity presents itself, I will succeed. I will push the boat out, hop onboard and get the motor running before the next wave threatens to turn the bow or swamp us. I have to make sure that, at the right time, in between swells and before my feet get lifted off the sand and I lose my grip, I have enough momentum to do that. No concern, no fumbling, no doubts. Just good, clear, definite action. It may take a while. It will take patience to spot the right circumstances. I must be sure of myself, my legs, my arms and a keen eye. There is no routine in what stirs before me, so I must be alert, constantly. The risks of doing this grow with each passing year, each unclear decision, each weakening of the body and the possible increasing brittleness of my aging bones. And they are balanced, hopefully, by each passing year's added experience, knowing and wisdom. It doesn't have to be a slide, I tell myself, to incapacity and fear. It can be continued growth, learning, education, power and burning passion for life, new discoveries and realizations. Why do it? To know that every time I push the boat out, I am a living miracle.

170

I am a young artist. I don't know if there is such a thing as an old artist. There are plenty of old non-artists, but a true artist is always young. 'Emerging' is another bullshit term used for artists who are starting to make their mark in the community. Aren't we all, always? Does 'established' simply infer a comfortable standard of living, high prices and the ability to get by without further 'emerging'? I don't know. Of course, young artists have a different energy—often not so well-managed. And they see the world from a point of view that I could not imagine. Yet we cannot really pigeon-hole artists so conveniently. That only serves the commercial machine, with its trends and darlings and deal-making and egos and money. Art is really independent of all that, yet has to interface with it to sustain the artist. I do, all the time. It's the least pleasant part of the work—unless, of course, discussion, recognition and interaction come from a different place. Then it can be exciting, because it respects the process and opens up new possibilities. Artists don't actually need support. They are the ones who see further. They simply need conscious recognition of what they are doing, the part they play in life and in society, and the space and time to create. The rest is simply the ebb and flow of energy, as it enriches lives. We do not get old, we are all young artists. We just change our clothes, our energies, our work, timelessly.

171

Today is a day to do nothing. I have those, now and then, but I am always conscious of not letting them become the norm. They are welcome breaks taken wisely, not continuous indulgencies that make my body and mind fade. Even on days like this, I want to make good use of the time. I am sitting at my favourite table, having got to the café early enough to nab it. I could almost demand that they reserve it for me on a permanent basis, but that would be unfair as I don't turn up for days at a time when the studio becomes my focus. I am content. Sunshade, sunglasses, coffee, local paper, sketch book. Why is it that however much I love my Gaggia at home, there is always something I like about the coffee at the café. Maybe it's simply the different ambience, the people, the view of the harbour and the sun on the road, the occasional whiff of two-stroke as a scooter goes by, the sounds and smells of the fishing activity, even the smell of the odd cigar and the pizza oven next door. Even on days like this, I don't slump (thank goodness for the gym) or lose myself in daydreams. It's a wonderful opportunity to observe, take notes, watch how light and shade and colour work together. Don't get me wrong. It's still very relaxing, but I realize that however much I think I want to do nothing, I actually don't. So self-management of energy has to be carefully observed. So when I come home, I have stories and plenty of energy for you.

172

Why do I paint? I'm not sure I can answer that question with any one, neat answer. I know that my relationship with it has changed, over the years. I no longer see it as a compulsion. "I am an artist, therefore I must be producing inspired work constantly." That has left me. Now, I paint for discovery inquiry, fascination – when and if those emotions visit me. Which, it seems, is most of the time. Yet there has definitely been a shift and, as a result, the work I produce now is less hurried, more deeply executed and more mature in some way or another. I find better relationships between shape and colour, and I am more considered in my actions. And painting, after all, is a part of life that connects other experiences. I have always felt that it must be impossible to be a full-time painter because I need a full life to feed it. David Bowie used to paint to feed ideas for his music when he was stuck. As a result, he not only produced incredible music but also gained profound insights into art that he expressed in his writing for art magazines. I have never seen what he painted, so I guess it was a private tool for him. I, on the other hand, cross over a line and reveal my very personal work for public consumption. It is never comfortable. It always feels somehow dangerous. That is what keeps me on track, out of the box and trying new things. If it doesn't generate those feelings and if it isn't born out of passion, it has no value in anyone's life.

173

The evening is going well. The barbeque is working well and the musicians are creating just the right kind of ambience on the deck. It's not music that either of us is particularly keen on, and some of the company is, well, a bit outside our normal chosen company. But, then again, this is what this evening is all about. Disruption. Opening doors to new things, deliberately going outside our boundaries for the sake of shaking things up a bit. Our life has become so perfect that I felt we could easily become detached, indulgent, even boring. Life presents its edges for us to grow. So that is what we are doing here. To us, the conversation may seem trivial, views expressed distasteful, or they are expressed by people half our age and we dismiss them as something old, that we covered 40 years ago, or they are too narrow to be valid, however much passion, intelligence and forethought went into developing them. It's not that we feel superior. I certainly don't. So any evening like this, where we are confronted, or ignored, or disagreed with, is a small test of our humanity and our ability to find the positive in everything. Same old choices, fresh opportunities. And it is exactly because we have come this far, learned so much, gone so deep, stood our ground in unpopular territory and succeeded on our own terms, that we can now be strong enough, magnanimous and generous in and of ourselves, and truly enjoy our fellow human beings.

174

There is nothing old in my studio, save for some favourite tools that I use all the time. Old paintings don't stay. My assistant and my agent make sure of that. Old paintings that haven't sold or that I no longer feel connected to get a fresh coat of gesso, so I can start again. I no longer use harsh artificial varnishes unless the client specifically wants it. Wax is the preferred medium now, once I am sure the painting has hardened enough to take it. Usually, I don't cover them at all. That way, if I need to re-use the canvas, it is so much easier. Nothing old. It's a bit of an obsession of mine as I myself get older. I don't want to leave dusty corners filled with ancient, irrelevant stuff that no one knows what to do with or wants. Every day is a fresh experience, every connection with you, every painting I do. If all of that ever stops, then I know it's time for me to go. After all, what use is life if I am not filling it with fresh experiences? Then it simply becomes a process played out for as long as survival is there. I think I'd also like to learn to play the sax properly. It has sat there for so many years and it is such a beautiful instrument. I still have my breath, and the swimming and the gym keep me fit. I wonder if I can gain the flexibility and dexterity in my fingers to make the music sparkle. Some new projects, new paintings, new writing. Push the envelope so it is no longer stationery! Look up. Look forward. Remember those seven key qualities[17] and live!

175

I have been attempting to incorporate the notion of time into the painting that I am working on. It has always fascinated me that, in my experience, time is not linear. How I experience time can vary. I can drive one way along a road and it is quick; drive the other way and time gets drawn out. An evening with friends can seem interminable or gone all too quickly. And it's not just about my engagement in the conversation or whatever is going on. Whole days can pass with me hardly noticing the time passing, or they expand and give me the opportunity to do more, or be still, or observe things more deeply. It feels as if time has sped up generally, but I know that is the experience of many people as they age, so maybe that is a different phenomenon. I know scientists have found out all sorts of things about time and have built various constructs around it, but does that really explain anything on the level of personal experience—that slippery, infinitely forgettable, omni-present ghost of our souls that plays with our minds, emotions and senses? So, it is a challenge to incorporate such an ethereal, fleeting thing in two dimensions with ancient tools. Especially when the subject itself is always moving and presenting different aspects—not just changing light but also all the changing aspects of me. Is a painting even possible? And would I recognize it for what I intended it to be? Or does every painting always incorporate it?

176

I am so glad that the work you are doing now makes you happy. Your face lights up all the time when you tell me of the effects your consultations have on people, and the fun you are having with your latest book. You no longer look concerned about the passing years and you have not once mentioned that you are looking older. You're not, as a matter of fact. Happiness and peace of mind have been rejuvenating for you. What I am noticing, for both of us, is a maturing of our work and a kind of quietening to it. Gone are the anxious protests, the feeling of helplessness in the face of an all-dominating machine that threatens our lives in so many ways. Gone are the floods of e-mails—the anger and tears that people cry, the symptoms and so-called evidence of so much that can be wrong—they no longer invade our inbox. Now you have connected only with true seekers, the ones who are determined to move up, not down. Your connection with the quantum field and consciousness has shown its subtle power in channelling the good towards you and the bad away. I feel its effects every day. The more you do it, the more utterly attractive you become. The more powerfully beautiful you radiate out to the world. The deeper I love and want you. It's kind of infectious; revealing and oh so attractive. And it opens everyone's eyes to what is possible, how much abundance and beauty there is in the world. You did it, we did it, and now we always will.

177

I have to focus on my art. That is how I play my part. It is not by argument and counter-argument with those who cannot hear or who are so set in a train of thought and belief that to change would threaten their entire identity. It is not by activism or intellect. It is by being human and part of my community and a love of life. And I can express that through art, the most powerful means of communication that has ever been. Because it can bypass the so-called rational mind and connect directly with humanity in whatever way the observer needs most. It's not always pretty, as it has a job to do, which can sometimes be confronting, uncomfortable and unwelcome. Yet it can illuminate those minds to new ways and, lovingly in its aggression, start to help a new vision emerge. The common consciousness is a superficial, ever-changing sea of confusion that bubbles up with occasional revelations that move us forward a little, in some part of it or other. Influences wax and wane, shock turns to boredom, intensity evolves to new norms. And still there will be those, by societal pressure or plain ignorant stubbornness, who will provide the colour of an ever-more irrelevant minority and stay stuck. At the other end of the spectrum of consciousness, the dreamers, creatives and seers create new minorities that bud and flower.

178

"Darling," I say to you as you hide behind the bathroom door, "you are huge. You are vast. You are interfering with flight paths. You stand as a colossus of mythical proportions. At least, that's how you appear to him. So what's the problem?" You poke your head around the door, smiling apologetically. I fall in love all over again. I just want to rush to you, take you in my arms and smother you with kisses. But I can see that this is a serious situation—which, unless handled deftly and speedily, could lead to some emotional fallout. Hands on hips, I peer over the side of the bath, feigning seriousness. The spider, at this point, is blissfully unaware of its impending fate. Doing its spider thing, exploring new territories, marvelling at this vast, white, seamless, skateboarding park, its surface only occasionally broken with bulbous drops of water positioned as slalom barriers to skirt around. He's looking at me now, while also curiously assessing his own distorted reflection through multiple eye sockets. Life was getting complicated for him, and is about to get traumatic. Suddenly, Boris, for that is his name, is enveloped in a restrictive white surface. It happened so fast there was no time to run. I carry him, being careful not to crush his fine legs, past you (as you back away from me), down the stairs, out into the garden. I choose a suitable bit of foliage and introduce him to his new home. He's safe. I'm a hero, You run your bath.

179

We seem to spend most of life finding our place in it. Isn't that strange? On the one hand, we attempt to expand our knowledge and expertise and, on the other hand, we tend to narrow our focus further and further. Is it that we are so daunted by the enormity of what is happening that we seek sanctuary in small places? Are we not designed to comprehend the vast areas of living and spirit, consciousness and even the geography of this tiny blue planet? What a strange phenomenon we are. At once given enough to be conscious, yet not so much that we don't end up in catastrophes of our own making, driven as we are by confusion, ego, lack of connection to the world and therefore our innate knowledge that can be used to harmonise our existence. I dare not stop to think about it too much. Just keep dabbling, keep enjoying and playing. Dangers lurk in too much thought. That's where man's weaknesses spawn on the dysfunction that has beset us. Yet, as I dabble, I am increasingly aware and I am giving much more credence to intuition and feelings, for my own guidance. Before I met you, my plan was to 'have fun', but I quickly realized—or maybe it was realized for me—that there is only emptiness without any sort of meaningful connection. So, as I sit in my studio and paint you yet again, it is another celebration of my salvation.

180

I take a minute. Or ten or twenty or thirty or as many as it takes to come back. The veil of reality shifts sometimes so that the perfect place I am in is not apparent to me. Nothing has changed, apart from something in me. Imperceptible and easily denied, because my perception has shifted and drawn a steel door across my vision, on which is engraved, in deep, immutable letters, concern, serious, stress, worry, unhappy, fear. A dissolving steel door that I choose to see as solid and vast, without end, stretching above and below me, and to the horizons on both sides of me. It disappears into the dark clouds above me and I look down into the chasm, thousands of feet below me, where it is rooted. Yet one minute, ten or twenty or a few more can remove it, taking with it all memory of its corroded presence, weight and sombre depression. As if it were never there. Yet here I am, back again in my perfect place that is real and filled with light and joy and a reality that, despite the occasional obscuring by my own choices, remains true. I cannot remove it because it is the reality, so I might as well just enjoy it, because danger lurks in becoming too attached to the other—as well as madness and hopelessness—and I cannot afford those useless conditions. And why would I want them, anyway?

181

John Lennon famously said 'Life is what happens to you when you're busy making other plans'. I feel my life has been one of purposely avoiding making plans. I wonder if that means that I truly experience life. I made a decision many years ago to work with my art in that way. The result has been that I have a pile of unrelated things that I have produced in my effort to work with 'a beginner's mind'. I still question that ethic, driven as I am by a need for success and concern that, unless I produce evermore polished work, I will be perceived as an amateur. Finding the balance between simply doing what comes naturally and creating from intention and purpose, has been something that has dogged me all my life. That and seeing the work of others who are doing it differently, on their own course, and whose work I admire. Yet, truly, I know I must go through this painful process repeatedly, starting from scratch each time. That is the course I am on, and it is just as valid as any. No plans, then. And isn't it ironic that, without planning, I have found some success? The doubters and the critics were wrong. The doubter and the critic inside me is just as wrong. I have proved that, time and time again, without intending to and having no desire to. It just happens. I still hold a vision of ease and energy that eludes me in my work to this day. Yet, at the same time, something inside me tells me I really don't want that.

182

We are lying on loungers languidly laughing, loudly and loquaciously. Although I don't really know what that last one means but, what the hell, we're laughing anyway. I should look it up, but that would mean getting up, walking up the beach to the house and searching for a dictionary. Never mind. Knowing what it means won't improve the situation. It's already perfect. We're doing the 'reach your potential' pose—arms out-stretched. But, rather than standing on a mountain watching a misty sunset, we are lying on our backs on the loungers, staring up at the sky, laughing. We managed to reach our potential from this position, outside our home on the beach. Seems pretty good to me. No hiking for days, staying in rough accommodation, blistered feet, bad hotel food, parched all the time, smelly socks, weatherproof clothing, annoying fit people along the way. We have reached our full potential and we are staying there. Exhausted from laughing, we decide that it's actually more comfortable with our arms down by our sides, and we have already tanned the under-arms, so we no longer need to lie in a funny way to even things up. I think those outdoor mountaineering types have misunderstood a fundamental truth. Full potential is inside. Not up a mountain. It's an internal journey, twit! Oh, I know they know that, as well, of course, but when you've reached full potential, what else is there left to do, but fall about laughing?

183

I'm beginning to get a bit of a 'Jack Reacher' attitude towards clothing, these days. Having hauled various twenty-year-old (and older) items across the world for each of our moves, it was great to simply dump a whole case full of them. We each have a walk-in wardrobe attached to the master bedroom. Mine has a few clothes in it, but I have converted it into a sound recording studio, for the most part, where I doodle on my sax and, occasionally, we make some worldly declaration. But what I really love is when you use it to sing. They say that music keeps you young. Well, in that case, I am bordering on the criminal with you. Your voice, so seductive and pure, really shines in this little space. We should start a record label! What could we call it? Closet Music? Could be good. After all, you've kept yourself and this wonderful talent locked away most of your life. Now we have the means, along with our musical friends and a bit of digital jiggery pokery, to bring it right out of the closet and feed the world's ears with something beautiful; something they crave and need to hear. As with any great art form, the lyrics of your songs carry your message with creativity, and your voice and words carry your eloquence, refinement and love, in ways that the written or even spoken word cannot. A perfect outfit to be worn with joy and thanks from the inside out.

184

For once, I am glad that I cannot sleep. I would have missed this, otherwise. I check you are okay. Yes, you are peaceful. I pause, not wanting to leave you, wanting to stay and watch the gentle heave of your breast as you lie there dreaming of who knows what? Hatching the next book, no doubt. I slip out of bed and walk downstairs, out onto the monochrome blue-and-white deck lit by a silver moon, down the steps and through the gate onto the beach. The cool sand is softly giving under my feet as I walk towards the smoother, harder sand and the gently nudging surf. If ever I wanted to feel alone and yet in the presence of the Universe, this is the best way to do it. Clear sky filled with myriad stars and twinkling planets. The vast and beautiful power of a gentle sea, breathing through its depths of history and presence, promise and creativity. So gently, whispering stories of the incredible and the possible way beyond my limited abilities to think up or even attempt to manifest. Blackness, brimming over with colour, held in place by gravity, the cycles of the moon and an enclosing surface so strong that it can retain the entire world's oceans, and yet so delicate that I can pierce it with a casual footfall, let it run through my fingers, or let it carry me in perfect balance in its embrace and eternal energy. There is just one thing missing. I look back. Should I wake you?

185

When it comes down to it, do we really want a hand print of a star on Broadway, or a hand print in the surf in a beautiful place like this? Do we want to enter into 'popular culture', so-called, or into a fleeting relationship with this planet and those we truly love? To me, the Broadway version is a declaration of huge ego, that we matter and that people need us in some way. The sand version is a declaration of me simply existing and being a grateful part of all this, that merges with it again in the action of a wave. I press my hand into the sand again. Again, there is a perfect impression for a second or two, before it fills with water and gets pulled back into smoothness. The perfect swipe, revealing for me the subtlety of life and my true part in it. Only I see it. Only I know. That's plenty good enough. And I am proud of what I am. I think of your words on a video I once saw, where you challenge us to call ourselves out on our lies. Just as a hand in a star on Broadway is a lie—the illusion created by the person to achieve greatness in the eyes of others, but not a manifestation of any real truth—I struggle happily with this every day. How do I stop lying? In moments like this, I cannot lie. The truth of me, of my significance and reality is imprinted for ever in the fleeting moment, in the rush of water, over and over again.

186

Too much has been taken out of our hands and given to technology and convenience. I see that, sometimes. At others, I am glad of it. I think it's a lot to do with connection. We float above the surface of life when we give ourselves to the machine and take from it whatever it offers. Consumers, not creators. Van Gogh would take a hollow bamboo and sharpen it to make a unique pen. I go to an 'art materials shop' and spend time choosing a range of pens made from steel, carefully designed to assist flow, create consistency of line, reserve enough ink to make several marks. I still have some goose quills from Suffolk. It was so long ago that Mike Carlo[18] introduced me to wild and uncontrollable feathers that changed character with every cut, until there was no longer a hollow space to retain the ink. I loved those drawings and must get back to that more natural way of working. It's remarkable, when I think now, that I am one of very few modern-day artists who have actually mixed pure pigment with oil—rock and medium—to make a paste and then apply it. We live in a world where being connected to the source of things is seen more as an inconvenience, a time-waster, inefficient and slow. Yet, in missing that connection, I feel we can often lose out, miss the essence, the pure driving force of our existence and who we really are. Such a shame.

187

It's incredible to think that none of this has ever been written before. Nothing that any of us does, thinks, dreams, has been done, thought or dreamt before. We are as unique as each moment that we live. So, if anything counts for anything at all, it all does. The magnitude of that is mind-boggling but, on the surface, it must mean that we have some significance, some lack of randomness, some path or other that we tread. And that means that all the introspection that I indulge in is, perhaps, a complete waste of time. Or is it? Ha! There I go again! Even the limited plane of the canvas before me baffles me with its choices. I do know that every mark I make is, to some extent, irreversible. I can wipe it out and replace it, but that doesn't expunge the previous choice that is lodged somewhere in the universal hard drive. And, even more superficially, how can I ever know the right choice, if such a thing exists, for the colour I am mixing now, to be applied where, in what shape, with what brush, in a way that will build on my previous choices and yield, at the end of the day, a thing, a product, a feeling that I will assess as having been worthwhile for this tiny slice of time, in my studio and all the way out to the bigger picture, that isn't simply massaging the feelings of others, but that will stand its test and make some positive difference?

188

Where is it all going? Has anyone really got a plan? As we crowd out the planet and devise empty ways of coping and ways to pass time and be comfortable and beat our neighbour to the next 'good thing', do we have any idea what we are really doing? Is the purpose still to procreate, amass, decline and die, to be completely forgotten by all but a few as the train wreck of progress sucks people along, ever more urgently, through their blindness? It's a bad joke, if you stop to think about it, pierced through by opportunists, chancers, manipulators and control freaks who find their utopia in the eroticism of their chosen dysfunction, driving the grey people on to inhuman acts and wants, their brains addled by the complexity and confusion that has been served up to them on a golden platter atop the carcass of history. Open your minds or open your legs, they'll fuck you either way. It makes no difference to them. And the wise and intelligent, the caring, the concerned, the sensitive of heart are all too soft in the head to even grasp the corruption or the machine, built over centuries to run it all—let alone do anything about it. Protest is victimhood, concern is a BandAid on self-annihilation, wisdom is for the dusty shelves of the agreeable and the agreeing. Art is the only true voice: when it finds its own language, it can surpass all this. That is why I search and think and experiment till I die.

189

The road is full of potholes that have suddenly appeared in a freak storm that, every now and then, has turned it into a raging river across my path, carrying branches and debris down towards the coast. I took a chance, leaving the café while it was still pouring, but now the rain has almost stopped. It's remarkable how suddenly the whole landscape can change—form benign warmth and peaceful rolling hills, to a dark, forbidding place where nothing is certain any more. It feels dangerous to chance the waters, but the other impetus in me drives me on, balancing risk against my destination—my precious love, my home and everything I hold dear. There is no replacement for you, for us, for everything we are together. I would risk it all to be sure that you are okay, that some freak accident hasn't damaged you, or worse. I cannot even think of that. I keep moving forward, inching through the battering tumult, feeling the grip of the tyres on muddy ground, willing the car forward despite the forces that would see me slip sideways. The urge to survive could not be greater if I were drowning. A moment like this, that I pray will pass without incident, shows me just how important you are to me, how much and how deeply I love you, and how urgently I need to be with you, locked in your embrace, filled with relief and the knowledge that we continue.

190

"Express yourself," they say. But therein lies a conundrum. To express yourself, I guess you also have to know yourself, so that you can know what to express. I guess that is why art is an infinite journey. Not least because knowing yourself is an evolution. It's not a fixed thing that you learn and can then sit back, all satisfied and replete. It's also interesting that you can only express yourself. You cannot express someone else, however much you try. So, there's another conundrum. With this portrait I am doing, how can I express the person without the image being primarily about me!? Is a portrait ever about the sitter, or is it always about the artist? The National Portrait Gallery is full of images of people, but it is the artists who get the credit for the image, not the sitter. I cannot express you or anyone else, without expressing me first, and that is always my own process of discovery. The person I am painting may be fascinating in so many ways, but I am always painting a reflection of me, seen through my reaction to that person. What a funny world it is. We can never get away from ourselves—although we struggle to see ourselves in a true light—let alone know ourselves. Even when I look in the mirror, it may be that what I see is different to what others see when they look at me. How am I to know? All I can see is an accumulation of time, behaviour, thoughts, judgments, prejudices. Where am I?

191

"What do you think?" I check your look as I climb down from the ladder in the dining room. You don't say anything for a while. Then, you frown slightly and say: "I like it." Your uncertainty is showing through. I feel it in the pit of my stomach, but I let it pass as I return the ladder to the studio. Even just a few minutes of time passing can make a difference. I come back. You are still standing in the same place, looking at the new abstract that dominates the area. Even though you have seen me working on it for weeks, this changes everything; having it hanging in our precious space. Is it right? It's all about change, again, isn't it! Sometimes, we grow into it. Sometimes, we force it; sometimes, we welcome it. With my art, we are rarely ready to welcome it. That is good, because the comfortable and the familiar don't disturb our souls and mobilize our feelings. We just slot them in to an existing framework of lazy acceptance. The best paintings are a little ahead of us, perhaps a little daring or uncomfortable; a little more revealing of a fresh depth that we were only peripherally aware of, but we are aware of it. We just haven't brought it to the fore. Perhaps we don't recognize it yet. David Bowie said that an artwork is only complete once those interactions have taken place. I can see that. It is, after all, a communication. Not one hand clapping. We prepare dinner for the client who is coming to pick it up. "Do you want me to put the old one back?"

192

It's been a long drive. I didn't feel like doing it, so Manuel kindly offered to drive me in the van. It was hot; no aircon and the smell of fish and motor oil. A great trip with a good friend. It's just not the same, buying my art materials online; so, every month or two, I have to make the journey to the big city—no, I choose to—to experience the things that I will use in my next batch of work. I spend a couple of hours in the shop. They like to see me, because I always fill the van with canvases, paper, oils and so on. Online, you cannot feel the weight of a tube of paint, or remove the top and smear a little on your finger to see how much pigment is among the filler, or how bright it is, or assess its strength or opaqueness. Online, you cannot talk to the owner of the shop about the uses and merits of various mediums (or is that media?) and how they affect the finished product. You cannot feel the bristles of a brush, or choose the best one from the bunch on display. You cannot feel the texture of a canvas or inspect its construction and check it for lumps and bumps, So much that all the technology in the world cannot bring you. And it can never bring you a rich conversation over a coffee with a good friend before the drive back, with new smells filling the van. And so it is with my work. You cannot even see it online. The technology is just so crude, so inadequate and childish in the face of the magnificence of what the world really has to offer.

193

We all want a voice, don't we? Whether we simply want to communicate with the person standing beside us or with the whole world. We want to be heard. What voice, though? We are distorted and moulded as we grow, we take on the preachings of others and they become our own. We draw inspiration from art, music, philosophy, and integrate parts of them into our story, our voice. So, what is our voice, in essence—rather than the imperfect conglomeration of all that we have been fed? Training, education, religion, ritual, customs all jammed into the psyche, as early as possible (ideally, before age 7) to make sure the character is set, societal integration is known, expectations and levels of self-worth are established. Then the mute being, pre-programmed and socialized for a place in the world that is designed to fulfill the desires of those whose accident of birth or freaky determination landed them at the top of the pile, is launched from the womb of the home and told to exercise self-responsibility; feed the machine. Yet, even then, there are those who find a voice—maybe not their true voice—and rise above the grey masses with influence and their own brand of inspiration. And the grey masses look up to them, filled with wonder, unaware that they have been duped and cheated and didn't find their own voice because they never really loved themselves.

194

It's all about relationships. That is also one of the aspects of art that I love to explore. And it always seems to be that the exploration is a metaphor for any type of relationship. When I start drawing the model, I don't know the model. I start with a feature or a gesture that seems to define the overall sense of the pose. Sometimes, I take the odd measurement; sometimes, I just follow my instincts. As lines and tones are drawn, I make adjustments for inaccuracies, make things larger or smaller, even up one part against another. Sometimes, it is best to not try to impose an outline before I have explored the surfaces and the way the light plays upon them. Delving into subtleties that I didn't even see when I started, taking into account slight movements or the way the light changes, working the shading and learning about the structure, the feeling and the mood of what lies beneath the surface. What is hidden from view, underneath and round the other side, defines the reality of the outer form. I cannot get to it any other way. Only when all this is done, can I choose—should I even want to—to enclose parts of the form with boundaries. Yet, even then, it is often best to simply show how the background interacts with what I have discovered. Even then, all that I have produced is a flat image, in lights and darks, perhaps colour, and lines, of something I will never truly understand.

195

It's eleven o'clock at night. We are both tired after a long walk in the sun on the beach. This time, we got halfway to the village and back. You could have gone all the way. In my mind, when I am with you, my age and physical condition are that of a twenty-five-year-old. Yes, let's go to the village, get a meal, dance all night and walk back arm in arm as the dawn breaks, fall into bed and make love for hours. Then, maybe, think about sleep. If I had known then what I know now; if I had had all that learning that you have given me back then. If I had come to you complete and able to give you the stars from day one. How incredible would that have been? To roll back the decades and meet you clear, strong, powerful and loving. Then roll them forward again in this perfect light, would that have been the perfect life for you? I don't know. What I do know is, at this moment, at eleven o'clock at night, your hair is right for a photo session (according to you) and we both know it's not going to happen. We laugh a laugh together that is so close, so a part of each other, that no perfect past could have designed it. This laugh, in this perfect moment, born out of everything we have experienced together over the years, our incredible journey together, trial and error, ups and downs, creativity, growth, challenges and tenderness. A rollercoaster emotional galactic shift, a life of incredible colour and deep, deep love. Why would I ever, in a million years, want it any other way?

196

I watch your smooth action as I swim behind you. I have always been in awe of the way you can swim like that. You seem to use so little energy and yet I sometimes struggle to keep up as you cruise effortlessly through the water. My mind is stilled at times like this—or simply filled with you. There is no room for anything else, just the detail of what is before me. I dip my head beneath the surface and watch the sun-dappled movement of your legs. You are flying among flashing, tiny fish that dart here and there, bright silver jewels accompanying their queen. I pull up my head. Above the surface, you are lost in your own thoughts. Your back is golden brown and slick with water. Those lovely shoulders, rising and falling with the rhythm. There's a different world out here, in the water. Silent and all-embracing, it's a place we are not designed to live in, but it's so beautiful to visit and play. I dive down and swim beneath you, twist onto my back for the full view. That lovely body that completely wows me, that I make love to in heavenly moments, that you have shared with me so exquisitely all these years. You are still as beautiful now as that first time I laid you down in Begnins, that time when you walked out of the sea in Langkawi, the days and nights in Vancouver and so many places when I photographed you in the hope of capturing some of your magic. In a way, I didn't need to, because it is always there.

197

We can choose to be small, or we can choose to be big. It just depends on diet—food and life. Good metaphor. If we take the easy, pre-packaged, convenient, unthinking, un-self-caring route, consuming stuff devised by others primarily for their own gain, we get fat and lazy, uninspired and empty-souled. And the sadness, or aggression, or sense of unfairness that we feel, we take out on ourselves and those around us. Consuming, not creating, is finite, unsustainable and unsatisfying. Surely, we know that—right from the start? Maybe not if, in the formative years, we have been subjected to deep programming that we feel powerless to discard in what should be our discovery years. Creating, on the other hand, is limitless and expansive, bringing with it the natural tendency to question what is, to break us out of old patterns that cease to serve us—or perhaps never did—and take us to a sustainable, joyous, meaningful existence that can satisfy our soul, broaden us in every respect except our waistline. Because, with creativity, our mind develops self-worth and harmonious habits that are good for us, keep us younger, and build healthy discernment. So, really, what's to choose? The automatic choice is to grow big in all the healthy ways. Staying small is the shortest route to annihilation and death without ever having lived. Creativity is the challenge, the best life, and the biggest.

198

"L'embarras de choix," you sigh as we survey the vegetable patch that has burst into life behind our backs. The irrigation system that we installed is working almost too well. "L'embarras de chou," I reply. Row upon row of green and purple cabbages like a field full of footballs. A far cry from our first attempts in France. Beans search the tops of the poles for somewhere higher to hold on, instead loping sideways, this way and that in thin air. Tomato clusters bend their bearers earthward, leeks standing like an army on parade. I dare not think about the carrots, parsnips and potatoes that must be swelling beneath, out of sight. "The funny thing about all this," I say, "is that we'll end up giving most of it away and then buying fresh stuff from the supermarkets and the market when they are out of season." "Not if I can help it," you say, with a determination in your voice that tells me we have a busy few weeks ahead of us. Making sauerkraut, storing potatoes and more in our earth cellar[19], squishing tomatoes into purée and preserving them in jars. I don't know what you plan for the leeks and some of the other veggies. Herbs will get finely chopped and dried, soft fruits will be preserved. It's actually all work that I have grown to love and cherish as we learn, year by year, how we are meant to be living in this world. Respecting the seasons, living in and working with nature, caring for and valuing its abundance and each other.

199

I still try, still practise slowing down. Yet it's more than that. It's more about being present. There's a delicate balance to it, I am discovering. To be present and aware of everything, and not, in the process, miss the dynamic progress of things simply because I am so focused on the now. I suppose that is why I could never be, and would have no desire to be, a hyper-realist painter. Fixing a hyper-observed object in infinite detail is admirable, impressive and awesome, but it somehow diminishes its subject by fixing it in aspic, so it cannot move or evolve. It somehow becomes a relic of a past event, rather than the continuing miracle that it otherwise is. For me, the excitement is in the dynamism, the unknown, the essence and the life. The lack of control in a swiftly drawn quill ink figure retains more of that for exploration and discovery in the future. The looseness leaves more to the viewer to be a part of it and for it to live beyond its surface. And I haven't sacrificed days and days, trying to stop time. There are temptations all around, from ego and others, to take the impressive path. And, even as I write this, tricks of the mind are asking if I am afraid to try and fail at being one of those artists. Yet here I am, digging out a few weeds from the plantings on the steps down to the gate onto the beach, and I can truly enjoy and really see each plant, and they speak to me of unknowns in the language of the universe, and I am at peace.

200

Time is the biggest luxury and connection is the best way to use it. When I look around our wonderful home and its beautiful surroundings, I can see that now, more clearly than ever before. Our home is a reflection of time spent connecting. Everything inside it, acquired and kept with love, is only meaningful because of the associations that they are imbued with. Otherwise, they are just things—tools, furniture, equipment, conveniences, consumables. Seen like that, they are empty and worthless in terms of heart and soul, but seen through the myriad connections through time that brought them into our lives, they are so much more. Our garden—a manifestation of the passing of time and our connection with the earth and what it can yield. Our environment, bigger than anything we can touch or influence in all of our lifetimes, given to us to play in, forged over millions of years into something that has such a deep and fundamental connection to everything we are, that it boggles the mind and we just accept and are grateful for all of it. We cannot even understand the beauty of a sunrise or a sunset, yet we are deeply connected to them. I guess that is one of the many reasons that people who have little can often be more happy than those who have a lot—driven by the empty promise of consumerism and accumulation. Yes, we have some of that too, but we live in luxury despite it.

201

I am in an empty space. It's even empty of emptiness. Should I try to pull myself out, or should I simply acknowledge it and be in it. Empty is an unfamiliar place where I feel out of place. Maybe that's why I need to be in it. It's not necessarily an ending place. In fact, some sort of logic tells me that no empty place can be an end, as something has to happen, before an end can take place, as it were. So, we cannot end empty. So, it must be a starting place. Even that thought, therefore, completely removes 'empty', because now there is an idea, sitting quietly in the space, lifting me a little, although I don't yet know where to. Even writing this is a denial of emptiness, a betrayal of it, as thoughts become scribbles and the page fills up. In fact, the emptiness, if it ever was truly there in the first place, cannot exist now. Other things—fear, uncertainty, confusion—may be there, to some degree, but not in emptiness. I therefore have a choice as to what I fill this faux void with. What will it be? If I search my mind, it has no answers, so I must return to the void and use other faculties to emerge and move on. Faculties that are beyond mind, which I know exist because I am the living evidence of them, but that I cannot comprehend, or think, or work out, because they are beyond my mind, which falsely gave me an illusion, an idea, a sadness that my emptiness existed.

202

The woman in the coffee bar took my money on this bright, sunny day. Eyes averted, tight-lipped, I could feel her tension. I sat and observed. Flashing glances, whispered asides to her colleagues, fussy, fast actions. I felt sad for her, to be wasting her life like that. I wondered how her face could light up if she smiled. I suppose we have all been where she is, in a world of serious drama all of her own that coloured everything she saw with dark shadows. How incredible is it that it takes so long to find ourselves, and all the time we are inside, somewhere so well hidden, that we don't even believe it. We don't believe in us. It took me decades and I know I am still a work in progress. I sometimes wonder if, once we have truly found ourselves, that's when it all ends. So there's another reason to keep me in the dark, attached as I am to so much of the drama myself. Yet I know that it is only in truly knowing and loving me that I can truly know and love you. So, the drama has its uses, and it plays with our emotions, perceptions and realities to push us along on this journey. I feel I am close. The decades with you have changed me, taken me forward, helped me realize my vision, given me the perfect friend and lover to make the journey with me. I am hyper-aware of you. Every sight, move, sound, nuance goes deep with joy. I tread lightly, with full attention; forever exploring the mystery of loving you.

203

I am amazed at our good fortune, but I also know we earned it. We paid our dues in ways that most shy away from. A regular job followed by a pension was, however, never an option for two such as us—creatives with principles and integrity. If that sounds superior, I guess it is—and it doesn't exclude all those who did it the other way with those qualities intact. You worked hard, selflessly and with huge integrity and high standards, poking minds in ways that were sometimes unpopular because you insisted on unmasking deeper truths. They are often the types of truth that we avoid confronting. In the end, though, we have to, if we want to clear the way forward and lead a life that we truly want and that is a perfect fit for us. Echoes of Frank Sinatra in my mind as I think about this, as I drive home from the airport, having achieved the privileged status of avoiding airport queues and petty officialdom; the Aston burbling softly as I glide at lightning speed down the autoroute, radar detector on green. There's no denying that the journey here—to recognition and rewards—was a long and tough one. Although, it just felt as if that was the way things were for us, that was our normality, and we laughed and loved our way through it. And then life truly bloomed for us. The vision we held all those years suddenly manifested out of thin air, it seemed, and now, it feels as if we can really get going. The best is yet to come!

204

I am so proud of you! And this session is yet another reason for it. You are so willing, so game, so happy to try new things. It's sometimes hard for me to focus on the job in hand, because I am so disarmed by you and the way you are. This was just a whim I had, but it is turning into a fabulous photo session with my muse. Our terrace catches the sunlight, the plants and concrete structure throw ever-changing, complex shadows, and the glass reflects and fills in, creating beautiful patterns all around. Your body, arranged in different ways in this landscape of light, adds such beauty and incredible forms that I am lost for words. You twist and turn, bend, spread out, close up, arrange yourself in symphony with the lights and darks, the man-made and the natural, bringing new life, strange echoes, indefinable structures and soft, powerful humanity to a space we see every day, and yet we miss so much. I guess that's the excitement I have always found in creativity, and in you, and all of life. And it is so wonderful that, even now, you are happy and proud of who you are, how you look and all aspects of yourself. No hiding, no self-consciousness, just 'look at me!' without arrogance or showiness, but sensitively knowing the beauty that you are and gracing my imagery with it, just as you do with the rest of your life.

205

It's a great exercise to loosen the art students up and take them out of their world back home and out of their heads before we get into the studio situation. Drawing with long sticks in the sand next to the surf, I can usually tell how the week is going to open up: who'll really get it, who'll find it hard, who'll want to give up and go home before the week is out. I try to hold on to them, in case they make a breakthrough, but it's not always possible. It's the morning of the first day. And it feels like that for some of them. There's a woman in a long sun dress, dancing in the surf, making broad, generous strokes, enjoying the nature and being part of it. She'll enjoy the course, but I don't think she'll be particularly inspiring. There's a man, rushing with each breaker to draw an impressive masterpiece. He'll be the technician in the group, probably doing careful, detailed drawings. There's another girl taking her time; T-shirt and shorts. She's arranging pebbles to augment the stick marks that come and go, building foundations to build on next time, that shift and open up new possibilities. She'll do well. We think we are mysterious islands unto ourselves. Yet we don't realize just how much we communicate in our unguarded moments, how much obvious signalling we do, how transparent we are to anyone who cares to look. I immediately feel like apologizing to you for the open book that I am, and my resistance along the way.

206

I will never understand enough about the ecology of our planet to be able to join enough dots and come to clear conclusions as to how and why things have worked out as they have. Nor will I understand the shifts in climate that heat and cool different parts of the world at different times. I have never studied any of it and I don't know if I would truly grasp the big picture if I were to devote the rest of my life to it. Like the rest of the natural world, all I can do is watch it, work with it, adapt to it—occasionally moving to find greener pastures, although I think I am done with that. We have become accustomed to violent 'anomalies' in the weather. Those have seemingly been accepted by people all over the world, as an inevitable consequence of the lifestyles the wealthy aspire to, and the framework of economics that rules, to keep those aspirations in place. Only those who suffer its horrific consequences ever want to return to something more natural and they are all too often the meek and sensitive, who don't shout as loudly as the others. All this makes me so grateful for our home, the community close by and the micro-climate in our area that has retained its abundant natural rhythms. Yet, even here, we see some of the consequences of a world gone mad, although some are magnificent. As I sit in the late evening on our terrace, he settles lightly on the wall opposite me. "Hello, Timothy[20]."

207

I need stimulation. The best art I produce seems to be as a direct result of an experience, however unrelated or distant, that awakens in me some sort of plan. And, I have to say, that the best pieces are planned out, to some extent or other. Much as I would like to think that there is some sort of magical process, some inspirational super-state that I get into and that theatrically bursts forth onto the canvas, it is not true. There is work involved, diligence, serious thought—as well as a letting go that stops my head from getting in the way of a flow, an experiment or a happy accident. The best work is when I get that balance right, and the universe provides an additive quality that I had not perceived. It's as if the universe is just waiting for me to show that I have serious intent, an idea and some sort of focus and clarity. Otherwise, what's the point of it stepping in, if the commitment isn't there? The stimulation I am aware of, although I need to pay more attention to it. I need to be more impeccable, searching, investigative of even the slightest nudge as it brushes past me when I am on the way to somewhere else. To give it the attention and let it grow, to allow a detour from a fixed path (that is most likely the Universal Creative dropping a subtle hint; carefully, sensitively and quietly while also hinting at its immense power and potential); that is what I must do.

208

What am I thinking about, today? I think, and then I think about those thoughts, detaching myself, observing. So much of the thinking comes from programming and from memories that pull you back into it, if you are lazy and don't resist. Where, in that case, does original thought reside? Is it something we have to build ourselves, from scratch? Yes, we can re-program, but even the re-programmed thoughts come from somewhere else—a book, a therapy session, or some sort of construct designed usually by others to take you from A to B. A new thought, then, like a new image, floats without edges to catch and grasp onto, in its own knowingness that I cannot meet, seemingly, without reference to something else that I do recognize, however slightly. The most mysterious art, to have an impact, always alludes to or evokes something we know, however obliquely or however well it is hidden. A thought without any anchor. What is that? Maybe it's the definition of madness for an observer in the cradle of collective normality. We claim to love creativity, yet we fear it and tie it down to fit it within the very boundaries we hope to break free from. And can we truly achieve it, anyway? Are we equipped to go beyond the ties of recognition and reference and copying in some way or other? I think I will have to change my terms of reference in order to go beyond.

209

Even after all this time, I still have to discipline myself to go into the studio and stay there, working through the thoughts, the doubts, the physical challenge, the arrangement of canvas, paints, media etc, and the first actions—the preparation of the canvas, the arranging of palette, thoughts on the image the search in me for inspiration to at least make a start, perhaps the re-energizing of an old canvas, the continuation of a piece that has been drying for a few days, the onslaught of potential distractions and the separation from whatever is outside my door. STOP. I have to stop all this. Sometimes, I just wish there was a seamless continuity through all aspects of my life, my day, my being with you, this place and everything I love about my existence. That's the way I feel it should be, yet every time I start again on this journey, it's as if I am forcing all my being and everything associated with it through the tiniest of holes in order to feel the sublime release as I emerge on the other side, floating in ecstasy. Sometimes, when the painting is done, I get that feeling, but even the anticipation of disappointment after all the work, can create yet another blockage. Yet I feel driven to produce in this hellish vacuum where there are no boundaries or rules; the only place where the man of action in me believes I can make some lasting difference; my legacy and expression of love for you.

210

There is a great delicacy and deep subtlety to this existence and how we move within it. The need to stay centred and focused on what is important has never been so apparent to me. I don't want to rely on routine and order to maintain my equilibrium, and I constantly have to check that I am coming from the right place, inside me. We are masters of our environment to a degree to which we are largely unaware, and we are masters of ourselves only to the extent that we are aware. And so, I constantly change the environment to keep my awareness honed. The act of painting is a measure of how strong I am within myself. And that is reflected back to me in everything that interacts with my being. A conversation with you, a mistimed word, a tightening inside, an avoidance, annoyance at things not being as I perceive they should be, are all essential feedback that I can learn from and use to build a better me. The biggest and most tragic conflicts happen when I am not conscious. If I ever upset the person I love beyond anything in this world, I am just as conscious of my own hopeless devastation as I am your upset or hurt. I strive to stay on track in mind, body and spirit. The track is not so obvious at times when clarity eludes me, so I hope you forgive the occasional swerve or jolt. They are just wake-up calls and, with the help of my perfect partner, serve to get me back there.

211

It seems as if it carries a certain cachet if people say they know us, or if they have spent time here on a course, at a concert or for whatever reason. One of the reasons inquiries are filtered through your assistant is to weed out the lookers—the 'social climbers', would you believe! And all because you loudly proclaim the truth and help people find it in themselves and in the world, and because I daub paint on canvas. That's it! All the inventions, wealth, success, commerce, politics, activism seem to pale in people's minds when they can disconnect from it all and simply be here and be themselves. It now appears to be the ultimate luxury and the Number 1 social trend out there. Remarkable. And we live it every day. There is nothing mundane about it and we appreciate every moment—and protect this gift we have. And so we have had to turn down many who have achieved so much in the opposite direction but who have a yearning, having discovered emptiness or who haven't had the number one experience to brag about. A high-ranking politician who insisted on bringing his protective detail with all their radios, sensors and phones, didn't quite get it when he was refused. And I didn't quite get it that a man who had followed his dream now spent his life in fear of being topped. What kind of dream was that? It boggles my mind. And I smile, for all the open hearts who do come for mutual enrichment. Who said you have to die to get to heaven?

212

Never lose heart, my love. Always know, whatever happens, you are better than all of them. By them, I mean those who would control and harm you. Those who doubt and disbelieve you. Those who think that whatever they are told to do or be, they must obey. Those whose spirit and minds have been dulled by pharmaceuticals, radiation and de-natured food. Those who live in a gilded cage, protected by wealth and devious power. Those who have never had the courage to dig deep into their hearts and sing their soul to the world. Those pale reflections, those automatons who have ceased to even know what it is to be human. Those who live constantly in fear and compromise at the deepest level of their being. Those dishonest charlatans who claim to be of value to mankind with so-called answers for gullible souls. Those who lack integrity and would sell out their closest friend for a baseless principle or simple greed or self-protection. Yes, you are better than all of them, and I see you. I am privileged to spend my life with you, because I know that, had I not met you at that magical moment, I would have continued to be one of them, getting worse as the years went by. So, today, just like every day for me, when I awake and see you beside me, I celebrate all that we are, together.

213

I'm sitting in the studio, paintbrush in hand, staring at a canvas I have just started, and wondering what I am doing. I am actually thinking of Michelangelo, and his statue of David. What a remarkable feat that was, to make that. To go to northern Italy (no motorways or trains) look at a huge mountain, choose a section of it and, trusting in its integrity and homogeneity, having a huge chunk of it transported (how!?) to his studio, and then chipping away at it with simple hammers and chisels until, with magnificent precision, he revealed the body of David in fine detail. All by taking away, not adding. As I sit here, I wonder if, by adding paint, I am also taking away in a different way. Through the years, perhaps I am actually stripping away the superfluous and will eventually reach a point of some coherence, a purity, a clarity that can only exist in this medium and in the interaction with its viewers. Maybe it is all for just one viewer. In a way, it always is. One viewer, one purchaser sets the value for one, and then others take note and feed off that passion or search for it in themselves. I suppose that I have always really known that my work only really speaks fully to me. It's really the biggest indulgence, being an artist, and yet I have always tried to make it a communication that enriches, in some way, the life of another. I just hope I have not spent a lifetime spreading the superfluous as I search for my own perfection.

214

I remember when I stopped repeating the memories of the past, stopped reacting as I always did in the past, and opened up to new ways of thinking and acting that open up infinite possibilities. It was today. Or, more specifically, it was now. Or is that an oxymoron? Never mind. And that's another good maxim. Never mind. Always be in the present. Don't get stuck in your head. Always now, always new. I guess that's why every day with you is like the first heady, blood-surging, exciting and sublime day of a new relationship. Your smile, so familiar and yet so new, so utterly fresh that it almost surprises me, is always just that. You never age, you never become familiar, and yet I know you so deeply and our life together is my whole life. Whatever came before has shrunk so much that I hardly know it ever was. And to paint you now, with your naked body spread before me, is an almost impossible task, overflowing with emotion and a kind of desperation to see you—really see you—and somehow get that down. Time will not stand still. Nor will my thoughts and emotions. I daub brush-loads of paint in abstract configurations and colours that I hope will somehow transcend the physicality of the actions I take and make a worthy impression, transforming the materials into something that comes close to reflecting all that you are to me, and for us both to experience the far greater art that is.

215

Feet must be one of the greatest feats of our evolution. They always fascinate me when I draw them—once I get down to that far-flung part of the body, having dealt with the torso, the head and getting the legs to look as if they are an integral part of it as well. Somehow, they often end up being the last to be drawn, and yet they are one of the most important, if unsung, parts of the body. These miracles of engineering with their auto-balancing toes, multiple hinges, soft pads and sturdy ankles carry us every single day of our lives. If they could talk, what stories would they tell? Some of them may not be pretty. Corns, bunions, blisters, smells and other hardships usually brought about by abuse of over-use and lack of care by a consciousness that sits in a head several feet up and rarely focuses on their lowly needs. Yet even that depends on them for their successful functioning and to meet its ever-generating demands. It's pretty stunning, if I think where my feet have been and what they have done—what they have enabled me to do. Had I logged every movement of a lifetime, I'm sure it would be a mind-boggling catalogue of unseen achievement, often not appreciated, usually not even noticed until, perhaps, later in life, they ask for a little attention. So, as I draw these feet, I appreciate and love them into being on my paper, so perhaps their owner will love them back.

216

I used to have admiration for Mike Carlo's[18] seemingly endless ability to reproduce the same scene—a narrow country path in Suffolk—over and over again. Each one completely different. A bit like Monet's haystacks[21]. Same, simple subject, infinite interpretations that go deeper and deeper, and discover more and more as the nature of the scene changes through the days and the seasons. I used to wonder how someone could be satisfied by that, because my aching desire to see more and more of the world could not compute such a still existence. What I found, though, was two things. The more I travelled, the less the world held magic for me and the longer I lived, the more complex I saw everything becoming. Even now, sitting here in my studio, that's all far too complex. I just want clean white walls, good light and a tight focus on whatever I am working on. They say mess shows creativity, but I think it also interferes with it and sets the mind on distractions rather than focus. Now, I see so many infinite possibilities to explore, right now, in this room, that travel seems superfluous, even a burden, and it certainly takes me out of where I feel I need to be, and what I can handle at any one time. I don't paint the same subject endlessly. I reject that safe place for me. If and when I travel, it is for a specific purpose that, once completed, I can tidy away in my mind. It all may sound intense, but really, I just want to be free to play.

217

I had to show up. Since I did, I am only amazed that I didn't do it sooner. And it's interesting how energies shift when you do, and when you do it with purpose. Help comes from the least expected places and in the most interesting ways. And people change, towards you. They appear to see you in a new light. I know this, from seeing others show up, and persist in showing up. Years ago, a guy with a guitar who could not sing, was embarrassing to listen to. As he persisted, though, he got better, and rather than seeing the imperfections, I began to see courage. I began to look forward to hearing him and, gradually, his effort transformed his skill. We all know it works like this, yet I have spent most of my life paralysed by a notion of unachievable perfection that I required of myself, that grew like a dark spectre, drowning me in the overwhelm of seeming impossibility. So I didn't move outside my box for years. Not until all the supports for inertia had been stripped away, and I had to start. And, when I did, look what happened! A fabulous home, play, excitement, discovery, surprises, miracles. A huge quantum shift. I didn't even know what that was, until I had experienced it. Like the experiences I now have, it was just an interesting theory, an idea that I agreed with, understood and liked— but somehow never acted on. My blindness was intact, comfortable, painful but familiar. And yet it only took one small decision, one choice made, to turn black into white.

218

I feel younger now than I did ten years ago. I have a lightness of being that carries me beyond what my mind used to think was possible. The gym helps but, more than anything, it is my attitude, brought about largely by my own work on myself, my meditation and raising of consciousness. It's just as well. I could not keep up with you, otherwise, or do all that I do. You carry your youthful spark and infinite curiosity with you all the time, lighting my way. I know that if I put the true effort in, constantly and consistently, I have it easy. Yes, there are challenges; yes, the body gets tired; yes. I still don't know anything much or understand how all this works. Yet that's fine. All of it. If it weren't for challenges, I would get lazy in my mind; if it weren't for tiredness, I would wreck my body and never rest. If I thought I knew, I would cut off the infinitely valuable path to learning new things and enjoying creativity. If I thought I understood, what magic would be left to enjoy and to wonder at every day. I have it easy. All these things are provided and all I have to do is surrender to them, without question but with curiosity. I hold up my hands and smile. I give up. Now, there's a nice expression. Giving—in an upward direction. Now I understand it is not defeat or an expression of despair, but a recognition of our safety and being loved in incomprehensible ways. Yes, I give up, with so much gratitude for all that is.

219

Silly Scrabble[5] has proved to have its use in the evolution of language. Your notoriety as a writer has led to new words being accepted into the lexicon and used in conversations everywhere. Language needed to evolve. Somewhere, in the early 21st century, it got lost. After centuries of dynamic innovation, subtle nuance, creative expression, it got stuck in the base, mechanical, even commercial idiom. It lost its music and passion and became a tool of convenience. We became fascinated by Shakespeare, we watched our favourite 'language' film, Belle[22], and we played Silly Scrabble for hours. We unlocked the language and gave it new life for a world starved of wordplay and no longer able to express itself in ways that truly communicated how it was evolving. Or, more importantly, new words and phrases were introduced that re-awakened linguistic style and showed people colour, shape, feeling and more in their words, which brought them closer to the miracle of their humanity, and the potential cradled inside every communication to draw us closer together in a sense of wonder that had, for too long, been given over to the sad substitute, the empty promise of technology. Which has no poetry, no song from the heart, no love or companionship, no soul. I sit opposite you and watch, as seven letters are arranged into a new universe.

220

What I love about our theatre space next to the studio is the fantastic new energy it brings with each new visitor. Whether it is a well-honed group of musicians, actors, poets, authors, I feel privileged to host, with you, wonderful talents and to avail of what they have to offer. It feels like an essential component of our rich, creative life. Constant input and inspiration that keep us sharp, young and open-minded. What I actually love most, though, is the new talents. Young or old, anyone who wants to develop something in the arts, they are the true artists for me. The ones who break out and use our space to learn and try things out. Sometimes they bring a tutor, sometimes a group, sometimes they are on their own. The difficult work is done by the time they get here—vetting, financing, travel arrangements etc, so we can simply enjoy having them here for a while. Sometimes we are involved in some way, sometimes not, but always we find time for heart-felt discussions, creative exchanges, fun and laughter. We feel blessed because we know that when creativity and the arts are not in our lives and the lives of others, we are no longer operating fully, our senses are dulled and we give up our souls and a huge part of our life potential. Artists are the true leaders. Everyone else follows procedure and politics. And when we are also leaders in our own lives, we have a world to celebrate.

221

I get up for a pee. It's 2am and there is a full moon. The stillness is almost palpable as, afterwards, I walk out onto the balcony. The sea still as a silver pond. Above me, the canopy of stars poke through the blackness as if the vast dome is peppered with pinpricks, with light shining through from another sun, way beyond. Our home is a latticework of geometric lights and darks in blue white duotone. It's a strange feeling, as if my being is now the centre of the universe and all this, this strange apparition, is my domain. I have a sense of being infinitely large and yet still a pinprick of insignificance in space. Suspended in time, there is no up or down, no forward or back. Nowhere to go but stay in the centre. Nothing to do or say. Nothing to think or even be. "Where did you go?" I feel your hand slip into mine. My anchor, my love, bringing me safely and oh so gently back with soft words and exquisite touch. I feel a huge wave of something, I guess you'd call it love, but it feels like something even beyond that. A feeling so clear, yet so fleeting, so present that it consumes all before it, so uplifting that I feel taller and more expansive. "I'm right here." I manage to mouth the words although I am not sure I speak them. Somehow, I turn my head and our eyes meet, and I am home truly home, right here in the place I love to be most of all.

222

In the art, there are so many temptations to go the easy, well-trodden path, take shortcuts and aim to impress. I'm not saying that art has to be an angst-ridden activity or that easy ways are all bad. What I suppose I am saying is that I have to be conscious of what I am doing, and the value of doing it a certain way. Just as it is at the gym. I can find ways to look as if I am using the equipment to get strong, whereas, in fact, I am not training the muscles that the equipment is designed for at all. The same in art. If I choose to take an easy route, it often manifests as an unsatisfactory route with little to recommend it in the finished work. For instance, there are devices that help you draw by visually overlaying the image on the surface before you. Great for illustrators on a deadline. Great for graphics. But disastrous if you want to be able to draw. It's a bit like trying to copy a photo. Not only is it pointless, but a photo holds no 'dimensionality'. You never get to visually understand anything from a photo. It carries limited, mechanical tonality and nothing of the artist—whether the artist took the photo or not. I find that when I grapple with an image with pen or graphite on paper, it reveals so much more than mere boundaries, colour and light and shade. It reveals the life in it and in me, it generates feelings, it helps me find its spirit and true three and four dimensionality. It gives me the truth.

223

Most of the time, we are alone. Most people don't walk up the beach this far from the village, and there's nowhere for them to park between here and the village. And when we don't have visitors in the accommodation block, the whole place takes on a deep air of relaxation. Clara feels it too, and on days like today, she works quietly and leaves sooner, usually having prepared some lovely little snack for us to enjoy. I have just walked back up the beach from my morning swim, and there is a beautifully arranged plate of fruit and edible flowers placed on the table on the deck, with a jug of cooled water. I throw the towel on the chair to sit down and take in this wonderful day. You are still out there, doing your wonderful breast stroke to and fro in front of the house, bright orange cap moving smoothly through the water. On days like this, there is simply nothing to do other than be a lizard on a rock, occasionally glancing this way and that, but all the time loving the feeling of heat on my body and a peace of mind that I have sought all my life and that has now been given to me. I think we have earned it. Not that it is necessarily something to earn. It just feels that way. Perhaps there is a little bit of ego in there that, in a self-congratulatory way, adds up events, challenges, tests, thoughts, meditations, actions, intentions, cries and laughter; marks them up in a book and says "Yes, you did it!"

224

It was interesting to see how the world changed towards us, once the momentum grew. And it was interesting to see how it happened. Just one article set off a chain reaction. A hook to catch a shoal. Undoubtedly, much of it was self-interest-driven, but it was interest that sparked curiosity in people all over the world, so it can't be all that bad. The inexorable drive to build and attract audience numbers became our friend. And how did that change us? Did our minds and actions immediately become corrupt and exploitative? No. It almost had the opposite effect. It was almost as if the initial shock of knowing that the world was suddenly listening to what we have to say, drove us inward, made us more reflective, given this huge new responsibility. Until, that is, we realized that we were actually awakening self-responsibility in others, so there was no burden for us to carry at all. And, thankfully, it was not economically viable for most of the press to beat a path to our door. Their methods have changed to getting material primarily online. Which was also good for us, as it gave us a measure of control of the messages, and reduced the tendency for some to trivialize or sensationalize them. So it has been gratifying that much of what we had pre-feared about becoming successful in our own unique ways, was actually baseless, and now we can really enjoy it!

225

It still holds true that political leaders are just servants with big egos. The problem is that they so rarely serve the purpose for which a naïve public elects them. Rather, they serve the special interests of those who got them to the top and who keep them there. Many times, we have only seen the truly human side of our leaders once they have left office. Often, we never do, so consumed are they by self-importance and the craving for acceptance. That is why we need more artists as leaders. True artists—not the illustrators and the commercial artists. The artists who stay true to themselves while pushing boundaries within themselves and in the world, driven from a sense of compassion, concern, a desire to elevate and educate, and a commitment to reveal truths—some of which may not be welcome but are better aired—and above all to move life forward by revealing new and previously unseen ways of perceiving it. Surely, that is the job of a politician, in an ideal world. So, to me, as I sit in my studio and ponder my next piece, I am seeing my work, through introspection and the acquiring of clarity—which, in itself is a huge challenge—as a commitment to self-responsibility and, therefore, quiet leadership. I have to dispense with modesty, hiding and cowardice, and allow the universe to place me, through the act of art, wherever I am meant to be in the multicoloured spectrum we call living our life.

226

The first time I met you in an auberge in Founex, I knew there was something special about you. I had no idea then, just how special, though. Or maybe there really is something inside each of us that, given the slightest attention, acknowledgment or brief acceptance amid all the junk that goes through our heads, we know. Maybe that ancient knowing of things beyond our conscious mind is still in there, preserved intact, an integral part of our being that time and conditioning have all but hidden from view. And look how powerful it must be! To have stayed true through all my foolishness and kept you there, gently caressing you deeper and deeper into my heart, so I could have a life I love. I think your connection to that magical part has always been stronger than mine. You have totally kept yourself intact, with huge integrity that has never wavered, and you have blossomed in ways I could never have imagined. And you still do, every moment, independent of time and memory and forethought. A beacon for all who can see you, you stand strong as waves lash your shores just as when the seas are calm. Now I truly see you, but I am so grateful that I never completely know you and probably never will. Because every day brings new revelations and understandings. Some of them, I may have seen before, yet they are still new as each new day. Thank you for this incredible journey, and for forgiving and totally loving me.

227

It took me a while to get my skills together as an artist. Actually, it took a while to really figure out what skills I wanted as an artist, although, in truth, I think I knew all along. The trouble was that they were skills that scared me, because there was a huge part of me wanting acceptance rather than skill. And the skill I always wanted was to work with a beginner's mind. That was the one constant. Why that should be so important only became apparent to me as I pushed myself into it. The world has changed so much since I was young and yet, even back then, I was determined not to become type-cast. I could also not see the appeal of doing similar things or using the same technique endlessly, to achieve financial success. Once I had done one thing one way, it seemed of little value to repeat it, refining the process for the sake of pleasing others, or galleries who lazily wanted similar, recognizable works to make their life and profits easier and to show some sort of progression to catalogue and discuss. The value of the beginner's mind has never been clearer to me than it is now. With the world spinning off its axis with so-called 'progress', that forces acceleration onto all aspects of life, even to produce one piece that is relevant at any one time is a challenge. So, if my work is to communicate at all, it needs to come from deeper and deeper inside. And that well is infinite. The only places I can go now, have never been visited before.

228

To borrow from Michael Crichton: "This life is a work of fiction, except for those parts that are real." So deeply programmed are we that we spend most of our lives in the fiction. Some never experience reality. And, even in death, after a lifetime of no religion, we are expected to succumb to it and go through the formalities of ritual as we are removed one way or another. The final insult—to us, to our humanity, to who we really are. Although, at that point, the only difference it makes is to sadly confirm to those who live longer, the folly of it all. This beautiful home, while in itself not reality, is confirmation of our reality. Its manifestation brought about by truth, love and all that is. That's why I love it. It's not the physical essence of it, but the incredible energy that manifested it all. As I stand on the beach with my back to the sea, I gaze in wonder at what we have achieved, who you are, and who I am. It's so incredible and yet intimate and so private, because it is difficult to share the celebration with anyone other than us. We are, I realize, alone in this universe, but completely connected if we breach the fiction. And, once that breach is made, and once we are connected, there is nothing to say, nothing to share, because it is all shared. It's a beautiful conundrum, the ultimate irony, the greatest gift that cannot be given and only received. And with it, I truly understand the incredible love I feel for you.

229

I sometimes wonder if the study of history is just a poisonous waste of time. After all, we know that the victors, politicians, religious leaders and other powerful people with a vested interest write it. And, of course, all of them have their own nutty conditioning, usually integrated through some equally nutty religion. So, there is no truth there, and I do wonder if it is even worth looking for it. And it pollutes the way forward with assumptions and heavily-loaded bullshit arguments. So, let's leave that for now, I think to myself as I ponder the blank canvas, and try to grapple with where I am now, if I can get that clear in my heart and soul. Leave the mind out of it. The best way I find to do that is to take action—whether it is physical exercise or frenetic writing or drawing in ways that block the thinking process and allow something else to stir in me. I am also amazed that, year on year, I go through the same process to find the beginner's mind. I guess that has to be. Or does it? Can I ever reach a point when I am just there—swayed and impacted as I am every moment by everything that is outside of me. The studio, you, food, thoughts, events in the eternal dance of duality and the challenge to discover unity in every moment. I know that sounds indulgent, a luxury of the rich, perhaps, but I also know that only art, for me, when produced from the right place, with sincerity and integrity, will ever write a history that will be worthy of souls to come.

230

Much of what we truly long for is what we had before we started trying to make it better. What arrogance! That we arrive here—by some mysterious miracle—and it's all laid out before us with seasons, food, drink and the resources we need to keep us comfortable. Not bad, eh? So, what do we do with it—this life that we know nothing about and everything that surrounds us that we had no part in making nor would we have a clue as to where to start? We try to improve it. We decide to own some part of it, and we start messing with it. 'Messing' being the operative word. By now, it has gone so far out of whack that we find it hard to even see the true nature of things. Our planet and our bodies have become a pale reflection of our failed interventions to the extent that neither have much hope of functioning properly, in ways that they were designed for. So, it is with what may seem to others to be a bit of lunacy, a completely exaggerated, emotional reaction, that I dig a new potato carefully out of the soil. It's gnarled and pitted. Its skin is flakey and falls off as I rub its surface with my finger, revealing a creamy white, clean and pure mass of goodness that I know will taste way more wonderful than any potato I have bought in years. We have been finding ancient, un-tampered-with seeds that have been cared for over the years like refugees hiding from invading forces, that celebrate the purity of life.

231

Certainty. I suppose I have been searching for that all my life. The world offers a pale, weak certainty through education, developed expertise, repetition and even mob agreement and consensus of authority. But those are not the types of certainty I have been looking for. Those kinds are hollow. Not all easy, by any means, but they are all the stuff of submission and compromise. I want something else. When I draw or paint, certainty of line or shape or colour comes from another place. An unthinking yet knowing place that goes by no rules and doesn't seek external opinion. How else can one move forward—with anything? If we always fall on the 'known' for our certainty, we simply build a solid wall around it, not knowing what we don't know, and restricting our access to new, creative possibilities. How, then, is one to act with certainty? And the answer is always the same. Surrender to what is—being, not thinking, working out or stressing over it. The tense line drawn on an unknowing surface only begins a process of reduction. The drawing may develop, but its limbs will be stiff and weak, and the end result cannot be beautiful. The relaxed line of certainty is expansive as it has no borders or fixed concepts to hold it down, and the image can flow and grow to magnificence.

232

It's easy to get locked into envy and admiration, and lose yourself in looking at someone else's art. In my time, I have gazed in wonder at art of all sorts. I have admired its complexity, the use of colour, the pure emotion, the reality that it tempts me with. Hyper-realism probably has the most impact in terms of losing myself. Abstract tends to simply inspire me with feelings of awe. So, there was a period when I delved into hyper-real paintings, to get it out of my system, to earn my chops, as they say. I think I lost myself in it because it was so clear and attractive on a base level, and I had simply never done it and doubted that I could. So, I tried it, and found that, if I spent the requisite time on it, indeed I could. And the results were stunning. You immediately reacted with expressions of surprise and awe. I felt I had produced something highly saleable. It had taken a long time to produce and left me feeling like a slave to an interminable process that would be exactly the same the next time I did it, and again after that. No, there is a richness in looking at things in different ways, in not trying to reproduce a fantastical reality, but delving deeper inside and finding new and unknown imagery, visual poetry that is neither base physicality nor mere decoration. That, to me, is the worthwhile path. The rest is just imitation for the ego. Gosh—judgemental! No, just searching for the truth.

233

I sometimes wish I had a much better memory. Like you do, I sometimes would like to remember the taste of a meal in a restaurant somewhere on holiday many years ago, or even the label on an item bought in a shop last week so I can get your favourite what-ever-it-is without having to check in with you. I always love to surprise you. Yet I only want a good good memory, not a good bad memory. I am so happy to have completely forgotten so much of my past, let it go. I'm sure it had its value, but as long as it brought me, by some meandering strange route, to you and this lovely place, that's all I need to know. Good good memory is lovely, though. To be able to bring up at will, when I am daydreaming, some delicious moment with you, in Begnins, the camper van, Portugal, Vancouver, France, wherever, is such a gift. I do remember many, and the feelings are always there. I am just greedy for more. And in my work, visual and spiritual memories are so important. I would love to be able to remember all of it, for long enough to get it down just as I want it. Maybe that will happen with practice. Maybe it won't. The journey towards it is always a bit fraught with frustration at my own limitations, mixed with the continuously new experience of the creation of each new memory, each new line and colour, committed to physical memory on canvas, as I attempt to create physical love in paint.

234

This time of day, after work in the studio and our lovely meal together—something I always relish for so many reasons—we often head out for a walk. Today, as the colours move to blue and the sea quietens down, we are choosing the upper path, along the low cliffs, south into the wilds. We could walk for miles on this ancient path and see no one. Sometimes we do see someone. Sometimes we stop and talk if the feeling is right. Sometimes we make new friends. Whereas, in the past, we used to tire of the same walks after a while, seeing the same houses, the same orchards, the same fields; now we never do. To the south, there are no manmade influences—other than the path. Just a gently rolling accompaniment to the sea below, with the land behind, rocky, deep and mysterious. It has its own abiding presence, almost threatening with its hidden secrets, usually moving us to turn towards the beckoning sea. This evening, though, I make myself turn towards it, speak with it, thank it for its rugged protection and uncompromising sturdiness. And the gifts it offers up at every step. Delicate plant life, small animals, myriad insects and birds. Its impossible complexity astounds and humbles at once. Its vast planes and dense mountains, a million years in the making and yet never truly known by man, are almost too much to take in. And this, by some miracle, is our home.

235

There's this strange mix of impatience and calm, speed and slowness, standing back and getting very close, loosening up then tightening up, that I have had to learn. The beginner's mind doesn't always allow for structure to be built in a 'structural' way, or for intuitive marks to lead somewhere else, or for broad strokes and detail to evolve in any logical way. I sometimes wonder why I chose such a challenging path, until I realize that, of course there is no real challenge; only play in the present. And when I surrender to that, all thoughts of building a construction in a particular way fall away. And the painting—the image—appears, step by strange step, before my eyes. It's almost as if I am not there, not doing it. Those are the best times, when the painting is given to me to pass on to whoever that period of connection and natural lucidity, appeals to. Like automatic writing on a page, the forms take shape of their own accord and usually quickly, as if they have been waiting somewhere in the ethers for a hand with a brush to release them into the world. And all I have to do is stand out of the way and quiet my mind. Just as in reading this, interpretations, judgements, prejudices and feelings are lurking in the negative or positive spaces, so on the canvas the same potential is there. I am learning to accept for long enough for the reality to show through—and then there are no arguments.

236

I didn't realize how valuable I was. Not for the longest time. I saw the business world as a dark grey place where I didn't belong, where what I said and thought and even did, sometimes, was not quite relevant. I didn't speak the same language of the collectively enthused. I didn't hold the same manufactured values of so many middle managers; held onto out of fear for performance, job security or advancement politics. I was always an outsider, the visiting consultant who wasn't tied by all those things, even though I played my own versions of them to some degree or other. The corporate world was always a bit of a mystery to me—or not. Actually, it was a place I didn't want to be. It was uncomfortable and full of false promise; a playground for manipulators and the manipulated. At heart, I was always an artist, but I spent my life hopping from the boat to the shore because I could not see, or find my true value. Not for the longest time. Until I did. And the strangest thing is that I am now sought out by those corporate manipulators and those caught up in their own betrayal, for the very reason that I am different; that I speak my own truth naturally and without training, qualifications or a trumped-up CV. I am simply me, and that, in this world, is a quality that holds more value than all the tea in China!

237

I often wonder where to find the impetus, the compulsion to do something. Where is the passion? Most of the time, I just want to be at peace, and I strive to be there. That often seems to be a place of inaction, meditation, rather than activity. One hears of so many stories where people have found their passion as a reflection—the opposite—of the experience they are having, or a way out of a difficult situation, poverty, a difficult childhood or some other downside to their life. I have always just got by, made a living having grown up with a similar mentality in an albeit dysfunctional family situation. One might think that my experience of strained relationships, lack of communication and such an odd upbringing might have engendered in me a desire to communicate and build bridges. Now, I don't feel that. I just want to heal myself and be comfortable. So, where is the passion? I feel it every day in my lovely, gorgeous relationship with you, but I feel little compulsion to share that precious gift with anyone. And how would I translate it, anyway? What tools and methods would adequately describe it, and to what end? So, on days like today, there are only questions. On other days, I know—because I have lived long enough—there will be an avalanche of answers. So, I sit, and wait, and do the things I need to do to open the doors to passion and everything.

238

20/20 hindsight is a terrible thing. It creates that most useless of emotions—guilt—and colours your way forward with baggage you can best do without. Yes, I know hindsight can be used to make improvements for the future—or can it even do that? There is never a groundhog moment when you can exactly repeat a situation and, in that moment, choose a better way. Each moment is unique so, however much I worry that I will carry the mess I made of my response to your eloquent, funny, wonderful wedding speech to my grave, I will never have that opportunity again, to redeem myself. So, I might as well choose fresh ways, every moment, to show you and the rest of our world, how much I love, admire and respect you. Even so, each memory of my clumsiness in that precious, perfect moment, haunts me to this day. I wonder why that is. I am sure that everyone who was there has forgotten their own experience of that moment which, really, was so insignificant in terms of their own lives. Some of them don't even exist anymore. Everyone else had moved on the minute they left the castle[23]. Maybe it is just ego, fed by a sense of unworthiness. Maybe it is nothing. And giving it energy is the worst thing I can do when I have you still, after all these years, every day of my blessed life. I must turn this page and make the best possible use of the time I have. After all, I am here for one purpose: only to love.

239

There are so many subtle factors that affect me every day. Today, I am noticing the air as I switch on the coffee machine while you sleep and I prepare, in the morning quiet, to go into the studio. It's a little overcast. The kitchen is darker than usual and the air is like a warm skin, smothering me a little oppressively, clinging to my pores with heavy, clammy wetness. It makes me feel heavy, slovenly, uninspired. Wishing for a stiff cool breeze to brush it all away, renew the air in the room and let me breathe again. I open the window to the patio. The yellow light, tinged with sad greyness, doesn't bring with it any change in temperature. It reminds me that, in order to maintain consistency in my mood and energy in my body, I must be greater than my environment. I cannot go into the studio under this flat shadow. Turning on the lights only serves to remind me of how I feel and that, like a spoilt child, I just want everything bright and fresh like it usually is. I don't want to project this into my work or meet you with it when you wake up. I want to stand in this clammy heat as the bright freshness in your life. I want to serve my painting with unperturbed positivity, clarity and presence, so my colours are clean and the energy on the canvas is elevated. What delicate beings we are, that a slight change in humidity and light can sway us. I am so grateful for this small lesson.

240

Nobody told me, all those years ago, that it would still be the same now, only better. Nobody told me that the feelings would never abate, and only get more intense. Nobody told me that I would never have to rely on sentimental memories, because the present would be so much better. Nobody told me that time would not dull the experience, and that its dynamism, energy and attractiveness would grow and morph and change and develop in so many exciting ways. And nobody told me that I would be more than happy, completely content and eternally thankful for one incredible person who chose to share her life with me, based on the thin promise of hands around her waist as we watched fireworks, a few written lines, the sound of my voice, a home-cooked meal and shared laughter across the south of France. I'm so glad they didn't, because I would have lived in fear of messing up and losing you. And even when I did mess up, it was met with understanding, forgiveness and giving. Often at a cost that I didn't really know at the time. I'm so glad nobody told me, because I would have lived my life in expectation and longing, rather than being here, with you, and loving you on this ride of a lifetime. Nobody told me that, at this moment, as we sit on the balcony sipping our wine at sunset, you would look up and smile at me in the silence, and release a cacophony of delicious emotions, unspoken.

241

Sometimes I get carried away by stuff, or the beauty of my surroundings and, very often, you. I know that, at such times, I have to allow myself that distraction, that appreciation, and simply enjoy it. Once done, for as long as it may take, I then must bring all this energy together in a different way, to allow inspiration to convert it to creativity. A new contribution arises when I can focus with clarity on whatever my passion alights on. I can never know what it will be, yet I am learning to flow my consciousness, somehow, into new spaces, where what results is not simply an interpretation in visual form, but a revelation of a deeper thing (I can think of no better word) that stands the test of time, is not some intellectual and maybe obscure construct, or merely the copy of a visual observed either in life or in my mind. I am becoming more and more interested in how to interpret, how to actualize such things in truthful, communicative ways that are universally recognized. I think back to the great designer, Milton Glazer[24], among others, who captured in images that were so bold and so simple, emotions and icons of his time. All the time I am searching to bring about that same certainty in my work, through channels of the heart and of the universe, because I do believe that there are, deep within all of us, universal connections fundamental to our existence.

242

Every day, I win. There is no doubt about it, unless I think otherwise, so I don't. It's important to go with the flow, keep the energy of the winning streak fresh and active. There is no time or opportunity to fail. There is no opportunity in failure. It's like the therapists used to say—you need to go into the dark places before you can start healing. In business, the buzz is to 'fail fast' so then you learn and can start to succeed. Bullshit. I don't believe in that any more. The more I focus—and I have done so a lot in the past—on failure, the more of it I get. 'Focus on what you want', they say now, and that's what I do. Years and pages of affirming my perfect life as now, make it perfect all the time. There are still lessons to learn, thank you, and these are important as well. But these lessons are only there to help me along, because that's what the universe does. It's what it wants for me. Success. Thank you for that understanding. Thank you for the colour and dynamism of everyday life. Thank you for the work and the spirit and intellect that bring me everything that I want through careful and specific magic designed purely for my benefit. May I forever appreciate the twists and turns, ups and downs and the love with which it is all given to me.

243

Today, as I face a new canvas, I have nothing in my mind. That's always the best place to start, but also the most disturbing. Because there is always something there and it is simply up to me to tune in, find it by some strange, non-logical, non-thinking way and, somehow, through actions of mixing colours, choosing media and brushes or other tools, start to apply it and release the image that is there for me. Even then, I know that time plays a part. The image shifts, changes, develops. There are surprises to come that I have to make choices about—bold choices with a clear head—that weren't there an instant ago. If I can stay with it, let it guide me and remain out of the way when I intuitively feel I should, it is a magnificent process. It's one that is always completely unique and revelatory. The only thing that is required of me is that I act without judgement. It's a journey of trust that, if I were to think or know anything about it, either beforehand or in the doing, I would probably never start. I would be so wrapped up in my heady processes that the creative process would never get a chance to move. And, what I have discovered over many years, is that it is all about letting creation happen—whether in our art, our life, on our planet or in our relationships. It is the only thing that keeps all this going so beautifully.

244

Sometimes I play music in the studio. It's usually to stir some feelings, make me feel a little uncomfortable—to disturb me! Sometimes I hear you playing music in the kitchen when I am not there. Your favourite Italian, or something swishy and relaxing. When we are together, we are together, though. Most of the time, I much prefer the quiet, or the sounds of nature. That's a big part of why I love this place. Sure, when we have an event, or people for dinner, we often crank up the sound system but it inevitably becomes a bit of a nuisance backdrop to a better conversation. The only times I truly enjoy it are when I am purposely listening when someone or a group is playing live at our place—and if there is a song as well, all the better. Live music forms a bond. Recorded music makes demands, when in company. It's always competing with something or excluding someone. Yes, the best music for me is the sound of some exotic jazz emanating from the beak of a bird in a tree nearby. Such clarity and originality, such intuitive knowledge of tone and rhythm, such creativity and freedom are hard to come by elsewhere. And if humans try to do it, it carries other things with it—ego, trying, learned skill that never allow me to relax into it quite so much. And the best of all, in unexpected moments, is to hear your laugh, so natural and pure: my bird of paradise!

245

The first million had been the most elusive but, once that was in place, it all just started to flow. It wasn't as if the first million was even the result of some cleverly-worked-out strategy, put into action with manic energy and huge teams of eager young people in exposed-brick agencies who had fashionably uncomfortable haircuts, piercings and awful tattoos. It just somehow tumbled into place. One day, we were just going about things as normal; the next day, it was all happening. I suppose that's what's called 'paying your dues' or something. All I know is that integrity, focus, staying in the moment, being true to ourselves and totally honest seemed to seep into the world like a leak in a dam. It slowly ate away at the crack in the concrete until the pressure differential between inside and outside was so great, and the boundary between them so weak, that it simply gave up the fight to keep it all in, and it released a flood of conscious awareness into the world. It was as if people all over the world had been secretly looking for your wisdom, knowing that was the key but so caught up in learned illusions that held them tight, that they needed some event or realization strong enough to meet the power of that concrete cage, and smash through it. For us, it was never about the millions, but now that we have them it is clear that we know how to put them to very good use. So, thank you, thank you, thank you!

246

I feel vindicated. About my approach to art, anyway. And possibly, by extension, other areas of my life as well. I only learn about it by doing it; and doing it with passion, with curiosity, with a beginner's mind, with gratitude and with immersion. The way the world has lost touch with this simple human way dismays me sometimes. The way that shortcuts and 'easy' ways are presented in the form of apps, courses by 'gurus', with the promise of quick results, wealth and satisfaction, belies a simple human truth that unless we approach something with the positive qualities I mentioned, we are wasting our time. We are humans, not machines, and we have hearts and souls, not cash registers or performance charts. The wealth of experience and satisfaction reside in us, and not in what we produce or in the admiration of others. Just as with any language, you can only truly appreciate its beauty by immersing yourself in it. And that includes the language of love. No theories, books, courses or people can give you the whole experience if it is not first in your heart—be it music, art, road-sweeping, astrophysics, food preparation, vehicle design, massage, truck-driving, teaching or anything. Yes, I feel vindicated, but I don't need to. Vindication is, after all, a reflection of the judgement of others who doubt or challenge your ways and, really, we do not need to give that importance. I make a new brush stroke, and that is perfect, as well.

247

Twenty-four/seven is a long time to stay present. You seem to do it a lot more than I do. I know, because I watch you. It's one of my favourite activities, to watch you move, contemplate, do things with your hands, stare intently at your computer monitor as your hands race to keep up with your head, or walk that walk, or stand naked, pink and steaming after a bath, or grapple with a concept in conversation with me. So many things. A kaleidoscope of entertainment. And you do it all so un-self-consciously and naturally. Does that mean, ironically, that you are present to yourself? Am I present when I am watching? Hard to say, really. I feel very present but of course my mind wanders to all sorts of juicy places. I've said it many times—you are relentlessly gorgeous. You never give it a break, and I am completely happy with that. So, I wonder, then, if the creative process is one of dipping in and out of the present. Creating: present. Thinking about it: not present. Yet, unless I go away from creating and enjoy the richness of experience that you and this place bring, I doubt that I would create as, in my experience, my creativity dries up without regular inspiration that I have to be present to, elsewhere. I guess I just have to accept life's little ironies, and ride with its ebb and flow, taking chunks here and there and doing what I can with them. After all, I seem to have plenty of time sort through the present and non-present, 24/7.

248

Where are the limits? What are the boundaries? Having set up a home and situation where everything is complete, comfortable and well-oiled, you'd think that creativity would know no bounds. Yet we build more limits and place more boundaries along the way. Limits by attachment, boundaries by fear. Are we never free of them? I have a lovely home and studio; I have the most wonderful relationship, so I don't want to mess it up. If I filled the living room with rubble, or painted masturbating chickens shitting on a Chinese granny, for whatever reason, that would not go down too well. Limits. If I even left the gate open for a week, my boundaries would be compromised and I may be wracked with worry that we may invite the wrong kind of visitor into our space. So they are good things, I suppose, and they change as we grow. Maybe the frustrating one is the limits, and good strong boundaries do, in fact, facilitate lifting limits. But in terms of art or self-expression or simply doing whatever the hell I like for no particular reason, or having a reason and fully realizing my ability and passion to act on it, where does that take me? The sky is most definitely not the limit. Yet, to go inside, get all woo-woo, get in control, be centred—does that necessarily birth fantastic and powerful work? So I still ask: Where are the limits? What are the boundaries?

249

I let the hood unfold, store itself behind me and watch the wind deflector rise into position as I glance in the mirror to make sure the gate has closed behind me. Things click into place and I gently ease the car, crunching gravel as I turn hard right and onto the road. There are dark clouds inland, lit orange by the morning sun across the sea as I pass through dappled shadows thrown by trees lining the road, protecting our wall. The chill air is fresh on my face as I ease my foot down on the throttle and the scent of leather gives way to sage and salt and pine warming. I become one with the machine as I grip the wheel and feel the road beneath us. The Aston is tightly set up, highly responsive and eager to please. And it does. We play together on the curves, rack up and down through the gears, light on the brakes, through this route that I know so well, yet still can hold surprises. Alert, therefore, to any change in surface, any approaching vehicle, any stray goat, we choose the level of excitement and dial it in to the driving style. Confident yet cautious. Enjoying the romance, the sounds and the physicality. Enjoying a space alone, a fantasy made reality—because, truly, it always actually was real. Enjoying that very fact. It's only a short drive—15 to 20 minutes, depending on my mood—but rich with a quiet pleasure, like the coffee that awaits me at the end.

250

We are born, we live and we die. Essentially, we do all this alone. Because however close we may be to another at any time in our life, we are living as a discrete, unified, independent being. Our attachments to the world are born from the need for sustenance. A constant interaction with our surroundings to sustain and maintain our body and mind so that we can continue on a quest for realization, whatever we may choose to pursue, until, at some point, usually within 100 years, sometimes a lot sooner, something deems that our time in this body is complete. So, we leave it at that point and, perhaps, continue in another way. Or simply stop. Along the way, as innocent souls, we lose track of our divinity and make the attachments real. We lose track of our independent purpose and make the attachments our reality. We simply get lost! In searching for clues as to a way back to me, I have read books, painted pictures from the heart, asked for help, aligned myself with those I perceive to be pure of heart and, sometimes, sat in silence waiting, hoping, believing that some clarity, some understanding, some knowing, the knowing would come to me. Because I realize that everywhere I look is merely another attachment, another illusion, often created by those, without knowing, who are also searching. Somehow, I have to know that I know, and that everything is clear, and I am absolutely who and what I am.

251

I feel I am on an endless journey of learning. Today, I am aware of the need I have to embrace change, rather than resist it, and to observe and not judge. Hunters' shots fired in the distance echo through the still morning air. The feeling of threat, the savage loss of life, entertainment and recreation in death. Yet these are simply my projections. Food on the table for a starving family, protection of essential crops, removal of threats to livelihood and many other things can be involved here, and who am I to judge? Why do I even rush into this vortex of thinking about something that is happening several kilometres away? The lives and actions of those people are no concern of mine and I have my own concerns to take care of, and changes to embrace. I look at the painting and feel my resistance to making a correction, a change. At this moment, I just want this painting out the door. Yet I know it cannot leave here with that kind of energy. I have to make the change. However much I don't want to do it at this moment I know, from experience, that I will eventually enjoy the process. It brings freshness and love to a stiffened, struggled-over image that somehow lost its way as my mind went off track. It happens. I am not a machine. I should know, having lived with you for so long, that only when the truth is outed—sometimes a difficult process that I resist—will the result be truly worthwhile.

252

The cool solidity of commercial achievement has always affected me in its various manifestations. Whether it is a fancy car, a beautiful home or the calculated glances of those with castles to protect and high roles to play. With my attempted blue-collar upbringing, those things were out of bounds and I felt divided from them. Mine was the road of a survivor who got by. It's interesting, therefore, that now that all that seemed impossible is now a part of my everyday existence, what place they have in my life. None of it was given to me through stress and long hours of work. None of it was craved as status or proof of my worth. Yet I feel comfortable and completely at home with it all. I simply enjoy it—the comfort, the relief and yes, the style. It feels like me and I think I wear it well. And I am incredibly grateful for all of it. In a sense, it feels like a home-coming. I have come home to my own truth, and that is that I am worth all of this and more. In fact, the physical manifestations of my worth are nothing compared to the spiritual realization of that reality. They are just toys of the truth. Trinkets and games. I am powerful. I am something that no man can possibly comprehend (just as all men are). And it's incredibly calming to have arrived here in this way. Surreal and yet more real than anything I have ever experienced before.

253

Passion. It takes on so many hues, so many forms as I move through my life. As my body changes, physical passion is still there, very much, but it has changed from the riotous, needy, intense and constant desire to a gentler, more considered and somehow deeper feeling that is laced with much more gratitude. Probably because I am grateful that it is still there at all when so many seem to live with so little of it later in life! For me, it is very much there. It just needs a little more nurturing and encouragement, intimacy and time. And it seems to be the fire that creates balance in me and in maintaining some part of my masculinity. A reminder that I am a man, when I lose myself in the mechanics of living, and that I am so fortunate to have you in my life, a beautiful female feminine goddess who keeps me on track, who keeps my flame burning and who keeps my heart and soul young and inquisitive. The passion I feel for my art and anything else in my life comes through that balance. At least, that is what it feels like. So I have to be aware of that, so that we can maintain our independence of soul, which in turn drives the engines of passion in our relationship. The pillars of the temple, as they say, must stand apart to be strong. And so we continue this passionate dance, getting closer all the time while maintaining our own selves as separate beings with ever stronger elastic bands[25].

254

I find myself more and more preoccupied with identity. Not in the external sense. I know a lot of people completely identify with ancestry, geography, traditions, religion and other things that appear to carry weight and add some sort of gravitas to an otherwise un-anchored existence. If anything, I find that a life of constant travel has freed me of so many of those ideas—ideas that purport to give meaning while being based solely on accidents of external existence. How can they possibly reveal true identity? Comfort for those who don't want to scour the depths, acceptable in their logic and some sort of continuity. Why do we seek continuity, I wonder? We are bigger than all of that. We are designed to be creative, to evolve, to move forward. So, I question the value of getting too obsessed with hooks from the past. They may hold some learning, but they are past. The present is new, the future is to be chosen, so the past must be let go. And yet we carry it with us in our learned behaviours in ways that so often do not serve us well. Some of it is good, of course, as it drives us forward. I don't know where the healthy balance is. All I know is that if I am truly to know who I am, I must turn inward and away from the known and the assumed and the popular traps. I am not there. I am possibly everywhere, and that is a tricky one for the ego that wishes to stand apart. Maybe I am simply energy in action, with consciousness.

255

Ask me what life will be like on this planet in 100 years and I will probably say that, in many ways, it will be just the same. The same people striving for power, the same people duped into fighting wars, the same people starving and eking out a living from whatever they can. Yes, the mechanics of it all may be vastly different. The earth will, no doubt, be under incredible pressure and environmental stress; the pressure on people will have increased enormously; technology—if it hasn't been put in its place—will govern whole societies. People attempting to live a balanced, healthy, natural life will be vilified and laughed at, forced into whatever chink of isolation they can still find. So, I am happy to be living now, although my short future shows signs that I don't like at all. A refreshed nationalism and aggression and impersonalization. My job, therefore, is to show resistance but, more than that, as an artist, to illuminate and suggest and show a better life, a better human existence, higher values and deeper qualities than we are being rushed into by politicians led by the nose by industry. And there is so much that, as human beings, we have done and are capable of if we choose to look for the best in us. There is so much there to mine and encourage into minds that are being closed, relentlessly and progressively or simply not allowed to freely form for fear of free-thinking and disruption. We need more of the right self-interest.

256

We are so caught up in the drama of duality that we cannot see the wood for the trees. Branches everywhere obscure our view of the clear sky. When people come to visit us, they bring their own branches with them. Well-meaning as they may be (olive branches?) they are branches, nevertheless. They are an integral part of the social web we have woven. Conversation, news, mind-bending exploration, niceties, flattery, criticism, gossip, politeness and so on. I sometimes wonder what it would be like if people left their branches at home when they visited. No conversation, none of the effusive communication, no baggage! Would it be boring? Would they feel unwelcome? How do we communicate real affection and have a deeply moving, wonderful experience with others? If we do not use words, do we use the other senses? Touch, vision, smell? I wonder what a week of that would be like, and if we'd even want it. Just stay at home. Leave us alone. But, no, imperfect as it may seem to be, I suppose all those branches have their place and we can welcome them for what they are, and learn to love the tree that they are attached to. After all, whether they know it or not, all branches are growing, interacting with their surroundings, feeding and giving shade and protection, learning to find their place and their way and, ultimately, every branch seeks the light.

257

What an incredible thing the human body is. I am thinking as I get out of bed, of just that one simple action. Almost every single day of my life, I have, after waking, stood up. That's 365 times the number of years I have been alive, the brain has engaged with electrical impulses that have sent messages to both legs to pull muscles into tension and cause them to straighten up and support my whole body, in balance, then walk me to wherever I need to go. That's a pretty good record of reliability. When you buy a car, made of stronger stuff, carefully designed and engineered for movement, no manufacturer gives a guarantee of seventy years or more. You're lucky to get a limited warranty of five years and a life expectation of no more than twenty. So, I think I can marvel at this body, that I tend to take so much for granted and that I expect to get over all minor ailments without me having to do much, relatively speaking, and understanding even less. That is incredible, as well, that we can live a whole life and remain essentially ignorant of the vehicle that carries us through it, and with seemingly no in-built knowledge as to how to maintain it. The insurance companies are clever with the deceit of 'life insurance', which is really money for others on the event of your death, which in turn is more likely to happen if you are stressed enough to believe you need it. I guess that, really, good health is the only true life insurance you need.

258

I am still here, still writing, still drawing, still painting, still learning—although these days I find I have to break through so much noise to concentrate on one subject at a time. I remember, when I was young, how easy it was, or maybe how natural it was, to compartmentalize different subjects and focus on each, totally, in its own allotted time. The school system of specific subject periods really helped me do that. And even now, if I am given a commitment to produce something for a specific purpose, I can block out all else, concentrate, and do it. The challenge, I suppose, is to find something, using my own free will, that I want to focus on and give all my energy to. Every minute on the internet can be awash with such variety that I become image-drunk and fatigued with the width of choice, the expertise and skill, and I can become disheartened at the thought that I could not produce much of it without months or years of practice at one specific thing. So, I wonder, does that validate my 'beginner's mind' philosophy? Is that the most relevant way of being in today's crazy world? Is there just as much value, if not more, in a roughly-put-together, hastily rendered work—the antithesis of the work that is designed to impress but that gets so easily lost in the sameness of excellence? I have to ignore all that, I know, and simply keep writing, drawing, painting and learning—for me.

259

We had a vision, and it came true. That, in itself, is an untrue statement. A vision is truth, so it always is true. There is no point where it moves from, say, realm of fantasy, to a different, somehow more credible state. It just is. That's the incredible part about it. A vision truly exists as just as much a part of reality as anything else. The challenge, for us mortals, with an over-inflated idea of our cleverness, wisdom, knowledge and awareness, is to be the vision when all our earthly senses claim it is something else. It's a bit like the joke about Christians arriving at the pearly gates and, having led what they believe to be a good and worthy life, they are told by Peter that, actually, God was only joking, but they were too dumb to figure that out. I feel as if my body is tired of all I have to do on a day-to-day basis, but my spirit is only just beginning. It's a child that wants to play but has difficulty finding the playground. But it has finally understood, in fleeting but ever more frequent moments, that the vision is it. Without a vision, I am just a tired old body, trudging through limitations set by others. With a vision in place, intact and at the core of my reality, I am limitless, playful, grateful, happy beyond my wildest dreams, and real. The vision brings me the solidarity that life otherwise lacks. We are this, we have realized this and we did it!

260

I had a dream. Long ago in a far-off land, I learned guitar and formed a band. At first there was just you and me, but then we grew to twenty-three. We bought a bus, found groupies too, did sex and drugs—that's what you do. We sang and toured, made so much money, we *bought* the land of milk and honey. And when there was no more to get, we sold the bus and bought a jet. A higher plane that made no sound, all we'd lost could now be found, and bring us back to solid ground. It took us gently by the hand, and showed us sea and rocks and sand, and brought us home, our promised land. There is no fore, there is no after, just perfect now, with love and laughter. And as I gaze into your eyes, I see pure truth, I've shed my lies. With you my love, my home, my art, there is completion in every part. And yet, in truth, this is just the start. The destination? I have no clue, but that's fine, as long as it's with you. So pop the cork, cast off the line, open the throttle for a youmeus[26] time; chocks away, unfurl the sails, we'll create some art and tell some tales. Stoke the fire, flex the muscles, break free of downers, negativity and tussles. Blast the conditioning, inspire the nation, fuck the Wifi and radiation. We are bigger than all that stuff, we fought through when times were rough and triumphed, because we'd had enough!

261

Tell me everything, my love. Your voice is music to my ears. I know that sometimes I am preoccupied, or I am moving to do something that I feel I want to or should do. Yet, I want to listen always. Tell me when you awaken from a dream, when you are rested and your eyes squint as you first open them to the sunlight. Tell me when you and I are out walking on the beach and you brush your hair away from your face to make way for the stories that are bursting to come out and be shared. Tell me when the quinoa is cooking on a low heat and the courgettes are browning on the barbeque. Tell me all those whispering thoughts that come and have to be spoken before they go on their mysterious journey back to the universe or onward to another soul. Tell me, because I want to know, I need to know, I love to know all the sweet ideas, all the disquieting concerns, all the joyous revelations, all the carefully thought-out causes and consequences, all the ways we can be better together. Because it is all important; it is only there, fresh and right at this moment, only flowing in perfection and natural timing right now. And each one is a jewel to be cherished because this is us and I want all of us, right now and for ever. So, tell me when you are filled up and overflowing, when you are happy, sad, afraid, concerned, and I will do my best to listen with my heart. Tell me everything.

262

It takes patience and some kind of flexible, non-directional vision to work the way I do on paintings, these days. It demands breakdowns (of the work so far) to go for the bigger breakthroughs later. Sometimes, wet on wet works but, more often than not, I have to wait a day or two—or more—for the surface to be dry enough to take another layer. And I have to be bold. It's a continuous process of letting go of things that I have cared for and loved into being; being prepared to let go, so that a new creativity can take the work further and give it new life, imbue the surface with greater depth and energy. In a way, I build a longer life into the painting through this unrelenting process that both fills me with dread and releases me to move on. And the image is never what I thought it would be. It swerves and meanders, darkens and lightens, blurs and clarifies along the way. It's truly an adventure, every time, forcing me to let go of concepts and judgements, prejudices and fears, knowing and thinking. At times, it is a purely physical act with no regard for aesthetics or image. And, from this maelstrom, somehow emerges something new. We call it art, we call it a creative journey, and we give it some random and incomprehensible monetary value, but I don't know what it truly is, although I am grateful because, in pouring my energy into this, I feel truly alive and universally at one.

263

I look at the drawing and think, "I didn't do that." It doesn't seem possible. I have no memory of doing it—the struggle, the flow, the adjustments, the rubbing out, the corrections. I do remember a bit of the seeing. That intriguing process of observation that grows with time, revealing more and more of the model. I remembered to remember not to dive straight in, but to wait until the first layers of sight had revealed something to me. The shapes, their interrelations and proportions. The shadows and how they fell, revealing for me details of structure unseen with a casual glance. The slight movements of the model—a living person who feels the discomforts of holding a pose—and the natural settling over the course of the pose that I must take into account as I draw; choosing vulnerable parts first, understanding, over time, how the structure will be affected by an inch or two of movement one way or the other. And, of course, there are the feelings above and beyond the physical form, the temporary mute relationship, the trust and boundaries time-honoured through the centuries between artist and model. Some models are naked when they are naked. Others, not so much. And then again, I make choices of tools and surface and, through it all, emerges a form that works on some level, that I had no control over, that was given to me honestly and with love. And I am grateful.

264

I am finding a lot of satisfaction in simplicity these days. A simple line drawing, perhaps with a wash or some small detail, gives me more pleasure than a complex image. In fact, many of the paintings I do now, while they take longer and longer to complete with all their layers, are really a search for simplicity—among other things. There I go, immediately complicating the argument, but maybe I can reduce it down again. Our minds seem to have a tendency towards complexity, while our hearts go the other way. My thoughts are often the starting point, which is why, I suppose, there is an impetus to create detail, impress or analyze. It is only when I let my heart through that I can simplify and bring the image back to some sort of purity. Even then, I have to keep my mind in check, hungry as it is to put layer upon layer on top of something simple and from the heart. It's a relentless awareness that I have to develop, so I can be truly aware in each moment, as to what is simply in front of me. In our relationship, it is easy. I learned, many years ago, that I can trust my heart. With you, the chattering monkeys are stilled. That is how powerful you are for me—in that and so many ways. Now I just have to find ways to apply that awareness to my art.

265

It's taken me a lifetime (so far) to figure out what life is about for me. And I still don't really know. What is my purpose? Do I even have one? You ask me such questions and, even to this day, they send me into a numb spin of concern. And I think back to people who I have known who died young, or who had a lifetime career. Did they ever know the answers to these questions? It seems to me that, for most, the question is never asked. And that works fine for some; those who accept the illusion that is placed in front of their particular eyes, or those who have an unflappable positive outlook on life, or those who are completely satisfied, energised and completed by whatever spark drove their existence. I am one of the lucky and unlucky ones. I question—probably far too much for my own good. I have some level of awareness of a deeper reality. I am an artist, a creative person who is always looking for alternative viewpoints, angles, arguments. That is all very enriching, so I cannot be satisfied by a comfortable day-to-day existence. Although part of me craves that as well, especially as I get older. Even here, in this beautiful place with everything arranged as we dreamed about, I am still faced with that question. Is it something complex? Does it change from day to day? Is it simply to love and be loved? That seems to be the best purpose.

266

How do I make each moment of my life extraordinary and wonderful? Moments like this were never designed to be so. I am about three people back from the cashier. It was the shortest queue I could find on this busy Saturday morning. I chose the one with more men in it, as men tend to buy less and don't chat as much when they are bagging up; which is what the woman at the front of the queue is doing. The cashier takes it all in her stride and there is a pressure cooker of muted politeness in her wake. She pulls out a cheque book and starts scribbling, checking numbers, scribbling again and filling in the stub. It's not a clean tear, so she fumbles with thumbs while attempting to keep an over-stuffed handbag on her shoulder. She hands over the cheque. Then, and only then, does she start filling the trolley. We men exchange glances. A tribal or animal recognition, a vague macho communication fed by years of experience, relationships and time spent in queues like this. I smile. He smiles, and the next man smiles. The cashier smiles and then the lady looks up from her bagging and quizzically smiles. She doesn't know what we are all smiling about, but that doesn't matter. A smile is a smile and it has value in her life. We men smile more broadly, knowing that her smile is for different, innocent reasons, to our smiles. And, just like that, a minor tension is changed to a minor celebration of simple good feelings. Extraordinary. Wonderful.

267

Today, we are feeling the force of nature. It's kind of exciting as well as a little bit frightening. There's a powerful wind blowing along the coast from the south west. The beach is a blur of stinging sand that I am so glad not to be standing in, right now. The breakers are roaring with sliced tops that fly off in white sprays away from us. Plants on our deck are rolling around in the grey light, searching for a place to hide. Leaves stick hopelessly to our glass window panes, pleading to be let in. And the trees battle with unseen forces to stay their ground. It all shows me how small and powerless we are in the face of what nature may choose to do. And we never truly know why this earth has such wildly fluctuating weather patterns. Is it our doing, or are we arrogant to make such assumptions—that this power can come from our misdeeds? Or are there simply variations in the earth's orbit that we can do nothing about? At the moment, we try to appease our conscience for the blatant disregard of our environment by blaming ourselves. And, like us, we find safe havens—those of us who can—to protect us from the frequent ravages of nature that are so unpredictable these days. Nature will always put us in our place, in no uncertain terms. So, I leave the shutters open in acknowledgment and respect. We are being shown this for a reason, and I am grateful.

268

If I am even able to start the next painting with a beginner's mind, how do I finish it? With a mind made up? Maybe there is no finish. Just the process. I start the canvas, searching for clues inside me as to where to go. I try to be at one, whatever that means to my mind. I act and wait for a flow to begin. Each step is punctuated, not by a beginner's mind, but by decisions and judgements, which seem to be the only mechanisms I have to take the next practical step, and the next after that. And so, I oscillate, from clearing the mind to filling it and back again. Maybe it is a pointless process and I would be happier copying and filling in with colour, making recognizable forms with varying degrees of skill and clarity. Everything I produce is abstract anyway—whether or not it is in some way representational. So, why put myself through this constant pain? I know why, though. I have been down this road so many times. That is why I am tired, looking for an easier way. I want my studio to be my friend, not my torture chamber. And yet I know that the worst torture is to produce blah work, illustrations, decorations that have no soul of their own, that go no further beyond a cleverly constructed illusional surface. No, I am more of a Pollock, a Rothko or one of the many who spent their lives breaking through to more meaningful worlds.

269

Cow shit. It's that time of year when the scents of flowers give way to the heavy, sweet stench of cow shit. Manuel's farmer friend does this for us every year at this time, as the amount of compost we produce from food, weeds and old vegetable plants isn't nearly enough to feed the land for another season. We farm it fairly intensively and, as long as we keep an eye on the amount of nourishment it gets, it provides most of what we need in the non-meat department and, as I have mentioned before, more for friends and villagers when the weather is kind and we get seasonal gluts. While the smell is really ripe, I don't mind it. It is a clear marker of the close of one season and the beginning of another. Just like all of us, the land needs its rest and good food to sustain it. The farmer weaves his way up and down with a timeless, unflappable steadiness in his rustic manner. Occasionally, he twists around on his seat and watches the spreader flying wild sods this way and that. His 50-year-old tractor looks as if it knows how to do this with no help from its owner. They have a close relationship and a similar fashion sense. The hrudder-dudder-dudder of the engine is like a meditation on the land that the small front wheels joust with as they slip and grip. All is well in the universe and in me.

270

Are we just completely fickle, or do we make progress in some way, from day to day? I notice that each time I return to a painting the next day, it has changed, or I have changed towards it. Okay, some paint is dryer, and there has possibly been a bit of a reflected colour shift, or it has dulled down a bit so I don't see it through the glare of shiny highlights. But most of it, I know, is in me. Just one night changes the way I see it. That's interesting. In some ways, it means that a painting can never be finished. Perhaps I should encourage my agent to whip them off the stand after a few days, maybe when I am pondering some detail, brush in hand, gazing at it blankly, as I do. If he just came in, detached it from the stand and casually carried it out to his van, maybe that would be okay. After all, each piece is unique. Most of them are pretty abstract, and no one, not even me (or is that 'I', Olga?) can say that if I had done this or that or added another layer, or destroyed and re-built some part of it, it is not complete. Because the image never finishes. It can move eternally, re-shaping, re-colouring and simply becoming a different image—either subtly or obviously. What is gained in each moment that I should keep and will anything ever have value in perpetuity? How can I ever know? I may be fickle, but all this is wonderful!

271

I make a point of not reading reviews of my shows. Having put all the effort in to produce the work, having worked with the gallery on the placement of the work, the catalogue and everything else that goes into actualizing the show, having travelled to wherever the gallery is, stayed in a hotel and trod the streets of a new or familiar city, having pressed the flesh, been introduced to all and sundry and made a short irreverent speech at the opening, my experience of my own show is done. Once it is all released into the world, people will think and do as they will. That, in a way, is the best of it all, but I cannot and will not get involved in seeking out opinion, gauging my reputation or harbouring celebrity. They know where to find me when the time comes for another show. And, when they do—assuming this carries on for a while longer—my responsibility and desire is to have remained in my own space, progressing with you in whatever direction (or not) I have chosen to take, or just simply being the best I can be. A strange and egotistical gift to the world, perhaps, but this is the only way I can come close to fathoming the purpose of it all. Of us, this place, the world, the universe and beyond. Opinion is just a cry for attention and recognition. Discovering a truth and giving it to the world is some sort of salvation.

272

Light, shade and colour. The infinite, dynamic interplay that has fascinated artists, particularly in the last three centuries, fascinates me still. We have seen how, from the late 19th century to the early 20th century, exploration into these relationships exploded with impressionism and everything that followed from that. The nature of light, the value of colours, the representation of shadows and the various qualities of light distorted or exaggerated. Van Gogh, Gaugin and so many more, many of them forgotten by history, particularly if they were female, spearheading daring ideas, way ahead of their time, totally sincerely, passionately and purely for the sake of beauty that stunned them, and learning that drove them. I wonder, as I apply another colour to a strange form that is of this world and yet not, if what I do has some value that is worthy of remembering. The beginner's mind, in a way, can never build a cohesive portfolio, other than it is cohesive in its un-cohesiveness. And then I wonder if this is just my ego poking its nasty head into the flow again. Where does denial start and mindless process continue? Does the mindless process have any sort of validity? In a world of illusion where nothing really makes any sense at all, though people swear by it, is the mindless process the most valid and valuable, relevant and revealing way to reach beyond? Funny. I can never know.

273

I should have been Italian. Maybe I was, in another life. So much of my vision of the perfect life has been tied up with that place—and still is. As I sip my espresso and look out over the beach, Phaedra pulls herself on to the boat, dripping passion and oozing sex as she argues with her lazy lover in the hot sun. Sophia was always there in my life. Maybe she pointed me to Italy. For me, that's where passion was born. In my teens, rattling through cobble-stoned hairpins in Mario's boxy Lancia, a permanent mischievous glint in his eye; or watching the village women of Saltara canning tomatoes in the dappled shade while, upstairs, he was having extra-marital sex in the afternoon. Or Mariangela guiding my hand between her legs, out of sight of her chaperone brother as my striped hipsters felt fit to burst. The language, the pasta, the bars. In Italy, I was Mastroianni dancing on every special day. It was my perfect escape from school and a constrained, conservative grey life in England. So much colour, innocent lust, a festival from dawn till dusk. There was real magic there in the simple things, in Fiat 500s; shuttered windows; airless hot village views; hard Italian bread; Carosello[27] spewing ads from precariously bracketed black and white TVs in tall, undecorated rooms; playing cards slapped down on tables; Amaro 18 Isolabella[28] in endless servings to unshaven old men in the bar. And I am still here, and it is still with me, and I love it all.

274

Other than a few who head off into space, or those who choose hallucinatory drugs, the only time we enter a different world is when we dive under the surface of the sea. Well, these days, I don't so much dive—although I do occasionally—as float with my snorkel, gazing down with my head fully underwater so the only sounds I hear are distant roars of breakers and my own breath. Other than that, it is all visual, plus whatever physical effort I make to change my view. There are days, like today, when the water is breathtakingly clear, and I have the sensation of flying. It can even make me feel I am too high and could fall, but of course that is something I quickly get used to. It's so incredibly peaceful in this quiet, unspoken landscape; and so completely different from the world above the liquid separating film that sways me gently to and fro. That we should be so close to this fantastic mystery and yet spend most of our lives watching only its reflected surface is, in itself, incredible. We see as far as the earth's curvature permits, from any point on land, and see nothing of the vast mountain ranges, caverns of colour, vast planes of sand and rock, whole communities of sea life, plants and strange animals. And we take it for granted. We don't even imagine it, so transfixed are we by the surface and what is above it. Time for some meaningful words? I have none.

275

I once wrote a novel called *Hominine*[29]. It received a lot of praise and modest sales at the time, with a few sales every year for a long time. Those who read it wanted a sequel—more of the same. But I felt I had told the story of *Hominine*, and anything that followed would have either been dramatized plots that yielded little more, or weak re-workings of everything that I put into that novel so intuitively. I felt the job was done and it was time to move on. Maybe it's a bit like a tsunami—once the huge energy has crashed through, it can take a long time for the next one to turn up, and it may well be in a different place. So rarely do they come again, in the same location. So, I waited, and worked, and lived my life with you. Each year, age was advancing and resistance to decay had to be fought ever more diligently. Periods of rest got longer and periods of intense energy got shorter. It was wonderful, therefore, that I re-found my mojo in art. The same for you, with your writing, although you never stopped, never wavered, building steadily to the throne you occupy now—never lost for words or ever-more progressive ideas. Fabulous! For me, it is so gratifying that I can do this for the rest of my life. Loving the process, enjoying some notoriety (that my ego loves), and gently—or sometimes manically—producing powerful, thoughtful work for eternity.

276

At the risk of sounding obvious, or trite, or saccharine, or daft or just plain sentimental, I still want to say something I know to be true. Love is truth. I see it every day. I even hear it embedded in popular expressions—'in my heart, I believe…', and 'from the bottom of my heart…' It's the ultimate reference point we have, as humans. And it is unique to us. In truth (there I go again), I didn't know this commonly-expressed fact until shortly after a curly-haired blond with dreamy eyes and a silky voice, sat down opposite me in an auberge in a small town in Switzerland. How random is that!? Or, how pre-determined, destined and meticulously organized was it? Blows my mind, just thinking about that. That this chain of events was somehow organized for me, so that I could be lifted out of all the non-sense that had gone before, given true and uncompromised love, to keep for all my days. And nights, of course. And that somewhere in my psyche I had foreseen her, years before—had that played a part in bringing her to me? I will never know. And nothing in the world can shake this truth that I hold so dear, manifested in beauty and forever renewed, each moment. My true now. Pretty incredible, huh? And we both know this truth, that is permanent, the solid foundation of all that is, doubt extinguished in a blaze of light. And I am forever just so grateful for you.

277

I have to remember and remind myself that I am in this for the long term. There are no quick fixes; no smart soundbite will ever express the complexity and deep satisfaction that come with time; there are no shortcuts, no automatic fixes, no apps, no labour-saving-time-saving devices that will appear in a burst of light over the horizon and come and do it for me. So, I might as well relax into it, do it, and recognize my enjoyment of it as part and parcel and a huge gift, of doing it. Doing what? Living. This, I realize, applies to everything. Whether it be painting, drawing, eating, playing, gardening, talking, writing, going to the toilet—anything and everything. Much of my life has been about escaping these experiences, rushing through them, getting them done and out of the way, glossing over things, feeling burdened by them, not appreciating them in the moment, the now, the only reality. So, I wonder, how much of my life have I missed? Stress, worry and self-deprecation have, I know, taken a toll. Useless activities that absorb my life, soul and heart, and give nothing in return, except for establishing negative patterns backed up by seemingly irrefutable evidence that, in itself, was created by those very things. Yet, I still know I can stop, reverse all that junk, and truly live each eternal moment in harmony and truth.

278

Every time I visit a new city, it completely boggles my mind. That there are so many millions of people sustained in these other worlds is beyond my comprehension. They do not farm, they do not produce their own food. They work in abstractions that generate other abstractions such as software and money. And now we have crypto currencies that are even more abstract. And people are swept away by all these abstractions. They live for them, desire them and hoard them until, one day, they cannot any more and they live out their days hoping that the interest on the nothings they hoarded will last them until they die. It kind of works for me, though, so I cannot criticize or judge; just be amazed that this actually works. At times, when I feel a little lucid, it all seems like pure, unadulterated madness. So, trying to find meaning, trying to nudge people's perceptions of it, trying to illuminate some of the cracks through my art is as amusing as it is disruptive. I am part of it, even here in our hideaway paradise, yet I feel divorced from it in so many ways. Maybe it is some sort of awareness, maybe it is a huge conceit, maybe it is disingenuous or unfair on some, but I cannot seem to help it. Once something is felt or known, it cannot be un-felt or un-known. And it always energises me, despite the challenges, to continue.

279

There is a perfect symmetry to everything that happens, if only we can see it. Sometimes, the reasons for strange things happening are so obscure and confusing for our ordered minds to comprehend that we despair and think that things are going wrong. The simple fact is, though, that we haven't aligned ourselves with what is truly happening, and we cannot use our minds to do that anyway. I can curse a clumsy brush stroke if I have decided that I want the paint to lay down in a very specific way, but that very intention precludes the possibility that, perhaps, something else is meant to be happening. It can be painful when the intention seems to be clear and good, but I have to keep reminding myself that this is creativity, play and just a game—that I am playing and that is being played with me. Move the line, change the shape, leave the mark that I think in this moment is a mistake. Enjoy the mistake. Loosen up. I know that the answers will not come if I am tight or tense. I know that I want to be flowing with energetic, free marks. So, let them be just that. I take a step back, breathe, see it all afresh and let the bigger picture develop with relaxed, sweeping lines. I take a strong shape and pull it back with a semi-transparent overlay so I can re-consider it, or just leave it as it is. Always searching for that symmetry, the connection in me and outside, where it really works.

280

There are clues all around us to the amazing potential of humanity. Much of it, we externalize and don't realize for ourselves. I am in our living room, eating breakfast as the sun comes up over the sea and slowly points out for me the amazing range of novels on the bookshelf near the door. It's not that all of them are amazingly inspiring stories. Some of them are merely candyfloss to occupy a tired mind at the end of the day, with intrigue or entertainment. No, it's the fact that all of them have been written and, before that, worked out and, before that, conceptualized by some author's mind. I wonder how many pages I am looking at in the whole bookshelf. Many tens of thousands, I imagine. Millions of words. Each carefully chosen to build a story, impart a fantasy, inspire a feeling, take the reader from one world into another. How amazing is that!? We are amazing animals. Not only has all that been done, but ways and means have been devised to create paper, print and distribute thousands of each one, so they can be enjoyed and digested wherever anyone wants to. Then, I listen to music. Same thing there. And as I eat my breakfast, I browse through a book of another artist's art and touch his world. Surely, then, the arts are the most important dimension of our existence as a community, the most powerful tools of our multifaceted existence and the greatest doorways and channels for self-realization.

281

So many things seem to have grown in my consciousness into huge and important and wonderful things. Maybe it is a reflection of how small my world has become, in some ways. But, then again, it could simply mean that I feel things much more acutely, now that I am more present and the stress and distraction of mind chatter and things to do have reduced to a level where I can put them in their place. And so many of those small things are so perfectly and uniquely you that they are amplified, even more, when they happen. We are heading out for a walk up the road from the house. The evening is cool. Distant headlamps weave their way through the scrub. A flock of birds weaves and dives, forming fluid, contained shapes that morph, split and re-form like a single cell on its journey to a bigger life. A light breeze brings the scent of sage to us as we walk. You hold my hand. Three of my fingers, actually, as only you have ever done. And my world is complete, sublime, happy and safe. Your hand is a little cooler than mine. I never want to let it go but, after a short distance, it's better to swing our arms. But the connection remains in the air between us and deep into my heart and soul. So, when I glance across at you, I cannot help but smile. The birds swoop over us and we duck instinctively. And I somehow feel some of your sense of awe, through you, to me. Electric!

282

A thousand years from now, what will all this be like? I tend to think in terms of an apocalyptic doom, but I do wonder if that's the way it will go. We are programmed to think in terms of an ever-evolving economy, largely driven by ever-evolving technology towards megacities populated by androids that are surrounded by wastelands. Yet, in fact, the human spirit is maybe what evolves. I sincerely hope it does. Whenever I travel away from home, the yearning to be back here consumes me. You, this place, our home, nature. Surely I am not unique in that? Privileged, yes, but not unique, I'm sure. Surely in the soul of each stressed worker, each unhappily married person, every drug addict and every child, there is something that points them upwards, a natural compass that tells them they are a precious being and true happiness and contentment are in a home, in nature and in love. Or are so many blinded to their natural, human birthright by the overwhelm, the shiny objects and the deep programming that they actually lose that? What are we doing? If that is the case, do we progressively become less human? The acceleration of change tells me that one thousand years hence will equate to ten thousand years of development by past standards. Humans don't evolve that quickly—or adapt to change that quickly. We are, in fact, fully evolved, if we could only tap into our full potential. We don't need 1,000 years. We need now.

283

The human face is so incredibly complex. To truly capture the person, in more than an accurate, superficial likeness, is a fantastic skill. When Van Gogh painted his self-portraits, they said far more than a sophisticated likeness ever could. Mind you, I have seen some pretty impressive, detailed likenesses of people like Keith Richards that say a lot about the sitter. More so than the usual subject for such likenesses—hill people from Tibet and so on. Tourist pictures. Squinty eyes, detailed wrinkles. On the other hand, some of the greats did such simple, yet evocative studies that somehow go further. Such as Matisse and his simple image of Paula. How to get beyond the physical and into the soul? How to choose which lines, shades, colours, shapes to play up, emphasise, even exaggerate, or let fall back? Each one is so different and each face is physically so different. We recognize the differences instantly, even though our visual memory is weak. It's something I have to work at constantly. Hand-eye coordination driven by quickly fading memories and a hand that is all too ready to be sloppy and inaccurate. To develop an ability to see beyond surface, into structure, and back to surface, in order to render a face (or anything!) with intelligence and understanding, would be a wonderful thing.

284

We are still quietly playing our part. The world has transformed, in so many ways, in our short lifetime. When I think back to the relative simplicity and healthy life of my youth, before technology accelerated at its dizzying pace, before people became part of the machine and before souls were gathered up and blasted with pervasive man-made radiation[30], interminable information and junk that they neither wanted or needed, some part of me is dismayed beyond the pale. Another part of me says that mankind has been subjecting itself to beautiful transformations since time began, and there have always been the seers, the activists, the revolutionaries, the intellectuals who cannot follow the madness and who strive against enormous odds to provide alternatives, reason, love and spirituality. The eternal joust. I wonder why it always seems to be set up in favour of dysfunctional masses. Maybe that's what it takes to motivate old souls to take action. I paint, you write and spread enormous wisdom. People take notice. And even if it is a brief article in the morning paper or an image that causes a pause in swiping on a phone somewhere, it makes a difference. I used to think it was about influence, but really it's all about energy: keeping our own in place and integrity, so that those who align recognize it, and are comforted and encouraged. There is so much power in that and, truthfully, in nothing else.

285

You look so small, lying there, all curled up and fast asleep. If I walk around to your side of the bed, I can just see one closed eye, caught in a frown as you are all bunched up in the pillow with your duvet almost covering your hair. In fact, if I couldn't see your blond hair when I am lying next to you, I may sometimes think you are not there. It's hard to believe how much power, love and energy is being re-charged by you simply lying there and relaxing. You are dreaming. I see a movement; your hand under the duvet, no doubt playing some cosmic tune—fingers playing the individual notes that accompany you on your dream journey. I do my five Tibetan rites[2]. When I have finished, you still haven't moved. Your breathing is silent and I instinctively watch, searching for tell-tale signs of life. A brief sniff confirms what I really didn't need to know. When I had been lying beside you, I had felt the warmth radiating off your body as you slept. So many ways you comfort me, and love me, even when you are unaware of what you are doing. Even when all I can see is a lumpy duvet with no signs of life, no smiles, no talking, no heavenly touch. Now, you would be getting embarrassed. I cannot take my eyes off you for these many precious moments. One eye, a tuft of hair. Incredible, isn't it, that we are capable of so much feeling, such love, such gratitude, in an instant, with so little information.

286

Dealing with the garden, the vegetable field and the herb garden has always been a bit of a mystery to me. I used to envy those people whose properties were always surrounded by leafy abundance. Now that I have one myself, it is a continuous source of wonder. My plants always used to die off at some point, leaving patches shrivelled up, dry, or dark and droopy. I still cannot name most of the plants we have and I certainly don't understand their needs. Yet here we are, thanks to local skill and knowledge, living in our own leafy abundance. I have renewed respect for gardeners who know their stuff. While I was soul-searching, looking for life's meaning, travelling and exploring creativity, they were nurturing life in and from the earth beneath our feet, creating a continuous celebration that, if only I had been the slightest bit aware of what was happening, was showing me something incredible and miraculous that needed no explanation, theories or tortured questioning. As long as it is looked after, it simply gives, in all its colour, complexity, and sheer beauty, in ways that I cannot comprehend. Just one single leaf is more incredible than anything I have ever done or achieved. That's not to put me down, but it's to recognize, in some small way, what we are living in every single day, and it's to be thankful and acknowledge the incredible power that is all around us that we cannot match.

287

I am so proud of you. Every time you smile, it is a victory; every time you laugh, I feel like celebrating. So life is full of victories and celebrations. Of you. That you have been through all that you have been through, that you have born the weight of so much disappointment, that you have survived the pain and everything the unthinking world has thrown at you, that you have felt it all so much more intensely than anyone I know, that you have shared your humour, conversation and love of life with others even when, inside, you were crying in pain; surely all these things are to be celebrated, acknowledged and written down in the history book of the world. And to shine through, and still be giving, in integrity and asking for nothing back, while forging a new, healthy life, a beacon in a world gone utterly mad, is surely worth all the worldly awards and decorations there are bestowed on those we admire, look up to and revere. And if, just in case, you are not awarded a Nobel Prize or a world medal or any other grey trinket or representation of normal people's inability to meaningfully acknowledge magnificence beyond their reach, all I can do is hold you in a warm embrace, kiss you, comfort you, touch you, love you, care for you, admire you, speak loudly through love, gawk, dissolve, laugh with you, play ping pong with you and simply be with you.

288

When the call came through from Manuel, we broke all records getting our lifejackets on and hauling the two-seater 'fat' canoe down to the water. The sea was a bit rough so we had to push it out a little way. You climbed on the front seat with your oar and I scrambled on at the back as soon as I had got it through a breaker and it was pointing out to sea. Manuel had been excited. It was a large school—maybe thirty or forty—coming down the coast in our direction. We paddled furiously to the clear, calm water, then got into a smooth rhythm—forging into the blue, creating a steady bow wave. I am distracted by your back and shoulders, your neck and hair. Concentrate. As we paddle, we scan the horizon for the smooth, glistening arcs of their backs breaking the surface. The sea gets darker as it gets deeper below us. "There!" you shout, pointing with your oar. I strain to see, but just catch the waves and the occasional seabird as I keep rowing. "Where?" "There—wow!" And then I see them. Like a vast wave of subsea energy, broaching the surface now and then. They are coming straight at us! Fascination and awe mix with apprehension and some fear—a potent mix we have to keep under control. Vulnerability in their territory. But they are kind and gentle and knowing. We are safe.

289

I am in awe of artists. When I see the love and care that go into some of the work, I am amazed at human diversity, spirit and skill. To stand in front of a painting in a gallery must be one of life's greatest privileges. To be given the opportunity to be part of someone else's life, their heart and soul, and to wonder at what they have discovered for themselves and expressed in such a powerful, non-verbal way, is amazing. Yes, there are artists and there are artists. Much of the work doesn't move me, blending as it does, into a different part of my mind. But that is just me, and that is the beauty of it. And I feel a bit sad for those who have never experienced that feeling, who have chosen not to allow their minds and hearts to open, observe and experience something new that perhaps they cannot understand, but may still feel, because that, thankfully, is the bigger, primal part of us. Our first responder. To compartmentalize art into boxes of prejudice, like and dislike, anger and love only hurts the observer and robs them of what may be gained. We are, after all, spiritual beings and, ultimately, we don't understand that. Yet that is what we are and there is no escaping it. Sometimes, to give up control of our conditional minds is a scary thing. Feelings can be frowned upon and judged, but the ultimate judgement is how human we are, and that can be magnificent.

290

I thought that, by the time we were fully installed in this wonderful home, life would slow down for us, days would stretch out like loose elastic, and there would be time to ponder for hours after a lazy lunch. Well, in fact, that does occasionally happen but, truth be told, we seem to be busier than ever. Today, you are typing as fast as you can to get an article ready for a press deadline. I am in the studio contemplating my model as I prepare for a long day of exploration and discovery. I know that we will both be exhausted by the end of the day, but happy to have achieved whatever we achieve. Jane is a favourite model. In her twenties, she is fit, healthy and not too slim. So, her toned body gives great definition, especially in the more energetic short poses. It can take me all morning to get to know a model's body enough to start painting. Quick, rough lines are followed by longer—just a few minutes each—poses drawn in charcoal and chalk to find the masses, angles, proportions and the light, dark, reflections thrown by the particular lighting of the day. And by the afternoon, I get started on the painting which, energy permitting, I will continue into the evening, with short breaks, so I have a basis that can be continued the following morning without losing its energy. And so begins another busy, beautiful day.

291

Just as I reach the supermarket checkout and the cashier has run my shopping over the scanner, the lights go out. Her till or computer or whatever it is, clunks and the drawer is locked shut as the screen in front of her goes blank. There's a general groan that emanates from the queue behind me. This was the only till that was working, up till now. It happens now and then. I think the village electricity supply is old and subject to periodic breakdown. I start unpacking my shopping back onto the belt. This could take a while. There's no point in asking, discussing or getting upset. Everyone in the queue knows. Time to hit the bar and have a beer. No coffee, of course. And maybe some tapas. Or head home to where we have our own supply. But, knowing this could be resolved in half an hour, I do the maths and decide the bar is a better idea. And, anyway, what's the rush? It's a nice opportunity to make new friends and catch up with old ones. Wartime spirit! I give an apologetic smile to the cashier and, as everyone else in the queue quietly puts their baskets on the floor (in line) we all wander out into the sun. And I am so grateful that something that, in the past, would have been an urgent concern, is turned into a social opportunity. I am even glad of this type of occasional disruption. We, in the second world, still have our independence. We are not chipped into a high-tech control society. We are still free.

292

I wonder why we doubt, so much of the time, that miracles exist. When I think about it, it's nuts that we ever do, and even more nuts that we demand proof of miracles. All I have to do is breathe, and there is proof. All I have to do is open my eyes and it's all around me. The fact that there is anything at all, is surely proof. And what is a miracle, anyway? For us spoilt creatures, it has to be a magic trick, because we have grown so accustomed to the myriad miracles that surround us every day, that we can no longer see them. The challenge, I find, is editing them out. When I, in a moment of crazy illusion, think it would be a great idea to do some drawing outside, in the landscape, I really see the problem. There is just too much going on for me to be able to take part of it and make any visual sense of it at all. It's a cacophony of shapes, beings, colour. Even one single square inch of it is overwhelming, whether it is a patch of earth, part of a plant, a section of sky, a small beetle, whatever it is, I feel I cannot do it justice—now or even after 100 years of trying. In trying, I make sweeping strokes that ignore millions of details. I go for an aesthetic rather than exploring the intricacy. I expect that's where hyper-realism wins out sometimes, forcing our attention to illuminated detail. Yet I know the answers aren't in the detail either. Because when I paint or draw, it is always an extended portrait of me.

293

I wonder how you create a state of satisfying permanence. So often, I immerse myself in a painting one day, all enthusiastic and fresh, and the next day I just want to chuck it out. What changes? Are our brains so limited that they cannot see, from one day to the next, what is worthwhile and what is simply rubbish, idle scribbling or mess? Or is it to do with the separation of heart and head—our two qualifying mechanisms that think or know how to evaluate? Or is it something to do with quantum physics—the observer changing what is there? How can we at the same time, be perceptive, inspired, creative thinkers and so utterly lost? What faculty can I develop to gain a sense of solid progress to satisfying permanence? And please don't tell me it's meticulous planning and forethought; those stranglers of intuition, dynamism, connection and creativity. I don't want to be an engineer of carefully laid plans. I suppose that's the risk I take with my particular approach that, maybe, at the end of a process there is nothing worthwhile—however I determine what that is. Maybe there is no even vaguely linear progress from start to finish. Nothing is guaranteed. Maybe I must find a way to celebrate that and express it in my work. At the same time as having all these concerns, though, something inside me loves all this chaos and this journey.

294

Georgia O'Keeffe[31] realized that life-long learning was the best way to have a fulfilling life. Well into her 80s, she was trying new things, working with a man in his 20s, for instance, to discover ceramics and make her art three-dimensional. She didn't stop till the day she died, producing sensual, beautiful work, even as she was losing her sight. Such a cruel twist of fate, akin to Beethoven losing his hearing[32]. I feel I am on a lifelong learning path as well, although I am not sure what I am learning. I try new things all the time with the painting, experiment with three dimensions, different media and so on. Letting go to let the new in, wherever I have the opportunity. When am I learning? What am I learning? I am not so sure. Maybe I need a mentor who can guide me, yet I feel I would not be the best student, unless someone can truly see me and illuminate my way, rather than simply replicating methodologies and ideas of theirs. I do love to learn. I remember, way back, at Kubricks'[10], Mike Carlo[18] encouraging me in his blunt yet loving way, and me making my own discoveries along the way. Inside, I still want to be the child guided by the wisdom of a great teacher, in awe of all that appears before me. At my age, though, I know the tables have turned, and that is my job now, to pass on all that I don't even know that I know, to others.

295

It's hard to remember, but I foresaw all this. The brain has a remarkable capability to block out the struggle, whatever hardships we endure, whatever health challenges; and transport us—figuratively and literally—to a better place. If we want it to. If we focus with all our heart and mind (using our brain) on the outcome we seek. Those who doubt that need only look at their own lives. What do they focus on and what do they get? What intentions are behind their actions? What is their big picture vision for their life? I know, all too well, that circumstances can block a vision and confuse the mind as to what is possible. Most of my life, I focused on circumstances. This is happening; therefore that. Reactive and victim mentality. The world was happening to me. How incredible it was, then, to discover that I am actually an active part of that world, fully integrated into the system that was creating all those circumstances that I saw as things being dumped on me. How incredible it was, then, to discover that I had the key to the machine, that I could go and tinker with it, rearrange the workings and decide how it would best work for me and for others. That I could decide on up and down, forward and back, round or straight, little or much, was all an incredible revelation that created a cosmic defrag and a whole new operating system.

296

It's all too easy to stiffen up with the art. It seems as if my mind is conditioned to seek out familiarity, safe ground and easy solutions. It is also conditioned (or is that my heart?) to seek out new territories, dive into unknown experiences and discover new ways, new imagery. Inevitably, that can lead to a lot of experimentation and sometimes a lot of mess before I produce anything that I or anyone else may consider to be worthwhile. Equally, there is little time (although there is all time, right now, and only time). But to keep a sense of urgency in the work, keep a flow going, not get hung up on the petty detail, is also an imperative. Detail means fixing things and making them sacred. Much as religion fixes a concept and then exploits it to hell (sic.), so the full potential, the full wonder and the infinite nature of it is suppressed or lost entirely within a comfortable and adequate paradigm or a frightful control system, the art is contained before it ever has a chance to breathe. Full expression, from a standing start—the beginner's mind. Am I asking too much of myself? Will I simply stop myself at the gate and never make a single mark, or stop myself in the process, by halting the process at an 'acceptable' place, judging it on technique or acceptability? I am actually not looking for struggle, but I have to be true to me, otherwise I am wasting my time and I am building a toxic religion from my life.

297

It's weird that the absolute luxury these days is nothing. No one watching you, tracking you, analyzing you, predicting your next move or your next purchase; no one fitting you neatly into another database or knowing so much about you when you simply touch a credit card onto a screen to buy some vegetables. We luxuriate in our anonymity at our home. No 'smart' appliances are giving away our habits or telling people when we are not at home. We cannot be completely anonymous, of course—and, in some ways, we don't want to be—but we have claimed most of our lives for ourselves. The private IP keeps us hidden from all but the most vociferous snoopers thanks to our VPN and our emails are locked down with all sorts of security. Partly, it's the cost of being well-known, but mainly it's simply our choice. And I find it so sad that humanity has reached such a low point that even a quiet walk on the beach by a couple in love can be monitored and recorded at will by those with their own interests at heart. What happened to us? Why is all this technology so important? Why did we not, at any point along the way, say 'STOP, this isn't what we want'. We are better than this. To be human is so much more than data, and we will never truly know another or ourselves through external sophistication. And, so, to come back to quietness, nothingness and peace is the true home everyone secretly yearns for, and that we have.

298

"Where have you been?" I see a distance in your eyes. A weary glance, maybe a tense mouth. Perhaps something you need to order in your mind before we talk about it. I feel at a disadvantage. Not being part of that process. Not sharing your journey. Knowing that, somewhere inside you, you are hurting. And I feel it all the more, now, after all these years, since it happens so rarely. I check the parts I can, somewhat narcissistically. Is it me? What have I done or not done? Armpits, teeth, breath. Everything looks well in the house. It must be something else that preoccupies your heart. These days, distances between us are not physical. Even when we are miles apart, we are still together. A visit to a shop or a coffee on the quay—all just extensions of our loving elastic band[25] that knows no breaking point. No, the only distances between us occur, very occasionally, in the heart. When they do, they are the worst—the bleakest, distant places with high walls and dark skies and no apparent ways to get back to the beautiful place that I love and value above all else. Yet these distant places always dissolve to nothing, without even a memory to taunt me, when we return. Simple words, a loving touch, a kind gesture, a recognition of the incredible reality that surrounds us—not just in the physical realm—is all it takes to realize the falseness in that distance, that is truly no distance but just an occasional old wobble. Because the truth is, our love is reality.

299

I want to retire, yet I don't. What is retirement for an artist, anyway? I think it's just a euphemism for not wanting to try anymore and to allow my body to go downhill and for my mind to visit its second childhood. Not for me. I am only just starting and I cannot imagine that I will be anywhere near finished by the time that, for some reason or other, I cannot continue. I'm so glad we have the gym in the basement that helps me keep up with you and my desire to keep all this going for ever, if I can. I have more to live for now than at any time previously in my life. Why is that? Why now? I suppose it is a natural consequence of finding the real me. It was no real surprise, because there was, of course, a deep knowing that somewhere inside me—was me. Sounds obvious, I know, but why the heck was I so elusive for so long? And look at all the consistent, loving effort you put in for both of us to get there—or here, is it? Blimey! I have arrived and I still don't know where I am! Never mind; it's all good. Keep on keeping on—with you and me as me, at last. What a relief! And it's so much easier than the tortuous effort I had to put in before, smothered in doubts and lack of self-worth as I was. So, why would I ever want to retire from being me? I reckon I have spent some 40,000 days of my life on a journey full of diversions and dead ends, so I think the rest of them are going to be the best. In fact, I know they are: with you!

300

I think that, for me, the richness of experience is directly proportional to the effort put in. I cannot get the same richness as a spectator. I'd rather be the actor than watch the movie, be the musician than go to the concert, be the artist than the viewer or collector. It's just the way I am. I think it is sometimes called the curse of creativity. Yet I am still not sure how creative I am. Do I even need to know? And what scale am I referring to, anyway? None of it makes any sense. The only sense is to keep on creating. That, for me, is where the richness of experience lies. And I see it in every painting. Especially the ones that I think I have finished, but then I wait, see them afresh and attack them again. Going deeper, going beyond. It's the same with you and me. I know I have often resisted change and depth in the past, but I also learned, fairly early on, to trust in what you say, even if it is just a feeling or something that may have been difficult to justify or articulate in any way that either made sense or that either of us understood. Yet those are often the starts of the bigger shifts. I guess that is why I have learned to trust them, because they are the foundation of all reason anyway. It's how our brains work—feelings first; the rest will follow in its own mechanical way, all in good time. And I am so grateful that, even now, we are still growing together, in our little paradise, and the feelings get deeper, and richer, every brand new day.

301

When you live in a world where the accepted norms don't apply, life can be a little challenging. With the personal development we have gone through over the years, I sometimes feel strangely isolated—from people leading so-called normal lives. One of the effects, which I suppose I should have seen coming, was that, while I hoped in some way to use the personal development to achieve what I wanted in life, what I wanted in life also changed. Gone are the energetic, focused, well-defined goals in business, ownership and lifestyle. I'm not sure they have been fully replaced with something I get passionately excited about. So, I often feel something is lacking in my motivation. Where am I going now? There is no one but me who can tell me. I even have trouble defining 'fun' any more. Adrenalin highs don't really interest me and I think I am more risk-averse than I ever was before. So, where are those qualities and are they necessary for me to be fulfilled and experiencing the full kaleidoscope of human experience? Where is the push to move onwards and upwards rather than simply survive and go through the motions? Having reached my vision in so many ways, am I now simply floating in my own unique space of sensory deprivation? All these questions still come in one tiny instant, until I return to the inside and be in the place where I know that it is all, actually, perfect.

302

Once I replaced other distractions with drawing, that was when my art started to take shape. Drawing, for me, is the basis of everything that I do. It's the connection that I needed to make between my thoughts and my hand. Observation has to be honed in order for me to train my mind into remembering what I have just seen a mere few seconds ago. I realize that I was observing, but not truly seeing. I was not able to even describe a person, a shape, a thing, almost immediately after seeing it. That began to upset me and limit my ability to even formulate ideas. After all, to formulate an idea is to build it in my mind, retain more and more detail and then have the capacity to transfer it onto a medium, a piece of paper or a canvas. Adding a third dimension, as I do on occasion, demands even more. So, the humble line, scratched onto a surface, in haste, with passion, is the basis for all good work. And I cannot do it through a computer. The relationship simply isn't there. Yet, forcing myself back to the basics of drawing was not easy. The easy solutions and distractions are all around us, but none of them nurture my soul, confront me with the essential learning on a primal level, or transfer part of my soul from hand to surface. That's the difference, and that's the reason why, however far we may have come, the very best tools we have are contained within us.

303

Yes, I can see the benefit of being ambitious at an early age, so you can accumulate wealth and comfort for your latter years. I was never driven by that kind of impetus. Working for others always seemed like a bad idea. I know people 'do well' using that model, but I could never believe totally in a boss or superior, and that's what it takes for me to apply my all. And I could not see how, by making wealth for another or an organization, I could be totally in integrity with myself. I never found anything that I totally believed in, in a way that I could devote all my energy to it. I called it healthy cynicism. And, although I could possibly have made life easier for myself if I had compromised, I am glad of the way life has led me to this wonderful situation. And it is interesting to see that the things that fire me up, inspire me and fill my heart and soul, are the very same things that did when I was very young. Before 10 years old, even. Art—the visual experience, the discussion, the breaking of boundaries, the shock of the new, the intensity of eroticism, the mystery, the eternal creativity in shapes and colours, the sounds of passionate music, the stretching of imagination, a part acted really well, words used in ways that fire up imagery and feeling and understanding fresh from the mind and heart of another. Yes, I have kept that wealth in abundance amid the noise of my life.

304

I pause. The alignment isn't there yet. It's not a rational thing, one born out of strategy or constructional thinking. It's not about thinking at all. It's more about aligning. Taking what is there, or apparently not there, and being in the right place to instinctively make the right move. A move that will establish, perhaps, just the beginnings of a greater form that works—on deeper levels. I surmise that it is the alignment process that produces or is the energy that resides in the work when it is done, and that passes from the work to the mind through the eye of the viewer and settles in whatever part of that psyche and body that it is meant to. Each to his own. It will be different for everyone. For some, it will pass un-noticed. For some it may cut like a knife through their soul, or their preconceptions, or judgements, or mind. For others it may alight softly in the heart or surge through emotions wherever the neural connections take them. All I can do is pause, and have an unspoken, unthought, connected certainty that I may not even know and that can pass in an instant, before I take the next definitive, irreversible step in this process. It's not as if I am on a tightrope, fearing a fall. It's calmer than that. More about caring and being real, and surrender to now and a future that I cannot know and don't want to know in mechanical detail. The magic is in the not knowing and the discovery.

305

There is a point to all of this. I have to be careful with this 'beginner's mind' philosophy. Maybe I have to mix it in with everything I have learned, or alternate between the two. I'm not sure where I am going with this, but I get feelings and flashes of clarity that only remain for nano-seconds. Not long enough for me to grasp them and log them, rarely even enough to see them or even feel them. Electric sparks in my consciousness teasing me with deep recognition and yet leaving me with nothing but a feeling that I just missed something significant and important; that I need to understand and be able to articulate—for me, and for humanity. I wonder if others have the same insights; rocking uncertainly from our dream world of foggy lostness into occasional seas of clear skies and total clarity of thought and vision. Released for infinitesimal moments from the self-imposed drudgery of reason, logic, 'common sense', physicality; yearning to capture the unformed, floating, seemingly gaseous reality that presents itself at those times and needs no proof or reassurance, but that gives us a glimpse into a world that we could be in. If only. If what? There is a point to all this. I know because I have seen it at such moments. I don't know what it is. All I know is that I have to let it come to me in its own way, as a frightened animal that is scared that if I truly know it, I may turn on it and destroy it.

306

What are heroes? And why don't I have any? Or is that wrong? I guess I do have a few. People I admire for who they are more than for what they have done. It seems that many gather heroes to fill gaps in themselves, use them as examples of who they want to be, to stimulate them to act in certain ways and shape themselves in the habits, attitudes and ways of others. Having mixed with some during my life, I chose not to. Seeing the famous without their masks on, such as in the BBC canteen, I could so often see their vulnerability and fear, the betrayal of hidden human qualities that I actually quite liked but were certainly not there to be admired. And I have been there when a famous hero to others has done despicable things, protected by their image, spin doctors and sheer manufactured presence. I don't need heroes, although I have one very obvious one. One who I love more than anyone. One who is a giver and a seer who, in her eloquent dignity and respect for all, has never taken advantage of or fed off the weaknesses of others. Maybe hero is the wrong word, but I can think of no other. I am not even sure what a hero is, and whether that title is earned through action, accumulation or stillness. Maybe it is different for everyone. If anything, the only hero I want is me. Sounds indulgent? Not really. If heroes are a substitute for personal greatness, I'd rather go straight to the point. And, with you by my side, I sometimes even feel it.

307

We don't know what we are missing until we drop the charade. First, we need to recognize and admit to the charade. That can be the hardest part, because once that has happened, we want to drop it as fast as we can. Being real, being true to oneself is always more attractive—and easier, in fact. But we don't know that, until we do it. Sometimes, something happens that cuts through it. Perhaps for a moment, perhaps longer, I can still remember the first time it happened with you, when I slipped my hands around your waist at the fireworks in Geneva. It was such a powerful moment, such a solid, real experience that I could not deny it, or ignore it, or be anything other than a melting, humble, thankful man. The feeling was electric and it stays with me still. No charade could impinge on its truth. Idle chitchat with other partygoers dissolved into clouds of steam as that connection lit up my being and love flowed through my hands, through you and back to me. A knowing so deep and attractive that it changed my life, right there in that golden moment. It defined my future and stayed with me, thankfully, so I could actualize that feeling into a long, so special, so beautiful relationship, an ever-expanding journey, the best learning of my lifetime and everything that flowed, and continues to flow from it. The charade removed, so the real me could live.

308

It's good to be making some new friends. I am actually aware of the way life has changed our situation where making friends is concerned. Sometimes I yearn for the simplicity, the naivety of youth, with its curiosity and flexibility of character, that didn't create walls and that opened our hearts and minds to a new presence in our life. With age, all that shifts. We are wiser, in some ways, life has endowed us with caution, consideration, calculation, a need for protection. And, on the part of the other, who is most likely younger and less experienced in the ways of the world, we carry authority, mystery, celebrity and experience that they may draw on. The balance, in many cases, becomes uneven. Closeness and understanding become rare commodities to be cherished and valued. And even when these things are apparent, experience keeps me separate, autonomous and alert to cracks in the flow. That's good, and bad, of course. I waste less precious time on fruitless discovery, and spend more time on celebrating relationships that have proved to be worthwhile. Even playing fields, no giving to get, no mind games and certainly no duplicity or even lazy assumptions. These days, it's all about quality. From that strong foundation, in any relationship, we can soar with ideas, dive into discovery, hold each other in dynamic excitement and relax with peace and laughter in the warm candlelight of knowing.

309

So much of my work seems to be about defining the indefinable in ways that our hearts and souls understand, more than our minds. This, I find interesting. I have always known that the limbic (feelings) system kicks in first, before the cortex (mind) starts to rationalize and order things. So, there is clearly some recognition, some intelligence in the limbic system that creates that feeling—that magnetism—before and so that the cortex can start to do its job. Yet, because it is not the cortex, that is precisely why whatever happens there is indefinable. It has to be, and it is perfect that way. That is the very reason we have artists—to poke and probe that layer of our existence and thereby poke and probe the cortex to stimulate it to think up different ways of seeing things, stimulate new neural pathways and complete the circle back to the limbic brain so that we act or behave differently, having been exposed. If the art doesn't, in some way, change a life, then it is doing nothing at all. That is why, for me, decorative art is pointless, dead and boring. After the first impression of awe, an interest perhaps in some detail, it dies and merges into the background like a too-familiar wall that it hangs on, merely filling a blank space. Although the difference between that and what I call 'real art' is a sliding scale that is different for everyone, and that changes if and as we grow.

310

Being here and staying here now; it's something I have yet to master. Sure, I can do it for minutes, perhaps even hours, but permanently? I sometimes think I have to find my child mind again. Isn't that what happens when people get older—they enter their second childhood? It feels like a nice place to be. No responsibility, no demands, no complications. Just now. Whatever I happen to be occupying my whole self with at this moment. Lying on the grass and watching an insect grapple with the terrain through the corner of my eye. Drawing a fantastical airplane with no concern for detail, accuracy, aerodynamic, practicalities, scale or anything else. Meditation helps, although practicing it can be a bit tumultuous, at times, as my head fights me before I settle in to it. And it can take years for us to truly appreciate a return to silence, if we ever do. Life brings so many rich experiences—and unwanted experiences too—perhaps in equal measure, maybe not. I have tended, through fear and confusion, to focus on the latter, which has stoked the fire to bring me more of the same. And the silence, my mind has told me, is unproductive, frivolous and a waste of time. But I have learned, and now I focus much more, in an effort to return to consciousness, sanity and being here now, permanently, because, when it comes down to it, I am actually nowhere else.

311

What do I believe? And does it matter? Does it ultimately make any difference? On the loony level, there are millions who believe in some brand of god, and will live and die in a story made up by those who want to control and manipulate lives, usually some long time after the supposed master has died. Napoleon once said that religion is the thing that stops the poor from killing the rich. I suppose that in a time before law enforcement organizations that was a very valid control mechanism. Poor = humble = heaven-bound. Keep that one going and the rich just have a debauched ball. Then there is science. The big one for us liberal intellectuals who would overthrow with reason but are kept in place through argument and counter-argument. One can never know all the science, after all. And it can be approached from so many angles and methodologies that decisions can be put off for ever, with the eternal promise of scientific evolution. Evolving to where, I do not know. Apparently, though, science is getting better and better, except when bits of it are proved wrong. Do I believe in my art? I don't know if belief is relevant here. Art is a huge experiment, driving forward awareness and making reflections on society and where we are. What is there to believe, rather than observe, have realizations and dream again? What do I believe? Why do I even ask myself the question? I am as I am, I do what I do and I definitely believe in me and you.

312

How do you do that? If it was anyone else, I would hardly have noticed. I would have passed the time of day, made some inane remark and carried on with what I am doing. But not you. You're standing at the table, by the window, arranging flowers in a vase. Okay, the setting is wonderful and the flowers are magnificent. That's a given. But the vast majority of what is given here is the feelings I feel, watching you. I'll have to think of something else to say to justify my gawking. It's yet another moment that must not pass without total acknowledgment, absorption and understanding; without full appreciation of all that is happening here. If I could just stop time, go and get my easel and paints and get set up, or at least dash upstairs and get the camera, and get this so I cannot overlook or forget this moment, I would surely do that. The shape of your body, the curve of your neck, the way your hands play with the stems and leaves, the smile on your face and the glint in your eye. You are focused on the flowers and talking to me at the same time. I can barely hear your words. "Pardon?" I say. You think I am going deaf, but I am simply in sensory overload. Surely no one can hear while taking all this in? Let alone speak. I am multitasking at lightning speed, but I cannot keep up. Trying to catch and store all that gorgeous detail and hoping I can reproduce it later. Unrelenting. That's what you are. And I love every single moment.

313

I worked late last night, so I am waking late this morning. As I come round, it's the pink inside my eyelids that tells me that the sun is streaming in. I gradually become aware of the gentle sea caressing the shore, and the occasional seagull contemplating the day, calling to friends. I can see it all in my mind's eye. The gull sits on the balcony wall with one eye on the ocean, the other on our terrace. Ever hopeful that some small part of our breakfast will be there for the taking in one of our unguarded moments. The sea is sleepy and the sand is cool underfoot, soft at the water's edge with just a few shells breaking the smooth, clean surface causing urgent rivulets. I cannot move. I can't open my eyes yet. There's a gossamer film between wakefulness and sleep that is just so deliciously delicate on a morning like this. And, of course, your leg is firmly planted over mine, holding me captive in sleepy embrace. I am conscious of your breathing beside me in sacred sleep and the busy creative dreams of dawn that twitch your hand incessantly under the sheet. I give way to the urge to wake up and take in this magnificent new day. I unstick my eyelids and the room lights up in warm rays of sunshine. I want to roll over to see you, but I know that would wake you and break the spell. So, I lie there and my mind drifts back to the studio and the piece I am working on. A new day, a new connection. It's amazing how that can happen every single day.

314

Bottoms. I have seen a lot of them in my lifetime. As an artist who loves to do life drawings and earlier as a photographer of nude calendars, among other subjects, I suppose I have seen more than most. It's miraculous how the human body comes in so many shapes and sizes—and all on a similar bone structure. Shapes change with musculature, diet, DNA and environment, I guess; but the end result is an infinite variety that keeps artists on their toes and blesses the world with a cornucopia of subtle and not so subtle differences. But I digress. The magnificent bottom, the seat of all sitting, the parting that reveals itself on parting and speaks its own language of cheeky, chubby, chortling chat as it recedes before our eyes, giving another perspective—that cannot be disguised beneath trousers or tights or even large dresses—of the person whose front may just be a front. Bottoms are honest barometers of life, of habits and disciplines or lack thereof. They follow us through life, embedding their cruel or flattering record, a receptacle of decisions made manifest. Celebration or consternation. No ifs or buts. A fabulous, flatulent, flabbergasting phlegmatic form. Shrivelled prunes or big balloons, continental shelf or tuck and mince, they are the heralds of our passing, inputs and outputs, what we gather and what we let go as we pucker and bloat our way through life.

315

All routine disappears. I know, after that late walk on the beach with you, that life will change again for the next few months. I love it! It started, again, just before sunset, as the waves calm and the little birds get busy in their dark-suited calamitous commute up and down the surf line, stepping deftly around spindrift and intuitively keeping their distance as we softly indent temporary pools with our feet. You released your hand so you could swing your arms as the energy of the idea fused with the light breeze. That is when I knew. Your mind is racing and, although I play a part in the conversation, you are way ahead, yet feeding me tidbits to keep me with you. "It's okay," I think, "let it run." You are kind not to overwhelm me with half-thought thoughts as the factoids and feelings jostle for attention in your mind. Your pace slows, then speeds up again. I watch you as your eyes scan the horizon, as if you are here, with me. I know not to comment on the vivid hues in the sky, or a seagull swooping for a fish. The ideas are coming thick and fast. I know you will be bursting to share them with me, and I want to hear them. I love to know, when you get so fired up you can hardly contain yourself. It's amazing, isn't it, how a walk on the sand can connect us to a kaleidoscope of fantasy that simply isn't there when we are acting out the day. And so begins another magnificent journey with my muse.

316

The creation of an abstract is a complex business for me. Today, I got started, after days of reflection and consideration, scribbling down thoughts and ideas, trying (and trying not to try) to achieve some intuitive connection with what may be subject matter, curbing emotions, generating emotions, stretching beyond tired old concepts of shape and colour, emptying my mind of things seen, other art, great works of the past, searching for a new voice and a construct that speaks clearly and powerfully, on its own terms, in non-words and deep emotions. I start with a blank canvas and a mess of imagery on paper on the floor. The white is oppressive, so I have previously washed it with what I believe will be a complementary colour to the image that will evolve. I scrawl the basis of the form or arrangement in charcoal in swift, broad strokes. Step back; drink some water. Face the other way, watch the image in the paint-spattered mirror across the studio. Be careful not to edit or 'tidy up', but see it for what it is, with its comfort or discomfort, aggression or reassurance, balance or disturbing vertigo. Whatever. I start to think how I can work with this and, at the same time, get out of its way so it can emerge in its own way. I mix colours, precisely, intuitively, in varying volumes. A palette develops as its own artwork. I choose a brush and start.

317

I sometimes wonder if I will ever reach a point of total clarity with my work. It is, at the same time, totally frustrating and extremely exhilarating to not have clarity. To be constantly in a state of discovery is a blessing and a curse. All these contrasts, I know, bring urgency, life and energy to the work. Yet, in the back of my mind, there is also—and perhaps it is pure ego—that part of me that wants to achieve some sort of mastery. Maybe it is peace and light-hearted enjoyment that nudges at me, while all the time I really know that the path I am on has no such neatly packaged ending, no final 'Aha!' moment, no absolute resolution. And I am well aware that such a state could be terrifying, as well. A sudden stop, a precipice, death. Because there would be no more me, or reason to be me, so closely identified am I with this process. Perhaps I have already achieved mastery, and I just need to acknowledge that. Mastery of discovery, of creativity in ways that are unique to me. After all, it could be no other way, if you think about it. Despite living in such constant uncertainty, life is good. Maybe because of it. So, you see, I have advanced in years and I acknowledge that I know so very little. And I enjoy knowing less and less so there is more and more to discover. And what is life without learning and creativity? Simply a process and a routine—if we are lucky. Food in, waste out. But we are so much more: to discover!

318

Life's achievements so often involve rejection and acceptance on a different level to what I expected. I am so glad that I rejected all the religions, gurus and other so-called prophets—in both the spiritual and my business life—in order to gain my own self, independent of the ideas and even the convictions of others. Sometimes it has felt like self-sabotage, especially when I had no valid argument for rejection, no thoughts of better alternatives, just a feeling that 'this is not for me'. Sometimes, to trust that feeling, in the face of a well-established status quo, crowds of people who have already 'bought in', intelligent and clever people with seemingly bullet-proof arguments 'for' or 'against' whatever, it was the hardest thing. Especially when I was young, and searching, uncertain and vulnerable. I could not know then that each of us learns our own learning and, like religious fanatics, defend what we think we have learned merely to support our own identity and survival. We ultimately have no reason or purpose in convincing others of anything, and what we have learned may or may not serve us on our journey, and only we can find out anything for ourselves. That's the rub of life. And that's why rejection is the most healthy way to lean, because truth wins out inside. The rest is just colour and confusion. And that is why I know I am an artist, whether I produce or not.

319

Time seems to be speeding up. I want it to slow down. Living here seems to accentuate that acceleration. Maybe it is because we are both busy. Maybe our ages have something to do with it. When I am in the studio, time stands still for as long as I am engaged. Yet, when I emerge from the studio, time has passed—sometimes to a surprising degree. Whole days pass that I do not see. While I love my work, I also mourn the passing hours that revolved somewhere else, outside these four walls. I miss the time spent with you—laughing, touching, loving. I don't want to say 'you can't have it all' because by anyone's standards I certainly have it all, and I know for myself that I do indeed have it all. I am incredibly fortunate. That is why I want time to slow down. So I can pay attention to detail, fully appreciate everything. And I mean everything. All too soon, the paradigm could shift, my frame of reference change for ever, my brain and senses lose their acuteness, my heart grow tired. The seasons are passing in the blink of an eye. Cooler now, for what passes for our winter here. Die-off and sleep for the land, before it starts its work again in just a few short months. Fires in the hearth in the evenings. The absence of cicadas in the blue light of dawn. Windstorms bring sea spray to our windows. More to see, and appreciate and be part of, before the warmth returns yet again for a summer that I hope lasts forever.

320

To paint the mystery. Now that is interesting! With maybe neat shapes, messy lines. It doesn't matter. What matters is the mystery. After all, if I paint something that I see, using reference and some degree of accuracy, and if not, some degree of recognition—then that is it. It's that thing or that person or whatever. It can be judged on the emotion it generates, or the technique, or the memories it evokes in the viewer. But it will never take the viewer beyond that. It will always hold them in its basic interpretation and maybe the comfort of the recognizable and the acceptability of familiarity. Clearly, that is the space that most people want filled so they can stop, relax and escape. However, to go beyond that, yet at the same time make the image and the experience of it solid—that's interesting, intriguing. We are infinitely creative and we recognize indefinable mysteries as somehow being relevant or powerful, emotional or even recognizable to our higher selves—the part of us that is not bound by physicality and logic, that encompasses our brain and is infinitely larger than it. The part of us that craves our attention yet is usually denied it, that nudges and invites us with clues every day, should we be paying attention. The infinite ocean of possibility and extended reality, the loving force that lives us. Now that is very interesting!

321

The power of juxtaposition is one of the world's greatest wonders. To have that power is to elevate language for poetry and art. To find, in the databanks for the mind, grown through the years of learning and humanity, completely unrelated concepts and constructions that, nevertheless, enrich a description beyond mere description and, by a common recognition that can be visceral, humorous, devastating or otherwise emotion-generating, bring a completely fresh, yet intimately recognizable, vision to the commonplace or the extraordinary, is the skill that I crave in my writing and my art. The obvious is leaden, logic is dead. As humans, we are blessed with humour and a consciousness that enables us to draw from the ethers in ways that, we believe, no other animal can. And when we experience that creative reality, that comedy of coincidence, it awakens feelings in us that are there because we know we are more than the sum of our constituent parts and that we need to break free, again, from the tyranny of the left brain that dulls us down to economic units and makes us trudge through want and greed to an unsatisfied death. We have so much more to give. Art is a feeble and much misinterpreted word that hides a magnificence in all of us that is closer to our power, our centre, our purpose, our love, than anything we know. Without it, we are dead.

322

Where does inspiration come from? Is it some peculiar quality that some people have more of than others? Is an artist, who is expected to or who naturally exhibits tons of it, a special case? Or is it environmental—kicked into action by circumstances, events, generated feelings or whatever? Or does it come from somewhere else? I guess the truth of it is all of the above and more. I always hope it is a trait in me, rather than a state. Something I am prone to, have a natural aptitude towards, something in my DNA; rather than something that is variable, that comes and goes. If it is a trait, then why do I feel it deserts me so much of the time? The eternal balance of action and meditation has been a challenge for me to master, and I know that plays a huge part in it. But, in terms of my creativity, I also know that some sort of special engagement is needed. I have only met a few in my life who stimulated that. And they weren't all about art. Some special teachers I can recall—very few artists, who tend to be immersed in their own track. Exactly where I want to be so much of the time. And it does mean, for me, that I form a cocoon around me and delve in with all my being to strange and private places that I have all but forgotten until and unless I am there, when it is timeless, and I discover that engagement is not separation from everyone and everything around me, but love.

323

We are either creating or consuming. Most of the time we are consuming. And it is not a good way to live. Mainly because it is not sustainable. And our spiritual selves, our souls, are designed to create. Creating and consuming in balance—I guess that is the very definition of sustainability—is the best way. Only those ancient tribes who have somehow managed to survive The Onslaught brought by so-called civilization, know how to do that, and are truly in touch with their souls in a practical day-to-day manner. The rest of us are living in denial, purposely creating want and need with absolutely no regard for the whole. Ego- and accumulation-driven imperatives that have no regard for Gaia[33], and therefore no regard for ourselves. And we are so steeped in the wrong way that even our efforts to correct it—and many put huge effort into trying—are confused, badly focused and often doomed to failure from the beginning. Because one cannot take one aspect of the problem and work out a unique solution for that one aspect. We spout rhetoric, we have convincing arguments and words, we gather support for our ideas and points of view, but we always miss the point, and the whole world that is now so small and technically connected in so many ways, is fundamentally more disconnected than ever. Seekers of the real truth are the only ones who can really fix this, and it just so happens that I am married to one.

324

Through the eyes of a child, it is all so different. A moment that I dismiss in an instant is the whole world, at that moment, for the little girl looking hopefully up at her father, as he stands and talks to a friend. He gives her no attention. He doesn't respond to her tiny touch on his trouser leg. And I wonder, for that moment, in that fledgling life where the vast world makes little or no sense other than whatever clear and immediate desire is bubbling up in her mind, what kind of life she will live. What is she learning right now that will mould her view of the world to come, her world and that of those who pass through her life? Will a casual turn of her father's head, at this moment, make a difference between a life of self-acceptance or a life of self-rejection? How will this moment play out and arrange the dominoes that fall in such complex patterns from this moment to the next and the next, and so on? It seems impossible, in this unremarkable moment for an adult, that the life at his side could change, be permanently damaged, or not—as may be the case, depending on the delicate programs already in place, learned or inherited or contained within her DNA or whatever is at work here. A child's resilience is remarkable, to absorb so much in the first few years, and still have the potential, despite life's lottery, to be happy.

325

It's my favourite canopy—by far. On a morning like this, to be beneath it, in this beautiful place, is the best. I have often tried to paint it. But it is too perfect. Brushes, rags, sponges. I've tried everything, but that perfect, subtle graduation, that physical depth and extension, through distance, to light years, the feeling and hope it engenders, the gift of home and belonging it brings, is impossible to reproduce or even represent on a crude, physical surface. Of course, many artists have approximated to this feeling, but always devising supports for the lack of ability to truly express its perfection. Clouds, trees and more are all indicators, to instill a feeling of what is being attempted, but still the pure simplicity and power elude. Each painting still stops at the canvas, still has the mark of mixed paste, technique and its application. A dead experience even after an emotional initial reaction. Something dies on the surface and, once recognized, can never be re-awakened to transport the viewer from their stepping-off point to infinity, to this solid void that envelops everything, that supports everything in its place from here to eternity and that we are hopelessly inadequately equipped to comprehend. So I look down again, to this little ocean and tiny land, at my own hands. And I wonder at the consciousness that is me and everything.

326

What am I doing? Going through this process of finding images, my images, my truth? Is it truth? Is it mine? Thoughts have limited use in this realm. The realm of action is king here. When thought dominates action, rationality defeats it—the action—with assessment that is always too soon. Because the mind is comfortable with logic and repetition and order. It feels so threatened by play and creativity that it can go into panic mode, or freeze, in an instant. Fight or flight. It's basic. It's been understood for centuries. Why, then, do we have to keep re-learning it if we are to step beyond, step outside the collective norm that holds us down and, in itself, makes no sense at all. We have systematized life into bearable steps and burdened ourselves with right and wrong, acceptability, grey conversation throttled by self-imposed conventionality—whether by coercion or by choice, it doesn't matter. We don't see the miracle because we only see life through the base lens of 3D. We are so worn down by oppressive regulation that our bodies and minds cannot function beyond survival mode. What a crime. Yet, inside everyone, I believe, the true life is still there, the infinite creative potential, caged and forgotten, suppressed and abused. And so wild, anarchic, passionate action is our only true choice for life.

327

Does it get ever more challenging to attain peace in one's life? And I am not talking about the comatose, couch-potato variety. There is no peace in that. If you don't have peace in the first place. In the short term, it's the balance between striving and relaxing, eating and evacuating, thinking and meditating. That's all doable, to some extent or other and total exhaustion can be a state of bliss, post-coital or after an intensive activity that you love or challenges overcome. In the long term, though, there's a longer rhythm that encompasses those waves within its own waves. The sum of all the parts, accruing and shaping a life, the parts of the cosmic jigsaw falling into place in four dimensions or more. And the final pieces seem to become more and more elusive. Is it that, as we grow and experience more and more, that less and less we see our efforts as being the 'clinchers', because experiences pale and, like a drug addict, we seek higher highs and deeper depths. Meaning flits tantalizingly from one game to another. Perhaps it is the very desire for it, driven through reading, art, sex, love, travel, doing, that is its own limitation, a trap for the mind and heart that opens into infinite choices, infinite actions, infinity itself with all its mind-bending impossibilities. Remove it, and do we become zombie automatons, or do we find peace?

328

No wonder artists are sometimes seen as renegades, antisocial misfits or obsessives. The world is set up, commercially and politically, at least, to distract us from truth. To keep us busy keeping the wheels turning. I spend so much of my time doing things that my conditioning tells me are priorities, to keep us economically afloat, to keep things neat and tidy, clean and wholesome, reasonable. And those things can be all-consuming. Even socializing can become something of a game of politeness-tag. The important things, the search for truth, the stretching of our spirits and minds into higher realms of discovery and experience get pushed to the sidelines of our lives. Even when we are 'set up' with an income that comes automatically, the perfect home and relationship, the perfect, fully-equipped studio, the conditioning to do or avoid or excuse is sometimes so strong that all the effort to achieve such a privileged position may, at times, seem wasted. Yet when we experience the results of an uncompromising dedication, unencumbered by the social disease, we stand in awe of it, we love it, it hits us hard in the mind and heart. We give it huge value and the markets go wild for it. So I still know that that is my path—to squeeze through the narrowing gateway, to pry open stillness, to receive clarity and awaken my dormant passion, over and over again.

329

We take five. It actually turns into 60. That's fine. There are times when our projects take over. That's fine too. We both have burgeoning creativity that has to be released and realized. So, now and then, we take five—which usually stretches out to timelessness for a while. Just as there is energy in our projects, there is an irresistible energy between us. And sometimes it just makes perfect sense to let that come to the fore and give it free reign. Because it rules my life, and I love it. Sometimes we just sit and cuddle or read. Sometimes we babble out some details or thoughts about what we are doing. Sometimes we walk along the beach and watch ideas flow from the ethers, sparkling and dancing between us, growing with intensity and ownership or simply floating back to the universe, made thankful for a brief airing. Sometimes we make love with such intensity, or with infinite tenderness, or wild, unbounded passion that even 60 is too short. We cannot rush away from the sumptuous aftermath and sleepy, replete bonding. So, we take another five. Who am I kidding? The maths and the measurements are meaningless in love. And we know that the more we are in this place, this perfect, happy state, the more creativity comes to us, and the more we can enjoy. So, we just manage the energy and the numbers take care of themselves.

330

Some things are hidden from us. For a long time, I held a vision of our home. I spent a lot of time there before it transferred from the vision in my mind and heart to the vision of my eyes. I am careful to not say that it 'became a reality' or anything like that, as it was always the reality. I had simply not realized it. I knew my home. I knew the structure, the spaces, the land and the sea that accompanied it. Sizes and shapes morphed and rearranged a little, but the feelings were constant. The sense of being there was and is the reality, and so I knew it—perhaps for all of my life. Just as I knew you since I was about 7 years old, before my chaos started, leading me in a crazy dance until I came back to my vision, let go of the ego and saw again the mountains and water and blond curly hair as you walked effortlessly, like the perfect song, into my life. Yet that was just a fresh start, a new beginning to guide me back onto the rails and take me forward, washing away stale memories and lifting me over mountain ranges, across the top of the world and over warm, sunny lands to let me know that I deserve. Yet, even then, my art was hidden from me. I could not see forward to its realization in pictures in my mind. And, so, I began another journey, to humbly understand and find the voice in me that yearned to be expressed in its own time, in its own way.

331

When I see you, I see beauty, love and grace. No argument. No doubt. It's a fact. They say that beauty is in the eye of the beholder, but that just isn't true. Beauty is in creation, and some creations shine with it more than others. And sometimes there are things in us that blur the reality. Well, I think that happens most of the time. It's not what we see; it's what we are inside that allows us clear connection with beauty, love and grace. A fleeting relationship may mean that we only see the superficial, and that may trigger automated responses that judge and assess a person on those things. I know I have been wrong about people many times. I have also turned away before I can appreciate those higher qualities in someone. And, with unwise judgements, I have closed doors that could have led somewhere good. But, in your case, thank goodness there was an immediate recognition, a spark that circumvented the negative qualities I held dear for so much of my life, that kept me focused and let me in to really be with you. Actually, it was you. You did it. You ensnared me with your energy and you dug and probed and helped me make sense of it all. And you gave yourself, and you continue to give yourself, unfaltering, constant and clear, in ways that I could never imagine I deserved. And I love you all the more for it, every day that passes.

332

How fortunate I am that you are with me every step of the way. You have always been with me from the very first moment. Diligent, unswerving in the attention you give me, infinitely generous in all your intentions and actions towards me. Loving in the best way—as an active phenomenon, not just softly spoken words but also physical actions. These too, arising from your love like a flock of colourful birds tip-toeing over my body, along with the raging torrents of passion that leave me sated and breathless. And in you I see such beauty. That, too, enhanced and grown through the years, a stockpile that gets added to with every day's passing. A mountain of beauty to explore and marvel at every moment, to swim in and gorge my senses with infinite new discoveries. And a wisdom of ages is integrated seamlessly in all that you are and all that you give to me. Guiding me, bringing me back on track when I stray, reminding my hapless mind, jolting my discarded, inconvenient memory, caring for all parts of me that I erroneously and carelessly forget, blinded as I am, eclipsed by all that you are, 'falling up' to my best me, carried by wave upon wave of timeless nurturing that sees in me all that I see in you, and more, such that I am like a drunk, wondering how it all came together so perfectly, and the answer is always: you.

333

It felt good to let go of all my books on business. They had been watching me from my office bookshelf for years. Judging me, telling me I had a lot to learn. All written by bright, smart young men in their 30s and 40s, at the height of their career, after they had discovered something—a formula, an attitude, a process or whatever—and found a catchy way to put it down and then get their clients and industry-leading friends to endorse it. It's a perfectly valid formula. It's one I could have carried out myself, had I had the urge or the focus to do so. In fact, I did do that with some brand and marketing stuff, long ago. I no longer want to trawl the net of my own ego. It's too late for that, anyway. No, now is the time for introspection, for my own learning. Perhaps I will share it. I have no plans to but, if I do, I'd love to find a more authentic way to do it. The modern way of business teaching has such an air of desperation about it. Same with art. Too much shouting and justifying, rather than connecting on a deeper level and giving the student the job of really finding out if it's what they want. On the part of the student, there is more desperation to learn quickly and monetize. Whatever happened to real education? I bought all those books from the same perspective. Read some, learned less. Real learning must surely be a gradual, organic process, involving the whole self, in balance and fully integrated.

334

How far do I push and how much do I let? The eternal question when it comes to making some sort of personal progress in my art. I feel I should know by now. It's a constant interplay with my head and intellect wanting more linear development, more detail, more sophistication—if not of imagery, then of reason and motivation. On the other hand, my heart is looking for intuition, a receiving of ideas and forms from an infinite universe with which I connect all too rarely, a passion drawn from my life, love, my relationship and the wonder I have for very existence. In both, there is an urgency that I cannot explain because all of it is to do with discovery, and they are both, therefore, unknown to me, as yet. And the other factor is physical. The need for rest and recuperation, exercise, good diet and a healthy bodily balance that enables all of the above and without which it is all just so much unimportant tittle-tattle. Whether ego or heart are the do-ers or the let-ers, I don't know if I have, through all my wanderings, squandered my greatest gifts and simply missed my vocation. Living here, in this beautiful place has, I know, given me another opportunity to be my best, as befits me at this stage in my life. First, I have to let go and receive. I know that. There is no push, because only the heart is the true source.

335

We live in a world of symptomatic division. We use symptoms to divide, rather than exploring causes to enable healing. I know that if I have a cyst in my mouth, there is a cause for that. Only when I discover the truer cause can healing begin. The symptomatic approach to 'healing' it, is to cut it out, destroying nerves along the way, with a chance of recurrence. Why would it not recur? If the reason for it being there in the first place is not known. And so it is with the world. A focus on symptoms of problems and issues leads us nowhere near healing, but simply perpetuates and encourages new symptoms to spring up in an ever-more complex pattern that becomes near-impossible to resolve. And so it is accepted by most that this is the way of the world, with all its imbalances, wounds and disasters. And we drown out the calls to find root causes in our efforts to firefight symptoms. I am left wondering what is the point of it all. Which symptom should I spend my life trying to heal, with a sense of absolute futility? Or should I look at causes and join the herd as a tiny voice, set up for ridicule and rejection by all but a few? I feel that the best thing I can do is to withdraw from all of that, try to be a good husband and lover, and produce whatever my heart nudges me to do, so I can sprinkle, perhaps, a few drops of positive dust for whoever may want it.

336

You come to me on the stairs as I am about to go out. One step above me, the perfect height for a full-length, sinky, soft, gentle yet passionate cuddle. We kiss. Soft, warm lips connecting in a dream. The first kiss—of the day? Of a lifetime? I don't know, but at this point it is the kiss of life. Not in the medical sense, but in the spiritual, all-meaning, all-knowing, all-loving sense. It consumes me as I feel your body next to mine. My arms reach all the way around you, drawing you into me, merging our beings into one soft light. Standing on the stairs, now. Out the door in a few moments. What is the sense in that? Why not stay? Why not take you straight back to bed and gently lay you down? Drink you in. All over. Yet, I am going. It's only for a few hours. Fish, eggs, quinoa, olive oil, hazelnuts and more on the note in my pocket. I am here, really here, for this moment, yet I am also starting the car, planning the trip, watching for traffic as I merge onto the main road. But I am still here. A few more moments before our lips part and I release you to your morning. I stay. There is no hurry. Hurry can come later. I can take shortcuts, watch for the shortest queue in the supermarket, assess the speed of the cashier before I line up. Now I am here, with you, standing, holding, merging, loving with a fire that could ignite a galaxy. And you are with me, as always, in a perfect moment that, in my heart, is eternity.

337

My heart is full. Today, you and I have taken a short walk along the beach and are sitting among the rocks as the afternoon sun dips towards the horizon. It's still hot, so we brought the big sunshade, so I could sketch as you read. I sketch, you read. You're lying beside me on a towel, bottom nestled against my legs where I rest my pad and scratch away. There's a slight warm breeze—but nothing to curl the paper, flip your pages or send the sunshade bowling along the sand. I can feel the tingling energy of the air and the sea as it lazily dances to and fro on the sand. Muffled thumps as each new breaker breaks, sending little birds hurrying up the sand—avian commuters on their daily rush to work. I draw. The contact with you is a heart-swelling distraction that makes me smile. My marks play on the paper with a dreamy quality that tells me all is well and this little piece will work beautifully. You brush your hair behind your ear, sigh a contented sigh and glance at the vista as you turn a page. I briefly wonder how many pages you have turned in your life. It must be millions. I find myself vacantly staring at the ripples in the sand. Perfect patterns that run on seemingly forever, made in silence with no input from anyone. Better, so much better, than anyone could have thought up. And we are content, living in this fantastic emerging artwork of life.

338

It was a wonderful meal; the wine was good and the company very welcome and inspiring. The heat of the day has given way to balmy cool breezes and the cicadas are waking up as a soft orange/pink bathes the horizon in the evening's finale. We sit back and talk about nothing in particular. An ancient rite that has been played out across the world, millions of times. No technology intervenes. Our visitors know that it is not welcome here because there are no empty places in this experience for such things to fit. So it is that we learn to re-discover the ancient customs that are naturally a part of our psyche. The stories around the camp fire in the wilderness when travellers meet and share their rituals, mythologies and life experiences. Simple stories, so often, that say more and are imbued with more feeling than an entire book. No dramatically engineered plots; just touching, real and heartfelt stories that may have sadness, may be funny, happy and wise, that may show us something we did not know to be true, but that we can trust as being true for the teller. Such is the quality of real communication, between friends who value each other, but more importantly value and know themselves and know to share with caring generosity.

339

To get fired up, to get into the zone, into that special place that defies definition, to be filled with something other that is new and strange and to be treated with care and respect because to not do so, or to even notice it too much, or acknowledge it with any amount of awe or even the least amount of interest, would be to break the spell and return me immediately to the drudgery of physicality and reason and judgement. To simply be there, to be a servant to the forces that move my hand, make choices of colour and form and application. To have no part in it but to be it entirely for the duration of the process—one that has its own surges and pace and knowledge that defines me and the image I am producing without edges or separation, without need or stress, anxiousness or consideration from the conscious mind. To throw the weight of the Universe at this miniscule point on this planet to, yet again, generate the magical, the incredible, the creative, the new, the ancient, the total seeing that reaches every part of the psyche so that the being, the id, wrestles with a fantastic awakening in recognition of a startling yet all too familiar apparition that is at once foreign, strange, heartbreakingly beautiful, home and here and now. Form without form, experience without assessment, complete in itself yet infinitely dynamic and evolving.

340

When Facebook imploded, everything was turned on its head. When people realized that the only information that was worth discovering was that which had been banned or hidden or marginalized by Google, the internet changed irreversibly. When the trillionaires and some billionaires were stripped of their wealth and assets so they could no longer dictate the way the world went, a massive re-balancing started. We watched it happen from our home by the sea. It was not that we were constantly online, eagerly devouring the next piece of news—what would have been the point of that when everyone now knew it was devoid of truth? No, we saw it on the beach, in the sky and the sea, and on our visits to the village. Colour was returning to life. People were regaining their individuality. The shops were stocking better, natural and local products; the air was cleaner, the fields no longer exuded a chemical odour, birds and other wildlife were returning to abundant hedgerows. There was a feeling of possibility where before there had been a beaten down acceptance. There was an energy of discovery where before there had been submission to rules and regulations. Social distancing had taken on a whole new meaning—distancing from social media and connecting with your fellow man. Where before, life had become a test of endurance, now it was a time of celebration.

341

There's a hole in the sky above our heads. Thanks to the Russians. We can still look up and see the heavens that man has wondered at, enjoyed, navigated by and mythologized since he first set foot here. That must count for something. For me, it is a core part of my humanity to be able to wonder at the night sky, the stars and the far planets. Thank you, Russia, for scuppering the SpaceX and American plan for all those low-orbit satellites completely encapsulating the earth. They didn't want an American eye in the sky and nor did most other countries. Thank goodness they had the 'Sat-Alight' technology already circling the earth, that could disable these snoopers with high-power laser beams. In the end, the SpaceX plan was broken and it was uneconomical to send up any more, so they shelved the project and had some massive lawsuits to deal with instead. Thank you. We can now lie in bed or on the terrace at night, and look up, with a magnificent and uninterrupted view of the heavens. A profound, rather than a shallow high-tech, connection, which reaches deep into the heart and soul of every living being—every man, woman and child, every bird, every bee, every creature on the surface of the world whose right to the infinite gift of a natural order has been upheld, not to mention the natural processes that can now flourish once more in the absence, the glorious lack, of man-made electromagnetic radiation.

342

Beauty is an infinitely private thing. An experience that I cannot transfer or communicate in its entirety however much I try. And it has many qualities—all of which I crave to keep, renew and remember. Whether a jolt in the heart when a door is opened to reveal an unexpected glow, or a languid, smooth absorption of a shared moment, the way the light and a particular position at a particular moment, in a particular place, in warmth or cool contact, or a particular melody it is all that we live for and cherish. Artists, musicians, poets and writers all make the effort—that essential effort to share and describe and reach for the true essence, with whatever skills and tools they have. Yet the beauty they aspire to showing can only awaken in each of us the beauty that is our experience, our feeling, our yearning—and no one else's. We must never close our hearts to beauty. Those who cannot see it, or who dismiss it as frivolous, or deny it or try to profit from it without first making their donation, are not alive. What an incredible gift to be given, to have in-built in every single human being, to know such feeling, to have access to a never-ending spectrum of indulgence that fills our senses, feeds our never-ending appetite, should we want it to, from the moment we are born to the moment we take our last breath and enter it.

343

I haven't been in the studio for a few days. Sometimes the journey from me to the canvas just seems too far. The route from blank to filled feels like too high a mountain to climb. The reason for doing anything seems just too remote. And where to start? What to paint? The choice is just too vast. These are the times I am in danger of going decorative; losing the plot and going for treatment of the literal, stepping back from the brink to where tea and biscuits are arranged on a table, with a mindless novel and a comfortable chair. That's where we go when we are tired and wired. And it's not for me. Those are the times when a nice decorative piece could gain some 'likes' or perhaps a minor sale, but they, to me, are a betrayal of my potential. I can only paint for me. Decoration is for others. And I may never know—I never know—if the work I am about to create will resonate with anyone. Even me. Re-painted canvases used to litter my studio, but now I am fortunate to have a big enough reputation that the highly personal work finds a sympathetic soul before I get a chance, or have the inclination to destroy it. Now I wait, through unforgiving days like this, until my mind and heart are back in alignment, when I can be okay with me and my ups and downs, until the muse comes back and brings me fresh inspiration.

344

I feel more separate. I don't know what the process is—whether it is my journey to death or transformation of some sort, or realization. The picture I drew of my father pops into my mind. 'That creeping death'. I still remember it, and the feeling I had as I watched him, slumped in his chair with all his sad secrets, dozing away another tough day. Why do I remember that so clearly? I am not him. I have so much more to be thankful for. I have the love of my life with you, burning in my heart like a first love. I have this life, this place, all the accolades and accoutrements of success. Yet there is a separation, somewhere, that takes me by surprise and with resignation, as I lift my brush to make a mark. What does it matter? Where will this go? How do I even touch the canvas with this loaded brush, ready to sing its simple, natural song in whatever way it flows or dabs or jabs into the surface? When, suddenly, there is nothing, a void amidst all that I have ever striven for and that has been delivered to my door, tax-free, free delivery, no charge, a gift a million times over, what am I to do? What kind of an idiotic monster am I? Instant, and eternal for that instant, the separation is there; solid, empty, burgeoning, real. Then it is gone. Birdsong, colour, form. And I continue in heaven.

345

'Back to the future' was a great title for a film, although I never saw it, so I don't know how great that was. But the sentiment was spot on. I am now in my future, that which I perceived many years ago—and I feel that, thankfully, I have gone back. We were fine back then, before all this crazy technology pulled us apart. Yes, it was messy, and of course there were challenges, but we all lived our lives with what we had, and it all worked to the degree we expected it to. We weren't nannied so much, or observed, or tracked and controlled. Does anyone honestly think that things are better now, thanks to all that? You may say that life has changed, there are more people, planetary resources are more strained and so on. But was technology ever a real solution, or was it just an illusory BandAid to make people feel better, or at least enable them to cope on some level, while the state and industry crushed their spines into data streams? We have gone back to our future, and it is beautiful. Back to a time when what you grow feeds your family and friends; when actions are private if we want them to be; when we move and spend and behave without some watchful eye monitoring us; when we can behave with honour, love or total disgrace and deal with the consequences on our own, in our own unique ways; when love between two people is forged from realities and spirit and wisdom received through our own learning, being, deep honesty and respect.

346

It all comes from inside. The confidence, the energy, the recognition. I have to recognize myself before anyone else can. That's the challenge. To begin this next canvas with marks applied with confidence and detachment, the right, unspoken energy, the flow from within. That's why quick poses at the beginning of a life-drawing session are so important. To 'get my eye in', as they say. Get the mind out of the way through physical urgency. Much as exercise does when worry kicks in. Clear the airways, untie and release the knot in my stomach that threatens to keep me captive, in partnership with a mind on a downward spiral. Lift it all up. Enter the realm of being, not doing. Be the painting; let it give itself to you. That's me talking to me, of course, in the second person. That second person I must learn to stand beside and support at such times as this, when the oppressive white of the canvas sends a pang of uncertainty through my heart. Before I realize this sea of pure potential is a gift, not a burden, and I let myself begin, yet again, on a wondrous journey of discovery, humour, love, intrigue, fascination, inspiration and more. Nothing stays the same. There is no chance of boredom or any type of repetition. Only newness. The kind of unfettered newness that freaks an ordered mind out. At least, I hope it does, so that it can join me in wonder at the new lands I discover. My mind is not my enemy but a tool and a friend that is forever being nurtured back to the heart.

347

I just want things simple, these days, so that I can truly enjoy the complexity. Life is complex enough, and now I want—need—simple so I can take it all in. So, don't bring negativity or political arguments into my home. Their nature is to perpetuate and expand on complexity by bringing argument and counter-argument so nothing gets solved and nothing is clear. They are the way of confusion that brings frustration and hatred, and I think I have seen enough of that. And if I am infected by it again, I know I will want to check out rather than check in and be truly alive. Every day, we are faced with a wall of choices, challenges, situations, relationships, bureaucracy and more. How do we find ourselves amongst all of that? We don't. We are not of it. It is just the external manifestation of our choices. So, today, I make fresh choices, just as I can any day. And, despite all those things that are pressing in on me—important things, things to be done—I am making a choice for me. To love me, to look after my needs, to be kind to me, to relax, to be true to me. It's a choice that I should make every day. It's the simple choice that gets buried under obligations, fear and greed that is full of empty promises. It's the choice that allows me to live truly as me, and be giving and loving to you.

348

The wind has picked up. I see clouds tumbling from the south. The sand shifts under my feet and starts to bite at my ankles. I shield my eyes as the sand whips up in a gust. The sea, a murky grey, is relatively calm, although fine mists are flying off the breakers. And, all around me, the sounds of wind and water increase. Hair slaps across my brow, my collar rattles my neck. I stand still and watch it all develop. Watch and hear and feel. My heart quickens as the waves grow to a sustained roar. Raindrops sting my face and hands. The horizon grows dark and blurred. Just a thin band of cold white light beneath the incoming clouds that bear heavily down on it. Up the coast, sand and rain mix in the air, obscuring the far mountain. I feel the cold damp of soaked clothes against my back and legs. I turn towards the dark visitor, crouching menacingly, cooling massive rock formations and panicking the waves as far as I can see. The sand and rain sting like hell and I let them whip into my body. I am soaked through. I feel myself getting colder but I don't want to leave. I don't want to succumb to hiding in comfort. This vast theatre, this fantastic show, this all-powerful phenomenon is one wonder that I want to be a part of, immerse myself in, relish and fully appreciate with my whole self. And, when I do, I feel alive.

349

We give people and things names; we talk in languages; we are judged on our knowledge of all things; we only integrate when we have the correct markers in place. It's pathetic. There are those good souls who look out for the misfits who may speak a different language of, say, autism or muteness or schizophrenia but, for the most part, we cannot tolerate another way of being, so we marginalize it, hide it away and say it is not normal or healthy. But, most of all, if we cannot recognize a name, we cannot assimilate it into our lives. This is a challenge for the human race, if it is to rise beyond the physical realm, because we cannot name what is there. The world of spirit, of quantum connectedness, is nameless. It resides outside of our day-to-day realm of left-brain thinking and right-brain feeling. We cannot even truly name the tools we have access to, to experience it. Yet this is the greater irony. That we are designed to go there. We are not designed for scrapping in the dirt; we are designed to journey back to our own wholeness. And I don't know the reason for that. I only know, in my heart, that it is true. I wonder, then, if my fascination with art and imagery is simply my higher self nudging me, giving me hints, bashing me over the head, to find my own unique way to breach the portal to myself.

350

We are here. That cannot be denied. It is a fact. I wonder what that means. Fact. It's humanity's way of loading an idea down with heavy weights so it is somehow fixed and solid, certain and irrefutable. So, if I say, "We are here", what makes that a fact? We can argue about physics, senses and time. But do we really know anything? Can what we term a fantasy be more real, more true, more 'factual' than the reality we perceive? Or is there a better word than 'fact'. Maybe 'true' is a better word. It is true that I am sitting in my kitchen writing this by hand. Yet there are parts of me that are elsewhere. Outside my window is the terrace and the sea. Inside my head, there is a log fire burning in a far-off hearth. That we are here, I have no doubt. But where is 'here'? I curse the physical realm that threatens my flight and influences my moods too much, and places restrictions on me that grow as my reality beckons me ever further into exciting new territory. The dull rhythm of a suffocated, sick society, add to the overload of 'facts' that weigh down on 'here' and 'now', which, I truly believe, is meant to be such a joyous experience. So, all I can do is turn away, turn inward and continue my search there, away from the cackles and criticisms, doubts and follies, and find my truth.

351

"Bon app," you say, with a smile, as you carefully lay a meal in front of me, on the table. I watch the curve of your fingers as they release the plate. At that moment, I want you, but I know that, for you, food and love-making do not mix well, and so I don't make any sort of move. Instead, I watch your eyes that fix me with their care and generosity and direct connection. "Thank you," I say, choosing these not-very-creative words with care, as much to thank you for the heartfully prepared plate before me, as to suppress the bursting energy that could launch me at you in an instant and send it all flying in a mess of clothes, vegetables, sauce, skin and sweat. I calm the beast and take in the meal that you have put so much love into. You sit, blissfully unaware of the ravaging you so narrowly escaped an instant ago. Although, maybe if you had known, you might have been flattered, and perhaps a little excited. You might have laughed your special laugh, and I could not have stopped, or I would have felt conflicted by the contrasting emotions I would have felt at that moment. I reach for the salt, and you are still there, relentlessly gorgeous with your slim body, shoulders, tanned arms, lovely neck, smiling mouth, shining hair. Sometimes, good behaviour is a curse. But the meal is an important expression of love as much as sustenance. So we pick up our knives and forks, and talk about anything but intense desire, eroticism and sex.

352

What is going on? The longer I live, the less I know. You may say I am losing it, that my brain has got tired and I am on my way to a few years of vegetation before I die. But I don't think so. I know, I would say that, wouldn't I!? Because I can only think what I think and, to me, that will always seem normal, whatever the rest of the world thinks of it. So, given that I have my own thoughts, my own visions, my own way of seeing things that is unique to me, I decided to take a trip. I don't need the car, and I will be back in an instant, despite the fact that I will travel thousands—maybe millions—of miles. My own personal freedom gives me that ability. I take off—vertically. The ground recedes beneath me. The coast, fringed with yellow-white, describes a lengthening, meandering line. The village becomes a pinprick of red ochre rooftops and the landscape blurs into a fantastic tapestry of textures that eventually fade to a bluey-green as detail disappears and the thin, bright curve of the planet eventually turns full circle. 'Vertical' no longer has a meaning as I shoot past the moon and the sun recedes into a mass of other suns and stars that form the Milky Way that itself disappears into a mass of tiny galaxies that fill my vision. The relevance and existence of man, lost forever. Yet I am here, and I return and touch the sand with my hand, and hear the sound of the sea, and see so much colour. What is going on?

353

I met a man when I was out walking, on my own, which does not happen often. He wasn't old, but he certainly wasn't young. Maybe in his late forties. Remarkable to think that, give or take a few years, he could have been my son. But I never had a son. With me, the buck stops here. We both stopped walking. Perhaps we were making way for each other on the path, but it didn't feel like that. He casually looked towards the sea before turning to me. Our eyes met in silent acknowledgement. We both stood still. In silence. It didn't feel appropriate to strike up a conversation or even pass the time of day. There was a cool connection, wafer-thin but not brittle. Two strangers standing fast in the breeze. What is your message? I found myself thinking, my arms hanging by my sides, my hands relaxed and open. There was no threat here, just a stirring, barely perceived, as the world turned and the skies showed us their infinity, filled with yet more questions and answers that neither one of us was equipped to reach or understand. All we had was light and sound, our bodies, ourselves and the rocky path beneath. Two meteors, not quite colliding and yet conscious of each other's presence and energy. A meeting that is not a meeting, that will pass and be forgotten, yet stored somewhere in me and in him, for a common eternity.

354

How close we got to the edge, to annihilation, our self-destruction. Yet, just as in nature, out of the wreck of society and environment emerged a new and more balanced, humanitarian and compassionate world. The reset button thankfully got pushed. But only when we were at the 59th minute of the eleventh hour. So deep was the dysfunction, the pain, the ill-directed manipulation, the concentration of power and wealth in a few hands. And, right up to that last minute, the spin was being spun, the abuse of minds and bodies had become intolerable, the media were still pumping out their half-truths, lies and ignorance; they were still drama queens, ambulance-chasers, corporately and politically pimped to serve the greater bad. The air was still unbreathable and the silent, invisible and deadly radiation had reached new peaks, generating new diseases and spreading them like wildfire around the globe. But then it all stopped. No explanation, no apparent cause other than that the system simply broke. It was never designed to be sustainable. That was its fatal flaw. Thankfully, such a system, born out of greed and so many dark intentions, is destined to fail. Because we are better than that, and each and every one of us knows we are. It's the truly sustainable part of us that cannot be destroyed or taken away.

355

I still have to catch myself, although it is easier now. Or maybe not easier, but I'm more used to dealing with it and seeing it for what it is. You come to me with a concern and there is something in your voice that tells me this has built up over time. Or perhaps it has always been there and has gone unaddressed. And you want to talk. Now, if I stop to think about it, if I can be mature, be a man, I know I can trust you with anything. Yet, still, sometimes, I feel a resistance building, like a knot or a cyst in my mind—hard, unyielding, defensive, childish—that purports to be my defender, my statement of strength and independence, my boundary that, if not defended, will open the floodgates to me being dominated or losing my pride and sense of identity. But, sometimes, I still don't stop to think, because I get caught up in that stuff, which is, in fact, complete nonsense. Because, if I stop to think, and then stop thinking at all, and welcome your concern with an open heart and mind, I know already that this talk will be good for both of us. So, I see some distress in your eyes as we start, and I know that whatever it is that you want to talk about is a new gateway, a new opportunity, something good for us, something that will take away pain—small or large—and that will help us live our lives even better. So, thank you for your courage, wisdom, integrity and love.

356

Welcome to our world! You are very welcome. We welcome you first with a smile and warm hugs, a refreshing drink after your long journey, with homemade nibbles and inquiry into your journey here, and soft light and sea breezes and a deep sense of peace. Welcome. We can do that because we are living it, every day. And all the challenges of our lives are held in their proper place, respected and welcomed as the agents of learning, dynamism and growth that they are. So you are welcome. Because when we have the opportunity to live in peace, in the present, in wholeness, that is our natural state. One of welcome, and gratitude and appreciation. This welcome is real, and here and now; and we know that you feel it because, even after your journey, whatever may be happening in your life, whatever crises you have to endure, there is a part of you that knows this welcome, it knows the truth of it and yearns for it more than anything, despite knowledge, understanding, bravado and unfortunately learned acceptance of suffering that overwhelmed your greater qualities for a while. But this life is not about all that. That is why you are here now, with us, to unravel your heart and rein in your mind through a better focus, and re-build your true humanity. So, welcome.

357

We are such amateurs, we humans, at simply being, that it astounds me. With all the faculties we have been given, we still make a huge mess of things, every day. We try to follow accepted paths in our lives, according to our upbringing. Mine was supposed to be: do well at school, go to university, get a stellar job, marry, have kids, get comfortable and then drift to death. Hmmm… What happened? I wonder. I think the problems start because of the structure of expectations, although many seem to manage in spite of it. Social norms, acceptable behaviour, imposed morality all play a huge part in restricting and distorting our lives. Unless we have fearless parents who know the game and encourage us to flourish in our own ways. So few have that, and their offspring often have a hard time bumping up against so-called normality during their lives that they may develop other psychological problems or die young because of some unhealthy excess or wild action. No wonder it took me years, following my blue-collar programming, to break free. And, for most of my transformation, I was like a cripple on crutches, always looking for something to lean on, support, answers out there that would lift me out of the dull confusion, the seemingly everlasting mire that held me down, questioning and berating myself as one who had the ability but failed to use it. It was hard won, painful and long, but I finally arrived at my pride.

358

More and more, I see that we can only communicate through art. It is the only way we have that has the potential to bypass the brain and get to the real communication receptors that are hidden under the layers in each and every one of us. I am talking about myself, just as much as anyone else. The thing is that, most of the time, we don't want communication. We just want reassurance, confirmation of what we think we already know, a feeling of belonging through consensus, a feeling of self-worth, even influence and power over our situation or others. And, when any of that is challenged, we so easily revert to fight or flight, aggression, ridicule, denial or withdrawal. Sometimes, we feel hurt or angry, rather than stepping back from our ego and sensitivities and observing, assessing afresh, investigating or accepting a new perspective or understanding. The age of innocent inquiry is over, in a time when our only credibility resides in rigidly-held beliefs—even if those beliefs cause us or others harm. So, where does that leave me, living here in this perfect bubble, where I can accept or deny access to guests who come and go? Does that mean that I am now closed off to all that is new, all that could take me further, make me a better person? Would I even have the energy or capacity to explore all that is to be explored? Not now. I have to let my inner receptors guide me.

359

We rely far too much on our intellect to inform us as to what is real. And look where that has got us! Not only are we easily manipulated, but we lose trust in ourselves and our own capacity to know. We know we have always known. That is why our intellect gets disturbed when what we receive and perceive is at odds with what we know. And I understand that making such statements is understood in a different way to what I mean, since there is no language, no words, no lexicon that can truly express it. We think we know with our intellect—the very thing that keeps us blind to our knowing. And so we are tricked into believing and thinking—two inadequate faculties that are driven by the intellect and that are far from absolute and clear—that what is real is the illusion we follow every day of our lives. Yet our knowing is still there, breathing us, beating our heart, showing us with every sunrise, every sunset and everything laid out in between, and even more so in our dreams, when we allow out intellect to rest. But do we take any notice? Do we ask to reconnect? Do we even care? So immersed are we in stuff that the 'still small voice of calm', our knowing, is masked and obscured. How do I paint that knowing? How can I move a soul in someone to see that they are all-knowing?

360

You used to be able to buy a new gearbox for a Trabant from your local supermarket. Imagine it now. Go past the school section, past the female then male preening sections, past the gardening tools, seeds and compost bags on pallets, and there they were—bottom shelf of the auto section, beneath the de-mist sprays, chammy leathers and wheel trims. Everything standardized, mechanical and cheap. The Trabant was a terrible car, but it was, for many, the only option in post-war Eastern Europe. I always saw a return to that mentality—of mechanical and easily replaceable (if it can't be fixed) as a good thing. A new world order—but not the version that is ruled by a super-rich, completely horrible coterie of sadistic buddies. One that realized the value and limitations of the planet, one that put environment first so people could thrive in a sustainable way, one based on love and respect, cooperation and understanding. Someone once told me that the only people he could really trust and care for were his immediate family. I always found that a bit sad, although, given the way the world was working, completely understandable, and it made a lot of sense. How naïve to think otherwise! But now, years later, I realize the urgent need to think beyond those terms, to marginalize what was once mainstream thinking and embrace higher thinking, to change the reality—and then live it to its fullest.

361

I believe I have a good argument. My friend believes he has one, too. After years of knowing each other and building a strong friendship, we are discussing a particular subject for the first time, it seems. We both completely believe in what we are saying. We each have forty-something years of experience in the subject, and learning and research. Yet our minds are poles apart. How can that be? In this world of so-called information and the vast technology that disseminates it; in a world of political manoeuverings, powerful special interests, money and power itself; we have nothing out there that we can completely rely on as the truth. We cannot possibly put our hands on our heart and say we know, even if we could physically know, even if we have read all of it—which would take several lifetimes, even if we could physically do it. So, where does that leave me and my friend? Do we 'beg to differ', knowing in our hearts that some part of our friendship has changed for good? Do we say "Oh, it doesn't matter—no one can possibly know, anyway", which leaves us both dissatisfied and hanging on to our beliefs? Is there a real meeting point, where our individual egos fade away and some deeper truth comes to the fore—a bright shining light for our darkness? Essentially, we live life alone, and the trick is to be happy with that.

362

When the muse escapes me, I have to take action. Is that a man thing? I wonder. When I lose the connection, I have to be aware that that is what is happening, and pull myself up. Otherwise, there can be days of grey, hopeless isolation that appear to have no end, like a flat, endless dark cloud on a rainy day. Today, I simply went into the studio and scribbled. No imagery, no intention, no aesthetic—whatever that is. Just action. Similar to going into the gym but on a spirit rather than a body level. To raise the spirit from the trip of negativity, which can gouge and tear at an otherwise wonderful day, with doubts, sadness and anger, trying to infect me with unworthiness, guilt, shame and whatever damaging and useless gift it brings. I should know better. I do know better, but there are still dark eddies in my mind where gremlins lurk. It's the oldest story in the world, I guess. That's the story that all stories are born out of, ultimately, with their heroic or sad endings. It's the human condition, the human conundrum eternally playing its hand. But I am tired of being tested in these ways. I want the easy route, the comfortable, uplifting, happy route. So, now, when the muse escapes me, I laugh at it and all the tricks it pulls, and I win!

363

I have long memories. The young will have their own when they get to my age. I hope they are good ones, or will their brains be so addled that there is no room for sentimental journeys of the mind? I have lived through what has been the fastest change in humanity that has ever been, and I find myself fearing for the future—something I am sure older generations have been plagued with many times. Life used to be grainy, fresh and exciting. There was room for interpretation in those soft edges, room to fantasize when there were no hard lines or hyper-reality. I was more in control and part of it. I'm talking of the time before friendships became social. When social was real interaction with all its challenges, feelings, sights, sounds and smells. When it was personal and messy and we dealt with the human condition. When passion was an exciting discovery, before it was supplanted by a toxic mix of porn, publicity, political correctness. Before Snapchat and cellphones recorded intimate mini-events, social markers for later embarrassment. When there was no eye in the sky, or instant worldwide transmission from tiny devices, when human interaction was private and unrecorded. Before intellectual banter was reduced to sensationalism, hard headlines, short paragraphs, shot attention spans. Overwhelm. And I continue to seek others who pick among the wreckage to find rare gems of humanity.

364

They say that travel broadens the mind. Does it follow, then, that staying still broadens the heart? Does the fact that, these days, I don't really want to travel anywhere mean that I become narrow-minded? Or if, after a life of broadening the mind, it's broad enough and I can now stop travelling without losing anything? In this so-called mature phase of life, is it my main purpose to broaden the heart? So many questions. You'd think I'd know by now. But all I know is that there is still so much to learn. And I want to learn, so I guess that's a good thing. But I don't want to travel. Travel used to be fun, and adventure. It doesn't feel like that any more. The experience of travel has been so commoditized and downgraded, and travellers aren't sharing in the same way. Not like they used to. I can remember colourful conversations on the road, hitch-hiking through Europe in my teens. Pre-social media, pre-cellphones. Before the experience was packaged and diminished, reduced to 'likes' and selfies. I don't know if travel does broaden the mind any more, rather than numbing it, frustrating it on occasion and generally digitizing and reporting it, rather than being in it and truly experiencing it. Now, I prefer to keep learning as I travel in my mind and in my writing and on canvas. My new reality is such a wonderful journey that I don't want to miss a minute of it.

365

The vision that I had thus far not dared to envision, that was so outlandish and seemingly impossible—unreasonable, even—was the one that changed everything, when I put myself in it and fully allowed myself to receive. Our home. Our perfect place and the means to live out our days in the way we dreamed about, was all simply given to us. If I think about it now, that is not so outlandish. Our vision was not to have world-shattering wealth or a desire to harm. It was and is to live to give in some cosmic way that lifts ourselves and others way beyond and above the maelstrom that threatened us and everyone else. To return to the arts, our higher faculties, and be creative in ways that help people re-connect and become whole again. Perhaps that is why we succeeded. By envisioning ourselves as a part of the whole, in love, gratitude and respect, perhaps that is all it takes for the Universe to more than match our desires from its own abundant resources of which we have no knowledge. We cannot work it out. If we think about it, using our limited faculties that we have aimed in the wrong directions for far too long, the only way to achieve what looks impossible is to be totally unreasonable. And then we can play in the universe that cannot be reasoned. So, all our visions must be outrageous for them to work.

One more — for leap years

366

I have never done anything great. I have never had great crowds following me, soaking up my words that I arrange into great speeches that become the stuff of educational standards for a following generation. I have never taken my mind and body to remarkable extremes so that I achieve something greater than any man or woman has done before. I have never pushed limits and boundaries to the point where I am challenged, condemned, incarcerated or attracted an assassin's bullet. And I will never do these things. Not now. If they ever existed, those times have gone. Yet, in some cosmic scheme of things, when I search my heart and look at my life past, present and future, I am more than great. Because greatness in the senses I have described are merely comparative measures that attract the common feeling of inadequacy and give meaning to struggle and aspiration. True greatness resides in each and every one of us, and it is indestructible and awesome, as well as infinitely humble, quiet and still. The journey that we are all on, then, is to find that greatness, appreciate it, love it and live it with all our hearts. Because it is the value, the incredible value, that we all hold inside, independent of comparisons and judgements of the mind. I, you, we are all incredible, in reality. We just cannot see it for all the distractions our lives hold; but it is there, nevertheless, for all of us to celebrate.

Notes

1. Milestones: on our first visit to Vancouver in 2003, I proposed to Olga when we were having a meal at a restaurant called Milestones, which seemed appropriate.
2. The five Tibetan rites: I have made a practice of doing these every morning when I wake up.
   https://en.wikipedia.org/wiki/Five_Tibetan_Rites
3. Berkey filter: For many years, we didn't trust our water supply, wherever we were living, to be free from contaminants, so we used a filter.
   https://www.berkeyfilters.com/
4. Easy button: a free gift during a promotion at Staples, if you want one, you can buy them here: https://www.staples.com/Staples-Easy-Button/product_606396
5. Silly Scrabble: Olga and I play this, rather than 'real' Scrabble, as a way of having fun and extending language beyond what we know. There are no proper rules. The idea is that words must be completely original and they are accepted by the other player(s) only if the made-up definition is plausible, original, funny or otherwise interesting.
6. Olga has gluten and lactose intolerance and is sensitive to other foods as well, so if you are planning to invite her for a meal, it's best to check first…
7. Dee Rowland is a very dear friend who has been incredibly supportive of our work over many years.
8. Emily Carr University of Art and Design,
   https://www.ecuad.ca/
9. Valentine's Day
10. Stanley Kubrick: during my latter years in the UK, I spent many weekends at the home of the Kubricks. It was a magical time that I am eternally grateful for, and where I was able to experiment with many techniques in my art.

11. Olga and I spent our honeymoon on Langkawi Island, just off the coast of Malaysia.
12. Gerhard Richter: painter, https://www.gerhard-richter.com/
13. Gerhard Richter, Birkenau series: t.ly/3Dvo
14. Gerhard Richter 'September': bit.ly/3iiT4ek
15. DFA: When I worked at the BBC many moons ago, the lighting technicians in the studios had their own language and acronyms. This one was used when a nit-picking and difficult director wanted, for the umpteenth time, to change something on the set before the shoot could happen. DFA = different fucking arrangement.
16. Japanese knotweed: a real pain in the neck if you get it in your garden. https://en.wikipedia.org/wiki/Reynoutria_japonica
17. Seven key qualities as defined by Jim Self: strong, certain, commanding, gracious, loving, capable, present, with seniority
18. Michael Carlo, printmaker and painter: The Suffolk laneway prints: http://michaelcarlo.uk/1990s/
19. Earth or root cellar: I first became aware of these in Horsefly, Canada, where friends stored food and kept it fresh for months at a time. https://en.wikipedia.org/wiki/Root_cellar
20. Timothy: When on holiday in Mexico, I fell in love with pelicans. I took endless photos of them flying, diving into the sea and walking on the beach. I even dreamt up a short story that I shared with Olga about one called Timothy. When I got back to my studio, I painted a pelican in bright colours and called him T-t-t-timothy. He had a stutter in the story. The original is now hanging in a client's home near Williams Lake in British Columbia.
21. Claude Monet—haystacks series: https://www.claude-monet.com/haystacks.jsp

22. Belle (film): https://en.wikipedia.org/wiki/Belle_(2013_film)
23. Olga and I had our wedding reception in Ireland at Killiney Castle in Killiney. https://www.fitzpatrickcastle.com/
24. Milton Glazer: he was among the most celebrated graphic designers of our time. He died in 2020. https://www.miltonglaser.com/
25. Elastic bands: in our relationship, Olga and I refer to elastic bands as the tension that keeps a relationship dynamic and alive. It is necessary, sometimes, to stretch the elastic band by, for instance, being apart from one another now and then or having differing opinions, in ways that ultimately spring us back together again.
26. *Youmeus*: Olga's word for expressesing togetherness—you, me, us... all together.
27. Carosello: an Italian TV advertising show that ran from 1957 to 1997. t.ly/QWDp
28. Amaro 18 Isolabella: a well-known after-dinner tonic, first produced in the 1870s, containing 18 herbs. Now available as a bit of a collector's item, I believe. t.ly/fKJ8
29. *Hominine*: my first novel—a geopolitical thriller. Available at http://hominine.info and on Amazon.
30. Read Olga's story in her book, *EMF off!*, and discover many free resources at https://www.emfoff.com
31. Georgia O'Keeffe: artist, https://www.georgiaokeeffe.net/
32. Beethoven's hearing loss: t.ly/gmNG
33. Gaia: in Greek mythology, gaia is the ancestral mother of all life https://en.wikipedia.org/wiki/Gaia

About the author

A prolific creative—artist, marketing communications consultant, writer and inventor, Lewis Evans is married to author and empowerment coach Olga Sheean.

Another book by Lewis
In 2009, as the result of a dream, he was inspired to write *Hominine*, a geo-political thriller with heart and a social conscience. In fictionalizing tough, real-life issues, political dilemmas and global crises, Evans depicts frighteningly plausible scenarios, while providing refreshingly sane solutions.
http://hominine.info

Art:
https://lewisevans.net

Marketing communications:
https://cogenicamedia.com

Further recommended reading

Tell Me The Truth
— a Code for Freedom

by Olga Sheean

Your antidote to the tsunami of commercial spin, social stimuli and bad news clogging our news channels and our consciousness. This book challenges you to remember who you are and to change direction in favour of humanity and life. See the spin for what it is; let go of over-stimulation so you can reconnect with the real you; and trade the bad news for the good news and the truth about you and your world.

Be inspired to live your life out loud! This book is an uplifting meditation on life, written with extraordinary wisdom and insight. Not limited to any age, but a 'must' read for young people who stand at the crossroads of their lives, seeking answers, direction and fulfilment. I wish I'd had this in my formative years but I'm very grateful to have it now.
—Elize Potgieter, lecturer, Informatics and Design
Cape Peninsula University of Technology, Cape Town

Available at https://olgasheean.com/books

The Alphabet of Powerful Existence
—an A–Z guide to well-being, wisdom and worthiness

by Olga Sheean

This is a practical guide to self-empowerment, featuring 52 themes (one for every week of the year) and offering simple, transformative steps for resolving conflict, positively reprogramming your mind, making powerful choices, and creating more love, money, ease, success and fulfillment in your life. Upgrade your relationships, finances and business; fill in your 'missing pieces'; activate your creativity; and enhance your self-worth and personal magnetism.

Olga Sheean brilliantly inspires us in practical ways to live a dynamic, healthy, fulfilling life on our terms. This book will enable you to change your circumstances, heal, and discover yourself. An enjoyable, easy read. I couldn't put it down!
—Bev Ogilvie, author of
ConnectZone.org—building connectedness in schools

Available at https://olgasheean.com/books

www.ingramcontent.com/pod-product-compliance
Lightning Source LLC
Chambersburg PA
CBHW070136100426
42743CB00013B/2715